MW00560785

Mazda Miata
Performance Handbook

Norman H. Garrett III

MBI Publishing Company

Dedication

To my better half, my dear wife, Candi, who has been putting up with me playing with Miatas since 1983, with patience and grace. God has truly blessed me with you on all counts.

Acknowledgments

No book of this nature comes out of one person's head by itself. I extend a debt of gratitude to all the members of the Miata Club of America for their tireless tinkering with this special car, and for all that I have learned from them. Special thanks go out to Rob Ebersol, who provided tremendous help in illustrating this book and fleshing out the many chapters, adding greatly from his vast experience running Miatas around race tracks ahead of others.

First published in 1998 by MBI Publishing Company, 729 Prospect Avenue, PO Box 1, Osceola, WI 54020-0001 USA

© Norman H. Garrett, 1998

All rights reserved. With the exception of quoting brief passages for the purpose of review no part of this publication may be reproduced without prior written permission from the Publisher.

The information in this book is true and complete to the best of our knowledge. All recommendations are made without any guarantee on the part of the author or Publisher, who also disclaim any liability incurred in connection with the use of this data or specific details.

We recognize that some words, model names and designations, for example, mentioned herein are the property of the trademark holder. We use them for identification purposes only. This is not an official publication.

MBI Publishing Company books are also available at discounts in bulk quantity for industrial or sales-promotional use. For details write to Special Sales Manager at Motorbooks International Wholesalers & Distributors, 729 Prospect Avenue, Osceola, WI 54020-0001 USA.

Garrett, Norman H.
    Mazda Miata performance handbook/Norman H. Garrett.
        p. cm.
    Includes index.
    ISBN 0-7603-0437-8 (pbk.: alk. paper)
    1. Miata automobile—Performance. I. TItle.
TL215.M45G37   1998
629.222'2—dc21   98-48733

On the front cover: As a project sports car, the Mazda Miata is unmatched in reliability, tuneability, and the availability of factory and aftermarket parts. With just a little care and money, any Miata can be made into the sports car of your dreams, be it a weekend racer or a super-hot street car. You're only limited by your budget and your imagination.

On the back cover: Under the Miata's skin lies a sports car whose sophistication has been compared to the legendary Porsche 911: light, technologically pure, and strong.

Cover & interior design by Rob Ebersol

Printed in the United States of America

Contents

Introduction

This book has been writing itself since the Miata's introduction in 1989. Hundreds of thousands of enthusiasts around the globe have been tinkering, fiddling, hammering, and generally messing around with their Miatas since then, and this has resulted in a particular wealth of information about just what can be done to this special little car. This book has been written to serve as a record of the current state of the Miata tuning world.

I had the good fortune to be present at the inception of the Miata. I was a studio engineer for Mazda's U.S. think-tank in Southern California, and the Miata was a project our team took special care in designing. I have since left Mazda to found the Miata Club of America and to start *Miata Magazine,* of which I'm the founding editor.

The basic details of the Miata make it a very special sports car, even in stock form. Like all good projects, however, as solid a foundation as the Miata is right out of the box, improvements can be made to tailor it to one's special needs. It has come to the point where Miatas are being modified so regularly that we felt this book would serve as a useful guideline for owners and enthusiasts alike.

The bulk of the information contained in this book comes from two main sources: the research and development conducted by myself and the Miata Club of America staff, and the input from thousands of Miata owners and racers over the last eight years. The Miata Club, started in November 1988, has actually served as a clearinghouse for Miata enthusiasts since before the car's introduction. It has equipped itself with the technology necessary to perform all sorts of performance measurements and studies. Modifying automobiles is both an art and a science, but performance measurement is most certainly a science.

I can't tell you how many times someone has called the Miata Club office, exclaiming that they'd just added such-and-such a part and that their car felt much faster, when, in fact, our own dyno tests showed the part in question to actually reduce the Miata's horsepower. Seat-of-the-pants data is no data at all. We at the club are very careful not to inject opinion into test data, but we will offer opinions on installation ease, overall performance "feel," and how well a modification integrates with the Miata's character.

The second—and sometimes more important—source for information on modifying Miatas comes from the enthusiasts themselves. Literally tens of thousands of letters come into the Miata Club office each year from dedicated Miata owners (seat of the pants notwithstanding). They relate their experiences, good and bad, with various products. Recently, we have been getting more and more dyno tests on various products from our work and from owners around the globe. In addition, the Miata has been heavily raced all around the world by some of the most aggressive and clever tuners in the business. This has taught us all some great tips and tricks. From this massive database, we've distilled down a reliable set of recommendations and put them down in this book.

I hope you find your experience with the Miata an enjoyable one—it's pretty hard not to have fun with these cars. I also hope the words and pictures in this book help you to avoid some wrong turns and encourage you to maximize your Miata's potential. The best piece of advice I can offer is to just get going and dig in.

Happy Motoring!

Norman H. Garrett III

The Miata Development Story

You almost had to be there to believe it. Mazda in the mid-1980s was riding high. Sales of RX-7s were topping 60,000 units per year. The 626 and 323 models were selling like mad. The trucks had a popular niche carved out for themselves. The yen was strong against the dollar. Mazda was running like an athlete—and looking to expand its position as the No. 3 Japanese automaker. Since 70 percent of its sales came from the North American market, the Hiroshima-based company decided to open a design studio in America, to staff it with some clever Americans, and hopefully to create some U.S.-specific automobiles.

One of the first ideas was to recreate the MGB. It had only been three years since that car had disappeared from the U.S. marketplace in 1980. In that final year, MG had sold 40,000 Bs, even though by that time it was heavy and outdated. The Triumph Spitfire was discontinued during the same period, and soon there were no British sports cars left in the U.S. market. It was ironic to the product planners at Mazda that the very cars that created the affordable sports car niche in this country were now extinct—and that this seemed to leave a wide opening for someone else.

Bob Hall at Mazda Research and Development (R&D) first understood that if MG could sell 40,000 lightweight sports cars in America per year, Mazda could easily sell that many. Mazda was one of the few manufacturers that knew how to make a profit on just

40,000 units, and Mazda had a proud front-engine, rear-wheel-drive history to work from. Thus, the Miata concept was born, initially referred to as the P729 project.

The initial design phase went pretty quickly—basic layouts and shapes were decided upon within 12 months. Since there were no direct competitors (other than the upcoming midengined Toyota MR2 and Pontiac Fiero), a small Mazda sports car could be designed without constraints other than cost and market position. The RX-7 was moving upscale, leaving a nice little corner of the market for the Miata to have for itself. Thus, Mazda was free to optimize the Miata for the passionate few, rather than compromise its design for the mass-market appeal.

Each design team member was a confirmed sports car nut. Among them, some 76 different sports cars had been owned, ranging from Austin-Healey Bugeye Sprites to Lamborghini Countachs. Designing a small sports car was simply a matter of each member suggesting his favorite feature of his favorite sports cars: a curvy hood; a short shifter with great feel; a twin-overhead-cam, four-cylinder engine (the rotary would have had the wrong character); a front-engine, rear-drive layout; and a convertible top, for sure. Item by item, examples of the best were brought to the table and studied for inclusion into the P729 project.

Miata project team members (left to right) Chin, Garrett, Hayashi, and Hall with the "P729" clay model at Mazda's Southern California design studio. Budgets were so tight that the viewing yard consisted of temporary tents erected in the company parking lot.

The soft top was modeled after the finest on the market, the Fiat 124 Spider's. The shifter was targeted to be the mix of a Jag E-type's "snick-snick" combined with the smoothness of a used BMW 7 series. The engine styling was inspired by the Alfa Romeo four-cylinders of the 1950s and 1960s. The exhaust note was tuned to mimic the MGB. And on and on. Without the need to carefully place the Miata in the marketplace, the P729 project designers had free rein to make each feature of the car fit the sports car ideal.

The styling was to be both classic and modern. Mazda wanted to evoke as much of the classic-car emotion as possible, but realized that some younger owners would be seeing the Miata as a totally new idea. Mazda designed the car so it would look two years old when it was introduced, and still look two years old when a decade had gone by. Tom Matano, the studio head, knew exactly how to accomplish this critical task. Aside from being one of the most skilled designers on the planet, he understood the process, both politically and mechanically, to get the Miata to where it needed to be. Without him the Miata would be a very different car, and probably a less appealing one, if it were to exist at all.

The goals were simple to define, but difficult to follow through with. In practice, designing a lightweight sports car for the U.S. market in today's regulated automotive world is a great feat, especially because of government-mandated or market-demanded necessities such as 30-mile-per-hour crash tests, 50,000-mile emission warranties, 36-month bumper-to-

The author at the wheel of a running prototype based on an early styling model. The undercarriage was from a Mazda GLC station wagon. The car was built by, appropriately enough, a British design firm. Note the right-side driver's position.

bumper component warranties, and so on. Fortunately, Mazda put enough engineering might behind the task and kept the cost-cutters at bay while staying true to the project's underlying goal.

The Miata's package is a study in engineering density. In a large sport car, such as a Corvette, packaging all the necessary hardware is difficult enough. Trying to do the same in a sports car with a smaller chassis throws compromises at the designers right and left. Fuel tanks, catalytic converters, spare tires, heating and air conditioning systems, and others all become very difficult to fit into a small package. Keeping the "sports car" soul alive is sometimes impossible (for examples of failure, look at the latest Ford Capri or the Honda Del Sol).

The end result of the Mazda's efforts on the Miata package was a lightweight sports car (2,182 pounds) with a willing engine (116 horsepower) that had a perfect front-to-rear 50/50 weight balance when the driver was in place, had rear-wheel drive, and a simple convertible top, that sold for $13,500 when it was introduced in July 1989 as a 1990 model.

Since that time, more than 450,000 Miatas have been sold worldwide—nearly half in the United States alone. It has spawned the world's largest single-model car club and has set class lap records at nearly every race track around the globe.

Stock Performance Values

Right off the showroom floor, the Miata is a great performer. Cornering, road feel, overall handling, and even acceleration are all excellent for the small sports car niche it falls into (or has reinvented). Here's a summary of how a stock Miata can perform, both in its 1.6-liter (1989-1993) and 1.8-liter (1994-on) forms:

Miata 1.6 liter:

Acceleration, 0-60 miles per hour: 9.1 seconds
1/4-mile acceleration time: 17.0 seconds at 81 miles per hour
Top speed: 112 miles per hour
Braking, 60-0 miles per hour: 137 feet
Cornering force: 0.87 G on standard tires
Slalom speed (*Road & Track* magazine): 62.4 miles per hour
Weight: 2,182 pounds
Weight distribution (with driver in car), front/rear: 50/50

Miata 1.8 liter:

Acceleration, 0-60 miles per hour: 8.4 seconds
1/4-mile acceleration time: 16.5 seconds at 86 miles per hour
Top speed: 119 miles per hour
Braking, 60-0 miles per hour: 132 feet
Cornering force: 0.87 G on standard tires
Slalom Speed (*Road & Track* magazine): 62.4 miles per hour
Weight: 2,293 pounds
Weight distribution (with driver in car), front/rear: 50/50

While many owners simply buy their Miatas for Sunday drives, most use them for daily commutes and weekend racing or touring. The cars have proven to be nearly bulletproof, with no single item showing up as a catastrophic weak spot.

As a sports car, it's been an unqualified hit—and as a basis for further modification, it's nearly unparalleled in today's market. From springs and sway bars to turbochargers and superchargers, just about anything that could be added to a car is available for the Miata to personalize and customize it from stock.

After the Miata had been on the market for nine years, Mazda updated the line with a new car for model year 1999. The core principles still apply: lightweight, affordable, well engineered, fun. The formula will play itself all over again as the sports car market flocks to its favorite poster child: the Mazda Miata.

Miata Engineering Details

To appreciate the Miata fully, you have to go beyond the stylish exterior and peer beneath the surface. While the shape is certainly pleasant to look at, the engineers were sworn to the ideal that the car should drive as well as it looked.

There was a phrase posted on the wall of the engineering department that told the story of how the Miata was to feel on the road: "Oneness between horse and rider." To create this "oneness," some critical decisions needed to be made up front. Mazda was committed to reducing the weight in all of its cars and had made great advances in the science of building lightweight automobiles. At this time, Mazda's R&D budget was greater than that of Porsche, Mercedes, and

BMW combined, so some heavy artillery was aimed at all the many engineering challenges that stood between the blank drawing board the P729 project engineers started with and the ideal sports car the Miata would become.

The first challenge came from the chassis department: A convertible has to be strong to prevent unwanted vibration. The Miata was one of the first cars to use computer modeling for the entire structure, resulting in a much lighter and stronger body-chassis assembly than that of any previous convertible. Strength was put in just the right places (front and rear bulkheads, door sills, and so on) to create a firm foundation for the suspension to work from. To reduce the final weight further, the project engineers liberally used plastics and aluminum. One of the largest front body panels, the hood, has an aluminum skin for light weight (just as many British sports cars did, including the MGA). To further reduce weight at the extremities, plastics were used in the bumper cores.

When it came time to choose the suspension design, a classical approach was tried. Up to that time the Japanese auto industry had been on a patent binge, creating more and more complicated systems to solve problems. This trend was reversed on the Miata, as Mazda went to the old school of double-wishbone suspensions both front and rear. These had

Tom Matano (far right) contemplates the second Miata clay model, during a studio presentation to management at Mazda R&D. Matano's dedication and vision pushed the Miata through some of its toughest times. The target price in 1985 was $9,000— back when the yen was 250 to the dollar.

been the choice of great sports cars for years and would provide the optimum camber patterns during cornering.

Then the decision was made to rigidly connect the engine-transmission assembly to the rear differential. This brought a few different benefits: The typical drivetrain windup and release during on-off throttle maneuvers would be greatly reduced, the total powertrain structure would be much more rigid, and the assembly time could be reduced. This type of torque-tube powertrain structure was previously the province of considerably more expensive sports cars, such as the Ferrari Daytona, the Porsche 928, and even the C4 (and now C5) Corvette.

The engine itself started life as a standard 1.6-liter four-cylinder used in the Mazda 323, but it received a number of improvements, thanks to the capable hot-rodders in Mazda's engine department. (Remember, these were the guys that got the rotary engine to work.) The rotating masses (crankshaft, rods, pistons) were lightened to improve throttle response. The compression ratio was raised to 9.4:1 for more power across the rpm range. A windage tray was added to the aluminum oil sump to reduce drag on the crankshaft from frothing oil. The four-valve cylinder head was ported for optimum horsepower and torque, and the camshafts were aggressively shaped to maximize flow at high rpm (and, on the 1.8-liter engine, they were made hollow for lower weight). As a result, the Miata 1.6-liter engine created 116 horsepower at 6,500 rpm and 110 pounds-feet of torque at

Under the Miata's skin lies a sports car whose sophistication has been compared to the legendary Porsche 911: light, technologically pure, and strong.

5,500 rpm—that's 72.5 horsepower per liter, pretty respectable for a factory production effort. As a historical, nonemission legal comparison, an MGB at its best made 50.2 horsepower per liter; an Alfa Romeo 2000 2.0L four-cylinder DOHC engine produced 61.0 horsepower per liter (1973-1988); and a 1963 Jaguar XKE engine (DOHC 3.8L) produced 70.1 horsepower per liter.

Multiport fuel injection was used to maximize power and decrease emissions, rather than a less-expensive throttle-body injection system. Carefully designed intake-tract resonance chambers were used to accentuate low-end torque. A tubular, low-restriction stainless-steel exhaust header was created, and the downstream system was treated to a high-flow catalytic converter and a well-tuned muffler. In fact, great care was taken with the exhaust note so that the Miata could be instantly recognized as a classic sports car.

The engine tuning followed a scheme to maximize power while giving an ever-increasing sense of acceleration. This makes the Miata fun to drive and gives the driver the impression of more power than is actually there. The rate of acceleration has a subtle increase to it, leading to a "sinking into the seat" feeling as you go up the rev range in a particular gear. This acceleration-of-acceleration is called "jerk" in engineering terms, and is used in the Miata to make it all the more entertaining. To quote David E. Davis of *Automobile* magazine, "I have never driven a Miata and come away wishing for more power, but every time I drive a Z3, I find myself hankering for additional horsepower." The two cars have similar power outputs (although the Z3 is 400 pounds heavier), but the torque and gear ratios of the Miata are matched to optimize driving pleasure.

In the overall picture, the Miata drivetrain has a definite Alfa Romeo influence in engine theory, even down to the cam-cover styling. But at the core of the system is a rock-solid piece of Japanese engineering that's proven itself well over the last nine years. Even after nearly a decade of heavy racing campaigns, the Miata is regarded as a long-lived machine. Owners regularly pass the 200,000-mile mark, and racers go season upon season without a major failure.

In the rest of the drivetrain, the gearshift is of special note. The goal was to have the smallest shift pattern and lowest shift effort possible. The end result is the most acclaimed shift mechanism in today's market. Mated to the gearshift is a close-ratio transmission that's well matched to the engine's torque curve. At the back end, a limited-slip differential using viscous couplings was optional for superior traction during sharp cornering and acceleration. Later, a Torsen differential was made available starting with the 1994 model year. These are the state-of-the-art limited slip differentials that use a complicated gear set to equalize rear-wheel torque and provide smoother and stronger power transmission than typical clutch-pack or viscous clutch differentials.

The final product of the project team's hard work was a car both beautiful in looks and beautiful to drive.

As the starting point of a project sports car, the Miata is unmatched in reliability, tuneability, and the availability of factory and aftermarket parts. With just a little care and money, any Miata can be made into the sports car of your dreams, be it a weekend racer or a super-hot street car. You're only limited by your budget and your imagination.

Miata Variations Year to Year

As great an effort as the Miata was when it went on sale in July 1989, Mazda has found ways over the years to make evolutionary changes to the car that make it even better. The following is a historical list of the significant engineering changes made to the Miata:

July 1989:   The 1.6-liter Miata goes on sale around the globe as a 1990 model.

Limited-slip differential and hardtop are optional.

'91 model: Antilock brake option added. Automatic transmission option added.

'92 model: Rear subframe brace added. Rear defroster and headliner added to hardtop. Remote trunk release standard.

'93 model: Minor logo changes.

'94 model: Minor facelift and new interior. Passenger-side airbag is standard. Engine size increased to 1,840 cc. Horsepower is up to 128 at 6,500. Camshafts are hollow. Alternator and water pump belt changed to a four-rib poly-vee. Fuel injection system is new, with a hot-wire airflow meter. Exhaust gas recirculation is added to control nitrous-oxide emissions. Fuel pressure valve raises injector pressure during hot restart. Oxygen sensor goes to heated style. Oil cooler added at filter base. Second gear gets improved synchronizer. Brake discs are enlarged front and rear. Front subframe brace added. Substantial rear subframe bracing added. Cockpit brace added between shoulder harness pivot points. Alloy wheels are now 14x6 inches (width increased 0.5 inch). Gas tank enlarged to 12.7 gallons, up from 11.9 gallons. Flash-to-pass feature added to stalk switch.

'95 model: Oil gauge changed to "lo-hi" type.

'96 model: On-Board Diagnostics II (OBDII) compliant engine control system added. Various sensors and control items are added to accommodate this change, including a second oxygen sensor behind the catalytic converter. Horsepower is up 5 to 133 horsepower.

'97 model: No major changes.

'98 model: No such animal; the redesigned Miata was introduced as a 1999-model car.

Driving a Miata (Fast)

Any book about performance should contain something about enjoying the fruits of your labors. The Miata is one of the most fun cars on the road, and for good reason. In the following chapters you'll see how careful Mazda was to design the ultimate lightweight sports car (LWS). Before we get into that, however, let's briefly discuss how to enjoy that car in any form, stocker to shocker. As good as the Miata is, it can be improved through the mechanical modifications described in these pages, but the one modification that will improve your Miata's performance most of all involves the nut that holds the steering wheel—you.

The Miata is all about poise. Designed to be one of the finest cars in a corner, it rewards smooth and deliberate driving. It also forgives foolishness and inattentiveness, which lulls many drivers into sloppy habits of early apexes and early shifts.

Even stock, the Miata has more potential than most of us can begin to realize. It starts when you get into first gear. Poor shifting in a drag race can make a Miata over a second slower through the traps, so forget improving the engine for a minute and let's concentrate on improving how you use it.

Randy Pobst, two-time national champion in a stock Miata, referred to the car as an ideal setting for a driver to learn. "Driving a Miata in a race is a finesse experience," said Pobst, "like sipping tea with your pinkie raised. Very neutral, no manhandling. Brakes are

Miatas have been raced around the world with great success. Here, Rob Ebersol, racing director for the Miata Club of America, drifts his 1991 model through a high-speed corner, showing the balance for which this car has become famous.

very firm—easy to modulate. Balance and light weight allow it to carry speed through corners. Great roll centers. Pure fun!" Randy echoes racers and owners across the globe.

Your first step in becoming a better Miata driver is raising your consciousness of what the car is doing. On the way to the store, don't fret over the white-or-wheat dilemma; instead, pay attention to how your Miata is reacting to your driving and the road. For the best drivers, this consciousness is second nature. Fortunately for the rest of us, it can be practiced on every drive we take.

Once you understand how your Miata reacts to your inputs and changes in the road, you can anticipate those reactions in time to do something about them. There's a wall at the edge of each car's cornering, braking, and acceleration limits; knowing the height and breadth of that wall requires study and investigation. Once you know where these edges are, you can eliminate most of the surprises and allow yourself to rise to your Miata's level of performance. And yes, you read that right: Most Miata drivers use only a fraction of the Miata's true performance potential, probably less than 50 percent. Don't feel bad: Most Miata racers only reach about 90 percent. If they were reaching 100 percent, they'd probably have jobs in Formula One.

As the driver climbs the performance-driving ladder, each rung becomes exponentially harder to reach. With every step, the time needed to act and react is nearly cut in half—not to mention that confidence drops off rapidly when the driver enters a new territory. But this isn't about reaching the full performance potential of the car, it's about driving the car as though you were at the edge. Driving the car correctly at

A Miata is happiest when in motion, as are its owners. Precision steering and suspension designs make this a very rewarding sports car to drive.

seven-tenths is challenging and rewarding enough, particularly in a Miata, and that's part of its charm.

One of the things that's so wonderful about the Miata is its neutral character. Some of the world's most revered sports cars are just as notorious for their alter egos—their nasty habits at the limit that can catch the average driver unaware. For example, all but the latest Porsche 911s are notorious for lift-throttle oversteer, meaning they have a tendency to swap ends when the throttle is lifted in a turn. Mazda totaled three Porsche 944s while studying what *Car & Driver* then called the "best handling car in the world." Go past the edge, and many cars bite—and bite hard. The Miata doesn't exhibit any of these Jekyll-and-Hyde traits. It's perfectly neutral, giving the

Three Different Approaches To the Same Turn

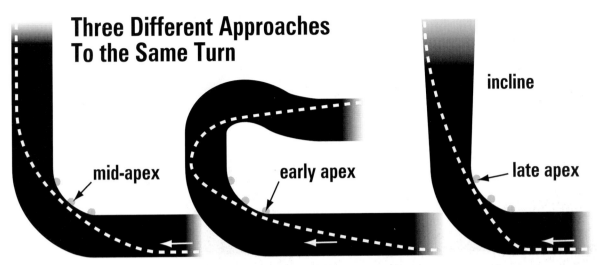

mid-apex

early apex

incline

late apex

1. Turn preceded and followed by a long straight— A mid-apex is compromise between retaining speed from the preceeding straight and allowing early throttle for high speed entry onto the following straight.

2. Turn preceded by a long straight and followed by a series of short straights and turns— The early apex allows the driver to maintain his high speed from the preceeding straight for a longer time by extending the straight into the turn. Since the first turn is followed by a tight turn, a fast exit speed is not necessary.

3. Turn followed by an uphill turn— A late apex allows the driver to begin the following straight sooner, thus accelerating sooner. This provides the needed speed uphill to maintain momentum.

You have to consider what comes after a corner to determine the best apex. It's all about momentum in a 120-horsepower sports car.

pilot fair warning when it feels uncomfortable. But for a generation of us raised on less-sophisticated sheet metal, learning this softer, more subtle language takes serious study.

There are a few fundamental issues a driver needs to remember in a performance-oriented situation. At any given point, the tires can only deliver a certain amount of traction—that's basic, right? Ideally, all of the available traction will be used in whatever function the tires are performing at a given moment. Under braking, it would be nice to dedicate 100 percent of their traction to slowing the car; in a turn, 100 percent of their traction would be great for resisting lateral g-forces.

But in reality, you're always combining these functions. During braking, you'll also probably be turning in for a corner—but asking the tires to use 100 percent of their traction for braking and another 25 percent of their traction for cornering means you've asked for more than they can give. The tire will lock up and slide. For this sequence to work properly, the driver must ease his or her demand for one function to "free up" some traction for the other. The adhesion released from braking duty (by easing off the brakes) can then be put toward steering the car into the turn.

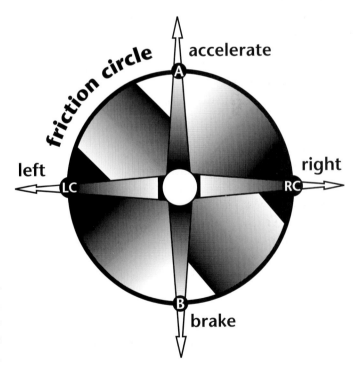

friction circle

accelerate

A

left

LC

right

RC

B

brake

A tire can only hold against so much pushing, whether it be pushing the car ahead, holding it back, or turning it right or to the left. Cross over that "wall" and the car will skid in whatever direction it was going.

*What happens when you take a Miata to 110 percent.
A moment's bravado can result in a world of hurt.*

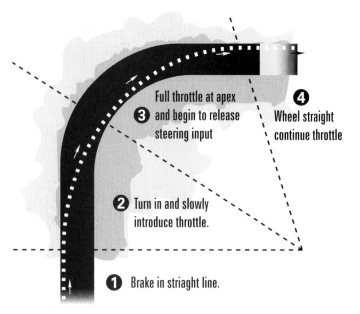

3 Full throttle at apex and begin to release steering input

4 Wheel straight continue throttle

2 Turn in and slowly introduce throttle.

1 Brake in striaght line.

Since tires have only so much traction, racers do their braking in a straight line and then carefully introduce throttle and steering inputs as they traverse the corner.

For this reason, it's essential to remember the following process when driving the car from a straight, through a turn, and into another straight: throttle, brake, turn, throttle. The beginning driver should try to segregate these functions to prevent lockup and potential spins, while still keeping the overall motions smooth and flowing. Also, keep in mind that the subtle driver is rewarded with a fast, controlled vehicle. A violent action usually produces a violent reaction or, at best, creates additional friction on the tires—thus stealing traction or decreasing momentum. Violent motions may look fast, sound fast, and even smell fast, but they are not fast! The noisiest driver around a course is also usually the slowest.

Make yourself comfortable in the cockpit. Sit upright to provide a good view of the track. Grip the wheel lightly, and keep your elbows bent. Always look ahead; if you're gazing at the turn you're already in, you won't be prepared for the next one. You need to take in all of the visual information, but concentrate on the road ahead, particularly toward the end of a straightaway. This will actually shorten the path you take.

Because the Miata is relatively low on horsepower, it requires the driver to follow these basic rules even more than a car that can make up for your cornering mistakes on the straights (you never re-create the lost time; it takes a minimum of three corners to make up for one messed-up corner). Conservation of momentum is the key. Study the track and take note of the turn characteristics and the straights preceding and following them, the hills and how they relate to the turns and straights, the surface quality, and the track width. A smart driver will take all of these factors into consideration,

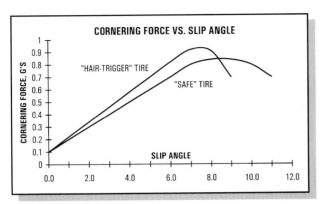

A tire makes its maximum cornering force when operating at a slight amount of "slip," meaning that the carcass is aimed in one direction but the contact patch has a degree of slip, or distortion. Go much past the maximum slip angle a tire can withstand, and the traction available drops off dramatically. Performance tires sometimes can corner harder, but their traction drop-off can only be described as "hair trigger" when their slip-angle limit is exceeded. A less capable tire might actually be more fun to drive because you can "play" at the limit more predictably.

and then drive through each portion of the course based on where the largest gain is to be made. For example, a very tight turn may be taken in a variety of manners, depending on what precedes and follows it. If this turn is preceded by a short chute and followed by a long downhill straight, then the driver should brake early and apex late (just to define terms, a normal apex is what is called an apex that occurs before two-thirds of the way through a corner; even hitting the center of the corner is an early apex), maximizing the length of the following straight and allowing very early throttle application. The more time you spend accelerating, the faster you'll be going at the end of the next sequence.

But suppose this tight turn is preceded by a long straight and followed by a short chute or more turns? Then the driver should brake late, maintaining his or her top speed for as long as possible. If this same turn was followed by an uphill section, the driver should brake earlier and follow a traditional line to maintain momentum up the hill. Although this would sacrifice some speed from the previous straight, it would allow a much quicker ascent up the hill—a real killer in a Miata.

A Miata at rest has the weight of its chassis divided equally among all four wheels. As the car accelerates, some of the weight transfers to the rear, adding grip to driving wheels—which most view as an advantage of rear-drive cars. When the Miata slows, weight shifts to the front tires, adding grip. Here's how to take advantage of this tendency while braking:

Load Transfer
The gray area represents the dissapation of the car's weight among the chassis. The darker the area, the heavier the load.

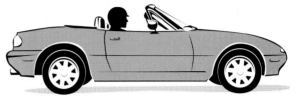

At Rest Load is distributed evenly among the front and rear.

Acceleration Load moves to the rear, providing added traction for rear drive cars.

Braking Load moves to the front, providing additional traction for steering input.

The gray area represents the dissipation of the car's weight along the chassis. The darker the area, the heavier the momentary load.

Maximizing slip angles is the name of the game in racing. The car in front has all four tires at optimum slip angles, in what is called a "four-wheel drift." The car following has its rear tires past the optimum slip angles and has lost traction at the rear, a condition known as oversteer.

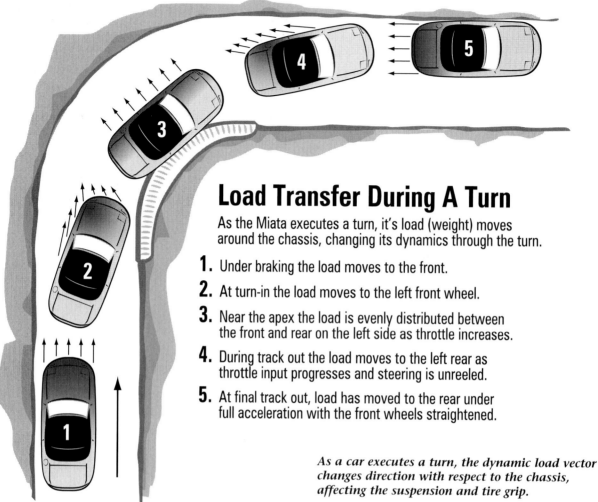

Load Transfer During A Turn

As the Miata executes a turn, it's load (weight) moves around the chassis, changing its dynamics through the turn.

1. Under braking the load moves to the front.

2. At turn-in the load moves to the left front wheel.

3. Near the apex the load is evenly distributed between the front and rear on the left side as throttle increases.

4. During track out the load moves to the left rear as throttle input progresses and steering is unreeled.

5. At final track out, load has moved to the rear under full acceleration with the front wheels straightened.

As a car executes a turn, the dynamic load vector changes direction with respect to the chassis, affecting the suspension and tire grip.

Upon entering the braking zone, slowly introduce braking, and progressively increase your braking pressure as you continue through the zone. This progressive braking avoids upsetting the Miata by gradually transferring load to the front wheels. Once the front springs are compressed, nosedive stops and the Miata readily accepts increased braking force. But if the driver jabs on the brakes all at once, weight is hurriedly thrown to the front wheels and quickly overloads the tires. If the tires don't skid, the driver will experience excessive grip at the front and a substantial loss of grip on the rear. The end with less grip (rear) will continue moving forward, causing the car to swap ends.

At the end of the braking zone, release the brakes slowly and smoothly. Immediately initiate the turn-in for the corner, taking advantage of the grip still residing in the front wheels. With most steering input provided at the beginning, aim the car toward the apex and ease in the throttle. The idea is to use a little steering input to get in and out of the corner, maximizing the allowable throttle input.

Now the weight begins a transition from the front to the rear with a preference on the outside wheels. This weight transfer will induce a drift and continue to rotate the car toward the apex. The advantage to throttle steering is that the vehicle is accelerating during the turning process. The sooner acceleration begins, the greater the speed maintained throughout the entire sequence. Think of this early acceleration as lengthening the straight. The throttle is wide open at the apex and the driver begins unwinding the steering wheel.

That's the drill for the track, but this entire procedure can be easily carried out on the street by understating all the actions. Your goal is to make the process second nature. At that point, the driver can concentrate on the details rather than the fundamentals.

Besides practicing on your daily commute, you can also autocross. This is a form of racing that resides in a parking lot decorated with pylons. Autocross may drill the driver in these procedures a dozen times a minute. The Miata is at home on the autocross course, and will prove the perfect assistant to furthering your driving education.

Modification Issues

With a car that's won as many awards in stock form as the Miata has, it would be negligent of any book on modifications not to discuss how to avoid messing up a good thing. Making a Miata better is a little like improving a good omelet recipe—subtle changes are best. Keep the following in mind when choosing which modifications to make and which aftermarket manufacturers to buy from.

Effects on Drivability

"Drivability" is an industry term that describes how well an engine starts, runs at idle, accepts an opening throttle, returns to idle after a full-throttle run, and so on. Most of us can remember the emissions-controlled carburetors of the 1970s and 1980s that had terrible drivability. Now that the Yugo is gone, all new cars sold in the United States have fuel injection of some sort, and drivability—at least on new cars—has become terrific. The Miata's drivability is even better than most, so before you start modifying yours, carefully plan the modifications to preserve the excellent drivability that Mazda engineered into it.

Many hot-rodders will profess a tolerance of lumpy idles, stumbly cold starts, hunting and pulling in the midrange, and occasional stall-outs at idle. We don't consider these traits normal for any level of modified Miata. Carbureted, highly tuned race engines that live at wide-open throttle may be forgiven these traits, but there's nothing about making a Miata faster that requires any loss in drivability. If a Miata has these symptoms, something is wrong.

Not every aftermarket manufacturer follows this dictum. Some tuners in the aftermarket may have gotten away with sloppy drivability for years, but today's emissions laws have pretty much stopped the abuse of the customer. If an aftermarket part meets emissions requirements, it pretty much follows that the drivability will be near or equal to factory standards.

EPA Issues

Fortunately and unfortunately, we live in a time when the emissions of our vehicles are controlled—and in some states heavily controlled. But in addition to cleaning the air, the regulations that have been imposed on auto manufacturers since the 1970s have also led to great improvements in fuel management and drivability in the 1990s.

Much of the Miata's impressive specific output (power per cc) actually comes from lessons learned in the fine-tuning of production engines to meet federal emissions regulations. The computer-controlled fuel injection system—which is more or less mandatory for a car to meet modern smog standards—is, unto itself, a vast improvement over the carburetors of old. When we measure the air/fuel ratios of a Miata engine throughout its rpm range, we find it to have near-perfect mixtures at all speeds at wide-open throttle. Certainly, there's no trick that will make a more powerful Miata by richening up the mixture—as many might assume, based on their experience with older cars.

As we look at aftermarket products that change horsepower output, we have to be sensitive to how these changes will impact the emissions of the engine. Particularly in California, emissions are regulated and measured on a regular basis, and it's illegal to install anything that will improve performance but increase emissions at the same time.

The California Air Resources Board (CARB) has become the gatekeeper of emissions regulations for the entire aftermarket industry. CARB has set up requirements that after-manufacturers have to meet to be eligible to sell their products in California, and their testing procedure is largely based on the federal tests that the EPA uses to qualify big-time car makers. It's a three-bag emission test on a chaise dynamometer where a car is driven "along a simulated city highway cycle starting from a cold start." The emissions from the vehicle are collected in one of three bags, and the pollutants are measured. If the aftermarket device causes a weighted increase of more than 10 percent in the production of hydrocarbons (HC), carbon monoxide (CO), or NOx (nitride oxides), it fails.

Currently, the remaining 49 states simply have an equipment rule, meaning that you can't remove any emissions-related equipment to increase the performance of a car. This is a much broader rule, but certain states, such as New York and others, are currently considering adapting the tougher CARB standards.

In general, it's the Miata Club's position that if an item can't meet the CARB regulations, there may be some question as to how well that system has been thought out. The

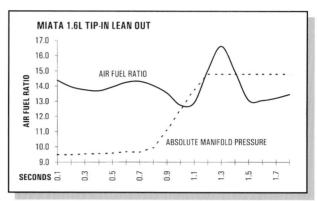

Drivability problems hide in odd places. When a 1.6-liter Miata's owner cracks open the throttle (called "tip-in"), the fuel injection system goes lean for a moment. The problem self-corrects in about a second. Aftermarket tuners don't always worry about these small details, or even know about them.

The EPA is concerned with how much additional pollution an aftermarket product creates when installed. Here, a Miata undergoes a certification test to qualify for sale in California.

last thing you want is a fuel-management system that doesn't reliably control the air/fuel ratio, and the CARB test isn't so onerous that a well-engineered performance system can't meet it. So we tend to look at CARB certification as a litmus test; as such, we'll, for the most part, be covering CARB-approved devices in this book. Of course, there are certain high-performance, "for-racing-only" devices that work quite well in the off-street environment, and we'll cover these as well.

Torque Versus Horsepower

For decades, we've all been fed horsepower numbers as the definitive measure of an engine's performance. The marketers have played into the myth that the higher the horsepower, the faster the car. Some clarification is necessary on this subject.

When it comes to moving a car down the road, horse-power is useful in creating a maximum top speed. As the frictional loads of the machinery, the resistance of the road, and the drag of the wind all pile up against the engine's output, it is horsepower that does the work. However, overcoming the inertia of a car and accelerating it up to that speed is a function of torque, not horsepower. To sum it up, torque is the pulling force against inertia that gets you up to speed, while horsepower is the pushing force against limiting drag that keeps you at that speed.

You see where this is going: For real-world use, you want to maximize torque in a street Miata, not horsepower. Torque will give you the low 0-60 times you're after, give you the passing punch you need, and make your launches from a stoplight more rewarding. Horsepower helps you going up a mountain or reaching top speed in a track environment.

More precisely, it's the area under a torque curve that best describes an engine's performance when it comes to acceleration. Peak torque values are nice to know, but you don't drive around at 5,500 rpm all the time. You accelerate by engaging the engine to the wheels and driving from 1,500 rpm, through 2,500 rpm, up past 3,500 rpm, all on your way up to 5,500 rpm. The total area under the torque curve shows the amount of "work" an engine can do.

The peak horsepower number, on the other hand, merely shows how much the engine can push at that particular rpm. If top gear is matched to the engine so that you're near the horsepower peak when you near your top speed, all is well. But this matching doesn't always occur—which is why some cars can go faster in fourth gear than in fifth.

Back in the heyday of the American muscle car, everyone compared horsepower, looking for best top-speed numbers. In today's world, the focus is more on acceleration, which requires torque. Don't mix the two up—horsepower in a Miata is good for climbing mountains. The thrill through the gears comes from torque.

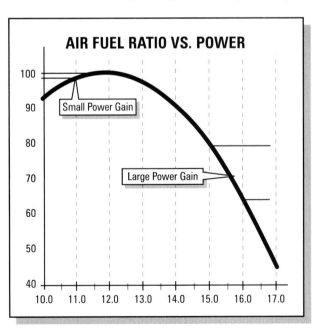

Peak power comes in at air fuel ratios between 12:1 and 13:1. Notice, however, how less-sensitive power is if you aren't exactly at the right mixture when running at 12:1 versus running at 15:1. Don't spend thousands hunting for half of a ratio point if you're already close.

We'd all do better to start thinking of this area under the torque curve as the true measure of an engine's output for acceleration. A single horsepower data point doesn't really describe what an engine will do for you out in the real world. Nor does expecting too much from a widget that improves your horsepower by four units. What does it do to your low rpm torque? To take it to the limit, the weight of the vehicle divided by the torque-curve area would give the most accurate comparison of how a car might accelerate.

Seat-of-the-Pants Tolerances

When you get down to it, 3 horsepower on a 120-horsepower engine is not very much. Avoid getting too excited about gains under 5 horsepower—the seat of your pants won't feel much improvement under this. Of course, cumulative improvements are important, so adding a performance air filter, for example, to a high-flow muffler would be a good strategy.

Statistically, most dynamometers have an error factor of at least 2 percent, which is 2 to 3 horsepower on a Miata engine. If a maker claims its widget adds 2 horsepower, question the testing method. It would take a test field of 50 cars to get a confident, reliable measurement of a 2-horsepower gain on a Miata. Regardless, you'd have to install around five items with 2-horsepower gains each to make any noticeable difference. This is not to discourage you, only to keep your expectations in line with reality.

Cost Per Horsepower

Nevertheless, horsepower figures can be a useful tool, particularly in measuring the value of a particular modification. Dividing the cost of the item by the horsepower increase provided gives you a good idea of where to spend your money for the most return. In general, we live in the time where the "sweet spot" of the cost/horsepower curve is around $40 per horsepower.

For a Miata, a $160 muffler can give you up to 4 horsepower, coming in at around $40 per horsepower. On the other end, a supercharger kit can give you 60 extra ponies for $2,400, or the same $40 per horsepower. Something like capacitive ignition wires might give 1 horsepower and cost $100 or so. With a cost ratio of $100 per horsepower, these might be something to put off for a long while. Of course, if an accessory has other benefits—and these can certainly include glamour appeal or bragging rights—hard and fast rules like cost per horsepower go out the window. Having the latest electronic gizmo on your engine has a lot of entertainment value, and that's what some folks are in it for. After all, it's all about enjoying your car.

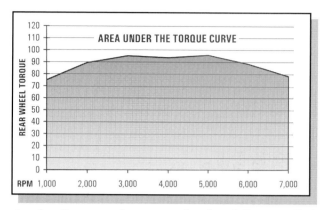

Accelerating a car from rest takes "work," as supplied by the engine. The total amount of "work" available is known as the area under the torque curve from low to high rpm. Since you don't run your car at a single rpm, your goal is to maximize the area under this curve to maximize acceleration. Peak horsepower or torque numbers mean less than you think for street cars.

An E Production racing motor. When you go racing, you have to stop worrying about cost per horsepower. Every little detail is needed to maximize power, because the person racing next to you has spent all his or her money, as well.

For this book, the focus will be on items that increase the performance of the total vehicle. There's an old question: "Speed costs money; how fast do you want to go?" It still applies. And keeping in mind the drivability, EPA and CARB legality, horsepower testing tolerances, the difference between torque and horsepower, and cost per horsepower of various modifications will help answer that question and guide you in making sure all your modifications are improvements.

Wheels and Tires

One of the best things you can do to improve the looks of a Miata is to change the wheels. The stock tires and wheels are 14 inches in diameter, and the stock tire size is 185/60x14. Going to a 15-, 16-, or even 17-inch wheel can improve the looks immediately. However, due to some severe engineering constraints, it's also one of the fastest ways to ruin the handling of a Miata.

The Miata wheel has three critical specifications: hubcentric collar diameter, weight, and offset. If you change any one of these three off from the original Mazda design, you can begin to degrade the Miata's fine handling, rather than improve it.

Hubcentric Collar Diameter

To ensure that the wheels stay centered on the hub, Mazda provided a collar, as is typical in the automotive industry. The collar is on the hub and centers the wheel as you place it over the four lugs. In the old days, we relied on the lug nuts themselves to center the wheels—which is not always the most reliable method. The hubcentric collar on a Miata (all years) is 54 millimeters in diameter. The first thing to consider when buying an aftermarket wheel is to ensure that the hubcentric collar diameter matches this 54-millimeter dimension.

Weight

The Miata's factory alloy wheels are some of the lightest wheels ever installed on a mass-production car. The original alloy wheel from 1990-1993 weighs just 12.3 pounds. In addition, Dunlop, Bridgestone, and Yokohama were commissioned to create special lightweight tires for the car (the original equipment Dunlops weighed 16.5 pounds—very low). All of these address the critical issue of unsprung weight.

The springs and shock absorbers in the suspension support the body and chassis as the car moves down the road, but they do not support the wheel, tire, and brake assemblies. Thus, it behooves the suspension designer to keep these "unsprung" pieces as light as possible, allowing them to react quickly to road inputs. A heavy tire-wheel-hub unit has a lot more inertia when it is deflected upward by a bump in the road than a light unit does, and all else being equal, this extra inertia will keep the heavier unit out of contact with the road longer, which of course is clearly a bad thing. Low unsprung weight also lessens the jarring effect that the tire-wheel-hub assembly has on the rest of the car. Like a light kid on one end of a seesaw, the motion of a feathery unsprung assembly contains less force to jostle the rest of the car than the motion of a heavy unsprung assembly. To this end, the Mazda engineers worked very hard (and successfully) to lower the weight of the tire-wheel-hub assembly. That's one of the reasons that the Miata is so surefooted.

So, if you increase the weight of the tire-wheel-hub assembly, the car's handling and ride will both deteriorate. As much as the suspension is controlling the 2,000-pound weight of the chassis in a Miata, the suspension is also controlling the 200 pound of wheels, tires, and hubs. Increasing that weight taxes the bushings, the shocks, and the springs of the system. The point of all this? That it's pretty hard to beat Mazda on this one, at least when it comes to performance.

The original Miata alloy wheel is patterned after the famous Minilite alloys of Britain. When we sent over the first clay model of the Miata (from the studio in Southern California) to Mazda's headquarters in Japan, we sneaked a pair of Panasport wheels (the Minilite knockoff) on one side to give the corporate guys a hint. They took it and ran, creating a wheel that was even stronger and lighter than the Panasport, thanks to the removal of one spoke (the Miata wheel has seven spokes, versus the Panasport's and Minilite's eight). The final weight of the factory alloy is 12.3 pounds— a very light piece. In addition, Dunlop, Bridgestone, and Yokohama were commissioned to create special lightweight tires for the car (the stock Dunlops weigh 16.5 pounds, which is very low). These wheels and tires help minimize the Miata's unsprung weight.

Beginning in 1994, Mazda created an even lighter sport wheel, the five-spoke alloy, weighing 10.3 pounds. These wheels are highly prized by showroom-stock racers because they reduce the unsprung weight and thus make the handling that much better.

Later still, wheelmaker BBS created a special-edition 15-inch wheel using a high-pressure forging process. This good-looking basket-design alloy weighs only 9.6 pounds. However, these are very rare and hard to find—and very expensive. The little-known fact from the racing crowd is that the absolute lightest factory wheel is the polished five-spoke

The hubcentric collar centers the wheel perfectly on the hub. It also makes for a good place to hang the wheel while you hunt for the lug nuts. Make sure this area stays clean, or the wheel will bind on the hub. Spray a light shot of WD-40 on the collar any time the wheel is off, but don't get oil on the brake disc surface.

alloy of the 1994 and later M-Edition (the polishing process removes considerable mass). So if unsprung weight is something you're concerned about, the 1994 and later alloys provide the best options, particularly when polished.

What will happen if you go to a 15- or 16-inch wheel-and-tire assembly that weighs more than the factory unit? It's often a step backward. As an example, one popular 15-inch aftermarket alloy wheel with a 15-inch 205/50 tire weighs roughly 48 pounds. This compares to the stock 1994 and later wheel-and-tire weight of about 27 pounds—that's an 82 percent increase in unsprung weight, which seems a pretty high price to pay for good looks.

This won't bother everyone, but for the serious enthusiast looking to maximize his or her Miata's road-holding characteristics, increasing the unsprung weight is the wrong direction to go. There's no denying that a Miata can be drop-dead gorgeous with 16-, 17-, or even 18-inch wheels, but you

The famous original Miata alloy, one of the lightest cast wheels ever put on a production car. These were factory standard on A- and B-Package Miatas from 1990 to 1993.

The engineers at Mazda sharpened their pencils for the 1994 facelift of the Miata and shaved even more weight from the standard alloy wheel. These wheels, installed from 1994 to 1997, make the best wheel for the money for Miata racers.

Wheelmaker BBS was commissioned to create a special edition wheel for the Miata. It was produced in a 14-inch diameter in 1992 for the black-on-red SE cars. It also appeared in a 15-inch diameter for the Merlot M-Editions in 1995. The 15-inch version is the lightest of all Miata wheels, but difficult to find.

Racers love this wheel, the polished M-Edition wheel, which is even lighter than the regular alloy. Very rare and expensive.

have to balance this aesthetic gain against the almost inevitable loss of performance. It's either show or go when it comes to Miata wheels; you can't have both in one set of wheels and tires. Of course, a few folks have a dress-up set of wheels for daily driving and some 1994-1997 alloys shod with race rubber for autocrossing or driving events. Maybe that's the best compromise of all.

Offset

The most difficult dimension in the Miata's wheel-design package is its offset. Mazda created the Miata wheels with a 45-millimeter offset to make room for the brake calipers and

to fit into Mazda's family wheel system. Unfortunately, 45 millimeters isn't a standard number in the industry. Most aftermarket wheels have 35- to 37-millimeter offsets, and therefore don't match the Miata system. These wheels will physically bolt to the car and even look correct, and to the casual driver, no untoward behavior will result. But to the critical enthusiast, this 10-millimeter difference will create unacceptable handling quirks. The salesman at the tire dealer might gloss over this point, but when your bushings are shot and you can't stand the way your car darts around since you got those hot wheels, don't blame Mazda—blame yourself for using the wrong wheels.

A certain amount of respect has to be given to the Mazda engineers who designed the Miata suspension. Some of the best suspension engineers in the world reside in Hiroshima, and they laid their best talents on the Miata. The Miata has so little unsprung weight and such good suspension geometry that messing up the balance becomes noticeable in a hurry.

Another critical area of front-suspension stability is the kingpin axis inclination line and the way it intersects with the contact patch of the tire. Now this all sounds very technical, but simply put, we're talking about where a line drawn through the center of the upper and lower ball-joints intersects with the pavement. That intersection should come in the dead center of the tire's contact patch when viewed from the front. This is called a "zero scrub radius" (see illustration next page).

If the contact patch's centerline is inward or outward of the kingpin axis' intersection with the pavement, you've effectively created a small lever arm in the system (see the illustration). Since the forces from the chassis enter the suspension through the contact patch of the tire, it's only going to be balanced when the geometry of the suspension intersects that patch evenly; an off-center intersection leaves the tire constantly trying to twist the suspension into a toe-out condition. This puts a continual load on the bushings and, in addition to introducing strange motions at the wheel, will simply wear out your suspension rubber more quickly.

On a manual-steering car, this small torque arm can become very noticeable when hitting one-wheel bumps. The steering wheel will literally jerk a half of an inch or more as the front wheel encounters the obstacle. Mazda spent millions of dollars developing the Miata suspension to avoid exactly this kind of bad behavior. With the simple choice of an incorrect offset on your aftermarket wheels, you can negate all that hard work. Power-steering cars are less susceptible to this characteristic, as the power-steering rack masks a lot of kickback. However, your bushings will still be feeling the ill effects, and the wear rate of your front suspension will be increased.

More critical than the wear considerations, the contact patch isn't kept in perfect alignment with the pavement, and the Miata will end up with wiggly, darty driving characteristics. It's not major or even dangerous, but it is tiring and

By far the most popular aftermarket wheel for the Miata has been the 15-inch Panasport. These have an offset of 37 millimeters, not optimum, but the looks are classic sports car.

unnerving. Mazda created a car that isn't tiresome to drive fast and frequently; in short, the wrong wheels mess that up.

Incorrect offset becomes an even greater issue when the unsprung weight is increased. The worst combination possible could be a heavy 16-inch wheel with the industry-standard 35-millimeter offset. Not only is the lever arm created, but now it has 20 or so extra pounds working on it. After about 20,000 miles of this, your suspension bushings will be softened up to the point that the overall handling will be noticeably compromised. Owners with stock tires and wheels, springs, shocks, and sway bars can expect 80,000 miles or more out of the stock bushings. As you change any of the previously mentioned components, the bushings degrade in a faster and faster fashion.

Experience with the Miata Club's 1990-model project car showed that even using lightweight Panasport 15-inch wheels, Koni shock absorbers, and performance sway bars has left the bushings pretty hard-worked after only 40,000 miles. Pay attention to the feel of your bushings, so that you don't end up with a rattle-trap car that you can't enjoy; if things get loose or "crashy" over bumps, change out those bushings.

So are you locked out of 16-inch wheels and tires? Not at all. Still, you have to realize that some performance sacrifices will be made. You've already decided whether your Miata is a tool for driving 100 percent of the time, or if you're willing to accept a small sacrifice in roadholding to have a

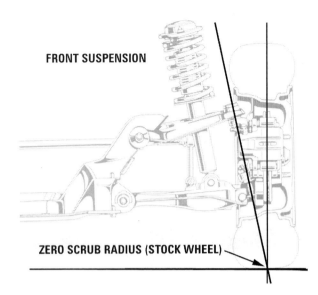

FRONT SUSPENSION

ZERO SCRUB RADIUS (STOCK WHEEL)

The scrub radius is carefully designed on a Miata's front suspension to be zero. This keeps road irregularities from affecting the steering precision.

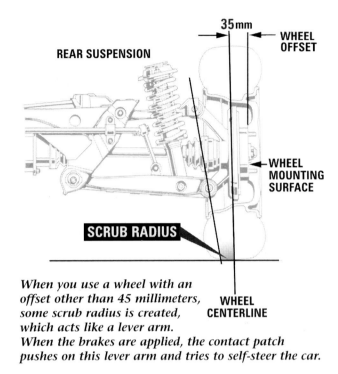

35mm

WHEEL OFFSET

REAR SUSPENSION

WHEEL MOUNTING SURFACE

SCRUB RADIUS

WHEEL CENTERLINE

When you use a wheel with an offset other than 45 millimeters, some scrub radius is created, which acts like a lever arm.
When the brakes are applied, the contact patch pushes on this lever arm and tries to self-steer the car.

more attractive car. This choice is simply something we have to live with because of the 45-millimeter offset of the Miata. It's not a handicap per se; with the factory Mazda offset, the Miata is one of the best-handling cars on the market. But with that handling comes the need to respect the original design of the car.

Discouraged yet? Sorry; it only gets worse. Just about every 15- or 16-inch wheel sold today comes with an offset of less than 38 millimeters. We only know of one 15-wheel (from Panasport) that is relatively light and has a 45-millimeter offset. Thankfully, it's an attractive eight-spoke wheel with a polished aluminum finish—a nice look. As for the others, many are great for the street, but keep your old alloys around for serious driving events.

Tires

The Miata comes with a lightweight 185/60x14 inch steel belted radial tire. It is the author's opinion that all of the stock tires installed by the factory are good for everyday commuter-style use, and more than sufficient for the day-to-day life of a passenger car. However, the only time you'd see these tires on a race track would be if they were laying horizontally and used as crash barriers.

Right off the bat, the best way to improve the Miata's handling is to change its tires. You can improve your roadholding by a demonstrative amount by switching to even an inexpensive performance tire such as the Dunlop D-60 or the Yokohama A509. The Mazda Club has been working with

these tires for years and has found them to have excellent performance on the Miata. Both of these tires can be purchased locally or by mail order for under $70 each, and sometimes much less.

If you want even more performance, you can upgrade to a premium tire such as the Dunlop SP-8000, the Michelin Pilot 4, or the Yokohama AVS. These tires will provide even greater roadholding and performance and work well on the stock tire sizes.

Wider Is Better?

It seems the first thing everyone wants to do with their Miata is put on wider tires. The widest tire a Miata really likes to see is one with about 195 millimeters of tread width. Due to the light weight of the Miata and its particular suspension setup, a wider tire doesn't automatically create more grip or response. You can get away with it, but there are diminishing returns for wider tires on a street Miata. There are two reasons for this. One is the mass of the tire—the increase in weight that comes with an increase in width. The other is the size of the tire itself, and this comes down to something called the heat content or thermal mass of the tire. The wider the tire, the more rubber it contains; ergo, the longer it takes to heat the tire up to operating temperature. All tires perform better at their operating temperature than they do cold, although we have been told recently by tire engineers that tires made

The RAS Engineering project car. It has 17 x 8 TSW Hockenheim wheels with Dunlop SP8000s sized at 215/45-17 (front) and 235/40-17 (rear). The rolling diameter is 23.5 inches which raises the overall gearing by 5 percent for greater top speed.

with today's newer compounds are less sensitive to this than they used to be. Even so, it's our experience that anything over 195 millimeters in diameter is window dressing on a Miata, unless you have made strong engine modifications that require wider tires and will also force the tires to get hotter, quicker, or if you are racing.

It must be remembered that a tire is a floatation device. The stock-width Miata tires inflated to 28 pounds per square inch (psi) are each holding up 546 pounds per corner, and each deflects against the pavement to create a 19.5-square-inch footprint. Changing to a wider tire won't increase this contact patch, but merely change its shape.

A wider tire will change the orientation of the contact patch, which will affect cornering ability. Up to a 205-millimeter-wide tire can help a Miata handle better, but to get to this width, most owners are using wheels that are heavier and have the wrong offsets. This negates whatever benefit the wider tire brought about.

Vibration Concerns

One more comment on the tire issue. Miatas are very sensitive to tire pressure. If your car has a 65-mile-per-hour vibration, the first thing to check is that you're running 28 psi in each tire. Twenty-six to 28 psi is right where the Miata likes to have it; above and below this sweet spot you're almost guaranteed to create vibration on some cars.

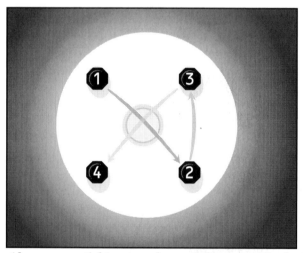

Always cross-tighten your lug nuts to prevent brake-disc warpage. Go in steps, getting tighter and tighter each time. Final torque is set at 70 foot-pounds.

The pre-1994 Miatas are particularly sensitive to this. Beginning in 1992, Mazda added some frame stiffeners to the rear subframes of the Miata, and in 1994 Mazda stiffened the chassis further, greatly reducing (but not eliminating) the vibration problem.

Go Large

One of the most common questions we hear around the Miata Club office is about the largest tire and wheel that can fit on a Miata. Since Mazda was generous enough to design all these cars with ample space for snow chains, there's a fair amount of room to increase the tire far above the stock 14-inch diameter. Tires as high as 18 inches in diameter can be

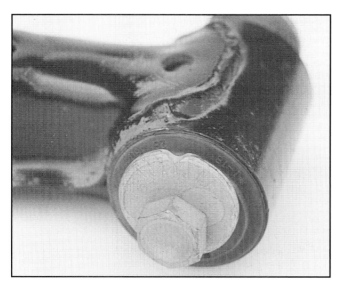

Here is one of those precious bushings that get hammered out of shape when unsprung weights go too high. These are made of rubber and are calibrated for 60,000 - 80,000 miles of dimensional stability with the stock wheels and tires. Put on heavier wheels and tires or drive on harsher than normal roads, and their life will be shortened.

Mazda created a special MX-5 just for kicks and called it the M2 1001. Panasports showed up again, but this time with the correct offset of 45 millimeters, as only Mazda would have them. These are still available in 14-inch and 15-inch diameters.

installed without significant scraping. Of course, when you use something as large as an 18-inch wheel, you have to have a pretty short (low-aspect-ratio) tire to go with it.

The rolling diameter of the stock Miata tire and wheel combination is 22.7 inches. As you increase the diameter of the wheel, you need to choose the tire with a shorter sidewall height so that you can maintain this 22.7-inch overall diameter. This is commonly known in the industry as a Plus One, Plus Two, or Plus Three combination. "Plus One" means

One of the most attractive wheels on a Miata are the Mille Miglia Glide IIs. Shod with 205/45x16 tires, these make for a stylish statement going down the road. Once again, however, the offset is 35 millimeters, and the weight is 20 pounds heavier than stock tires and wheels.

you've increased the stock wheel diameter by 1 inch and lowered the sidewall height a similar amount. "Plus Two" means 2 inches more wheel and 2 inches less tire, and "Plus Three" of course means 3 inches both ways. You can go as much as a Plus Four (18-inch wheels) on a Miata, but by then you're going to have to have a very specialized tire with a minimum of sidewall height.

The sidewall height (described as "aspect ratio" or "series rating") of a tire is the number following the slash in the size designation. A 185/60 tire has a 60-series rating. The 60 number relates to the sidewall height as a percentage of total tire section width. Thus, a 185/60 tire has a sidewall height that's 60 percent of 185 millimeters, or around 111 millimeters. This is an approximate measurement that's mostly used as a guideline, since inflation, load, tread depth, and other factors will all affect the actual sidewall height on the car.

To go to a Plus One tire-and-wheel combination on a Miata requires that you reduce the sidewall height by going to a 50-series tire. Therefore, if you want to use 15-inch tires on a Miata, you'll be changing from a 185/60x14 stock tire to a 195/50x15. The rolling diameter of the tire of this configuration will be somewhere in the 22.6-inch range, which is more than close enough. The rolling diameter of each tire can be obtained from the tire manufacturer's specification sheet, which is available from your retailer (see the sample from Dunlop).

It's important not to go much past 23.2 inches in overall tire diameter on a Miata. Anything taller than this will upset

Round and black, and so much mystery. Making tires is an art more than a science. Finding a tire that works is not as easy as it seems. Here is a shot of one of the best tires for a Miata coming off the line, the Dunlop D-60 A2 series.

While they may be pretty, wire wheels are among the heaviest wheels on the market. Along with the classic looks you can get classic handling (bumpy ride, skittering around corners) to go with it.

your speedometer accuracy and affect your gear ratios to a noticeable extent. The larger the rolling height, the taller the effective overall gear ratio will be and the less brisk the car's acceleration will become. On the other hand, a taller rolling diameter will increase the car's top speed, assuming you have the horsepower to attain it. A stock Miata runs out of horsepower long before it runs out of gears, however, so increasing the tire size won't make the average Miata go any faster on the top end.

A problem arises when you get into the 16-, 17-, and 18-inch tire sizes (all else being equal) in that the minimum width available is generally 205 to 215 millimeters. Pursuant to our earlier arguments about tire width, going to a 17-inch wheel with 215/45x17 rubber is purely a cosmetic decision. We won't lie to you; it will be a gorgeous combination. But from a driver's standpoint, you will have lost some of the handling characteristics that came with your Miata. You will also lose a lot of the Miata's inherently pleasant ride characteristics, as one important contributor to ride comfort is the flex in the tire's sidewall. As the sidewall becomes shorter, more bumps and harshness are transmitted to the wheel and ultimately the rest of the car. The tire itself has less air inside of it, so there is less of a pneumatic spring to isolate you from the road and less air for cooling off the tread. The larger tire usually has more mass, and therefore more material to heat up before the rubber gets to its best "stickiness."

Shake, Rattle, and Roll

The Miata, for all its strengths, does have one particular weakness. Its chassis is very sensitive to what might be called the "radial spring-rate variance" of a tire. When the belts of a tire are laid in the core carcass, there's one point where the belts will overlap. This overlapping area creates a stiff spot in the tire.

All manufacturers deal with this, but certain tire makers are better at controlling this stiff spot than others. In a car as light and sensitive as the Miata, this stiff spot can wreak havoc, particularly in the rear subframe bushings' natural vibration harmonics. In other words, they shake. To avoid the problem, buy tires that have a jointless nylon band (for example, Dunlops). These have a minimum number of belts overlapping to start with.

Since the introduction of the Miata, a percentage of owners have complained of a vibration at 65 miles per hour. Some cars—maybe four out of ten—are more sensitive to this than others. If your Miata is one of these, it's critical that you choose your tires carefully. We have found that the tires mentioned above tend not to induce vibrations. This applies to the stock sizes as well as larger-diameter models.

Unfortunately, if you go down to your local tire outlet and buy an off-brand tire, chances are the new tires will cause a

vibration in your Miata. At the minimum, get a guarantee from the installer that there will be no vibration and, if there is, that they'll change the tires over to a different brand. This is important advice that can prevent untold hours of sorrow or great expense if bad choices are made, so get the guarantee or buy from a dealer who will give one. Tires with a jointless band (Dunlop uses nylon) construction will have much less tendency to vibrate.

On 1990-1993 Miatas, vibration problems can be significantly improved by the addition of chassis stiffeners, as discussed in Chapter 5. But make sure that your tire pressures are near 28 psi to find the optimal compromise between ride, handling, and resistance to vibration.

If you buy a set of high-quality replacement tires, you will see a red dot on the tire sidewall. This is placed by the tire manufacturer to denote the high spot of the tire. To minimize your chances of vibration, have the red dot lined up with the low spot of the wheel. How do you know where the wheel's low spot is? It depends. For stock Miata wheels, the valve stem hole is cut into the rim at the low point, so line up the red dot on the tire with the valve stem hole. For other wheels, consult the manufacturer to find out the low-spot designation.

Make sure to have your wheels balanced on high-speed computer-controlled equipment. Every balancer has a rounding-off feature. Smile nicely and ask the technician to override this—you want your tires balanced to 1/10 of a gram.

TIRE SIZE MATRIX

SIZE	RIM WIDTH	MAX WIDTH	TIRE DIA.	LOADED DIA.	REVS/MILE	WEIGHT
185/60-14	5.0	7.3	22.7	20.40	932	17.4
195/60-14	5.5	7.9	23.1	20.80	916	18.3
195/55-14	5.5	7.7	22.4	20.60	938	19.4
195/50-15	5.5	7.7	22.7	21.00	920	20.3
205/50-15	5.5	8.1	23.1	21.20	906	21.4
225/40-16	8.0	8.9	23.1	21.60	901	20.4

All dimensions in inches or pounds   Source: Dunlop Tire Corporation

Not all tires are created equal. Here are some comparative weights and dimensions of various tires popular with Miata owners. When calculating speedometer error, use the loaded diameter.

Footprint- 215/45-16
Contact Patch=
19.64 Square Inches

Footprint- 185/60-14
Contact Patch=
19.64 Square Inches

Tires float the weight that's on them, according to how much pressure is in them. All you can change with a wider tire is the orientation of the contact patch, not its size.

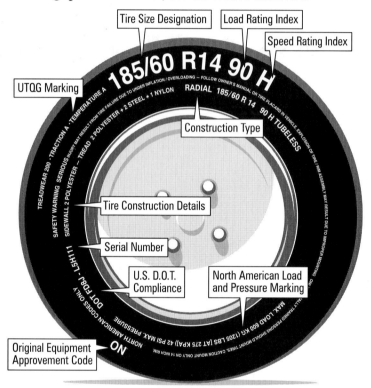

Each tire comes with a set of codes imprinted along the sidewall, according to Department of Transportation (DOT) regulations. Deciphering them will help you know what you are buying.

When buying a tire-and-wheel combination, take a minute to ask the weight of the tire you are ordering and add it to the weight of the new wheel. See how far the total weight goes over 26 to 28 pounds (weight of the stock tire and alloy wheel). Granted, the stock tires are not the best handling, but they are the lightest available. Better handling tires than the stock ones will also be heavier than stock. By comparing the weights of potential replacements tires, you can minimize the weight gain.

Go cautiously into heavier weights. Your total unsprung weight is greatly affected by every pound you add. It is possible to nearly double the unsprung weight on a Miata with a poor choice of wheels and tires—a decision that will greatly degrade the handling of the car.

Now as a point of reference, the mostly new 1999 Miata has 15-inch tire-wheel combinations available from the factory, again in very lightweight forms, and a handful of low-volume Series One Miatas also came with 15-inchers. The bolt pattern and hubcentric and offset dimensions on these 15-inchers is the same as on the stock 14-inchers on all Miatas. These wheels and tires can be retrofitted to earlier Miatas for greater performance without any of the potential headaches of poorly chosen aftermarket wheels.

The Sad Truth

Over the years, a lot of owners have made a lot of changes to their cars and, in the end, have degraded the performance in such a way that they've come to dislike their Miatas. When they sold their cars and looked back on the experience, their final memories were of a noisy, harsh, little car with lots of rattles. Generally they blame Mazda for creating such a vehicle, when in fact 100,000-mile Miatas in stock condition are usually still finely tuned road machines. Careless aftermarket modifications can ruin the character of a good car. With that warning, proceed with caution.

Suspension and Chassis

The core of a sports car's appeal comes down to how it looks, goes, and handles. But even if it's ugly and has mediocre acceleration, it can be forgiven if it handles better than the rest. Sports cars should out-corner regular that's a given. For the Miata, that goal was met and exceeded. Mazda began with a clean sheet of paper, especially when it came to the chassis and suspension, and used all the classic rules to make the car great on the road: good weight distribution, low overall mass, and carefully thought-out suspension geometry. The end result is pretty impressive.

Unequal-length A-arms and coil-over shock absorbers are the most timeless of all suspensions for sports and racing cars (look under any Ferrari). The Miata designers chose this classic combination for a number of reasons. Instead of focusing on patents and marketing schemes, they spent their time designing and tuning a perfectly balanced combination of road grip, low harshness, and predictability at the limit—features that A-arm suspensions have inherently.

The lower arm in the Miata's front and rear suspension is nearly parallel to the pavement, but the upper arm is tilted down toward the center of the car. This introduces camber into the wheel as the suspension compresses, counteracting the lean of the body (more on that later). Another subtle but important point is that the track width in the Miata doesn't change appreciably when the suspension is compressed. Less-sophisticated suspension designs allow large changes in wheel track as bumps are encountered. That might sound like a minor point, but when you hit a dip at 100 miles per hour, having your front or rear track grow by 10 millimeters and then shrink back instantly can spell more than trouble—it can spell w-r-e-c-k.

Mazda had become a master at suspension-bushing design by the time the company introduced the second-generation RX-7, whose rear suspension alone included over 100 new patents. For the Miata, Mazda used some of this hard-earned wizardry to keep the camber patterns on target without ruining the ride. The Miata's bushings are rigid laterally (when pushed toward the car's center) but compliant longitudinally, which keeps ride quality acceptable. This allowed the designers to use stiffer-than-normal bushings without ruining the ride or making a noisy car.

Acceleration and engine braking forces are fed to the road through the rear wheels on most sports cars. These forces act on the rear suspension bushings to create their own set of problems. The infamous hair-trigger nature of early Porsche 911s is due to a toe-out condition during braking or throttle liftoff. Additionally, the forces of engine braking enter the rear suspension at different points than the forces created by the brake disc, greatly complicating the requirements of the design. Mazda's solution to these problems was to design a suspension that has natural toe-in during cornering, which creates a more stable suspension under neutral conditions and tends to damp out the forces of both engine- and brake-induced deceleration. This toe-in is accomplished by locating the upper control arm ahead of the wheel centerline, creating a torque arm when side forces are introduced.

For the tuner, all of this means that the design has to be treated with respect. It's far easier to ruin a Miata's suspension than it is to make it better. Nevertheless, the Miata's suspen-

sion can be improved through the right modifications, but make sure you don't throw the baby out with the bathwater.

Many tuners approach the Miata as they would other cars, and that's their first mistake. Most suspension parts available today are centered around restraining the bad habits of cars, but the Miata comes with almost no bad habits of its own. Suffice it to say that very few compromises were made with the Miata's underpinnings.

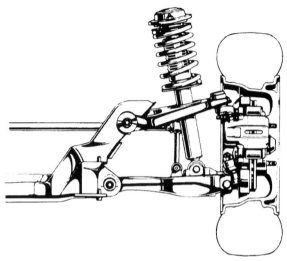

Unlike its competitor, the BMW Z3, the Miata has no carryover suspension parts from other car models. Each part is unique and optimized for a lightweight sports car. Double-A-arm suspension is the classical way to go. The Miata gets this at all four corners.

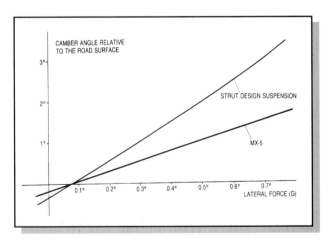

Some of the minor details that suspension engineers worry about. With a suspension having an aggressive camber pattern comes increased tread change during bumps. This can lead to instability. The trick is finding a balance between all the components, and this was done with the Miata.

TREAD CHANGE

When looking at how a suspension keeps the tires perpendicular to the road, the Miata's suspension does a better job than a strut-type suspension. You can see why a strut-equipped car would need a lot of roll control to fix this camber "gain" in a corner.

The bad habits most cars need to have restrained come from heavy unsprung weights, poor suspension geometries, and less-than-rigid chassis. Cars with MacPherson struts up front and solid rear axles (or even semi-trailing arms at the back, as on most BMWs) require the tuner to keep the body from leaning during turns. Thus, they respond well to higher spring rates, super-heavy sway bars, and strange alignment settings. None of these strategies are particularly successful with the Miata. Fortunately, the Miata suspension is actually pretty simple to understand and modify. All the parts are simple to work on, and performance parts are easy to come by. With a little knowledge and a small budget, you can easily tune your Miata to be more in line with your own style of driving, whether that is street or track.

Chassis Rigidity

First, let's talk about the structure that holds it all together. The Mazda engineers who dedicated themselves to designing a new-from-the-ground-up convertible back in the mid-1980s were among the first to use high-powered computer modeling in developing an automobile's entire structure. As a result, the Miata has one of the most rigid chassis of any convertible ever produced. This is particularly important in a sports car, in which the chassis is asked to resist cornering forces and provide a firm base for the suspension.

Adding greatly to the Miata's overall rigidity is a structural beam that runs from the engine-transmission assembly to the rear differential. The purpose of this beam (the Powerplant Frame, or PPF in Mazda-speak) is to tie all the major drivetrain components together. This eliminates the "rubbery" feel that a drivetrain can produce when you're hard on and off the throttle, something a sports car might be doing in a set of twisty curves.

The PPF also isolates the points at which the drivetrain components attach to the chassis. In a Miata, the entire drivetrain is supported by just four points—two on the front subframe and two on the rear subframe. The front and rear subframes, in turn, are mounted to the body in specifically strengthened and isolated locations. This is much more stable than having separate mounts for each of the drivetrain components, and lends a lot to the Miata's overall stability on the road.

Beginning in 1992, Mazda added a rear subframe brace as an evolutionary improvement to the rear subframe. This brace had some effect on reducing the Miata's sensitivity to that infamous 65-mile-per-hour vibration induced by imperfect tires (see Chapter 4). More importantly, the brace made the rear subframe more resistant to deflection under

The Miata's rear suspension has a set of clever bushings and linkage arrangements that prevent rear-wheel toe-out during cornering. When the suspension sees a side load during cornering, the rear suspension actually makes the outside wheel toe-in, greatly improving stability at the cornering limit.

Mazda put the steel in the right places—right down in the floor pan. Here is a cross-section of the rocker panel showing the large size of the beam and the inner strengthening plate.

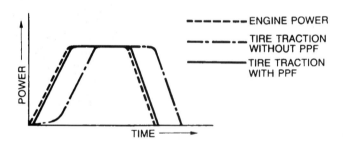

The PPF contributes greatly to the Miata's "connected" feel with the road. Responsiveness is greatly improved.

cornering loads, which keeps the rear wheel-tire combination better aligned with the pavement.

In 1994, along with a minor facelift to the interior, Mazda made more advanced changes to the chassis of the Miata. Front and rear subframes were stiffened and braced, greatly improving rigidity and reducing the flex in the platform. Fortunately for owners of 1990-1993 Miatas, all of these changes can effectively be replicated via the aftermarket. Many aftermarket suppliers sell rear braces that simply bolt onto the existing pre-1994 subframes. Cockpit braces that run between the shoulder-harness pivot points are also available to help stiffen the rear passenger-compartment structure. Also available are front subframe braces that reduce deflection by closing the open tunnel near the control-arm mounting points. All of these updates can be performed at nominal cost on your pre-1994 Miata.

Another way to increase the rigidity of a Miata's chassis is to install a "sport-style bar." These used to be called "roll bars" until the lawyers got involved and everyone had to start calling them something else, just in case someone put one in his or her car and got hurt in a rollover crash anyway. These "style bars" have the effect of stiffening the rear bulkhead to a great degree and can help reduce the 65-mile-per-hour vibration sensitivity at the same time. They generally attach to the towers that support the shoulder-harness pivots just behind the seats. Some also come with rearward supports that tie into the frame rails surrounding the fuel tank. The latter type are used by many driving schools, but they are less popular for street use because they are difficult to use in conjunction with the soft rear window.

If you want to go for ultimate stiffness, a full roll cage (as used by SCCA racers) will tighten your Miata to the nth degree, creating an exceptionally stable platform for the suspension to work from. But for most of us using our cars on

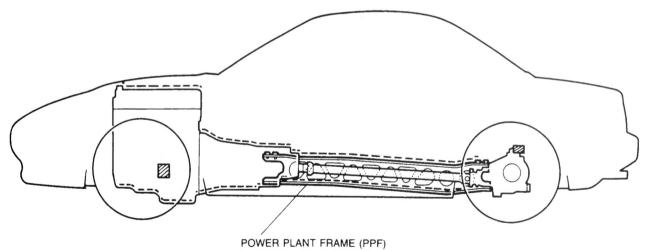

POWER PLANT FRAME (PPF)

One of the nicest style bars is this one from Racing Beat. It has an attractive cover and does not interfere with the soft rear window.

Most style bars hook into the shoulder-harness pivot tower, a very strong part of the Miata's structure.

the street, a true roll cage simply isn't practical, since it complicates entry and egress of the car and operation of the soft top.

The simplest way to improve the structural rigidity of the Miata chassis is to buy and install a Mazda hardtop. A side benefit of the hardtop is that the highway noise is reduced about 5 decibels, which makes for a quieter car on long-distance trips. Many road-warrior Miata drivers taking long trips install their hardtops for the highway portions, and then take them off and store them in their hotel rooms while they enjoy driving around their final destinations.

Strut-tower crossbraces (steel bars that connect the shock tower mounts together across the engine bay) are very popular in today's performance aftermarket. These braces work great on cars with MacPherson struts (thus the term "strut-tower crossbrace") because these suspensions have no upper control arm. The entire lateral load from the upper portion of the wheel hub, plus the shock loads, plus the spring loads, all enter the chassis at the upper strut anchor point. That's a lot of force for the sheet metal of the engine compartment to handle.

As good as tower braces are for some cars, they aren't as useful on a Miata. On a Miata, the hub forces are contained by the upper control arm, and the upper shock mounting point only sees spring loads and damping loads. These are markedly less severe than the lateral loads imposed by a strut suspension, and therefore the Miata sees considerably less flexing at the tops of the shock towers. The double A-arm suspension allows each component to do its specific job—the coil-over shocks damp the ride and hold up the weight on the corner, while the control arms are free to take the massive

Closing the "box" of the engine bay is not as critical on a Miata. Not only is the box already well supported, but the suspension doesn't put its main loads into the shock towers to begin with, because its suspension does not use struts.

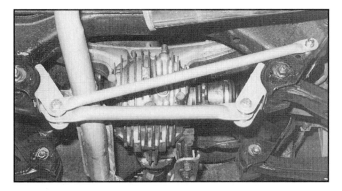

In 1992, Mazda began closing the rear subframe structure with a support bar. Technosports brought out the first retrofittable unit for the 1990 and 1991 cars to update their rear subframe. Note the well-triangulated design. This bar is no longer available.

Brainstorm Products sells this simple subframe brace that does the trick. The bend in the bar allows fitting various aftermarket exhausts—an important consideration.

If you want to really improve chassis stiffness, here's the way to go. A full cage welded to the main crush tubes in the unibody ties everything down solid. Great for racing, impractical for the street.

One of the easiest ways to increase a Miata's chassis rigidity is to install a hardtop. Flex is noticeably reduced and the weight penalty is under 50 pounds.

side loads of braking and cornering. Left to their own specific tasks, all these pieces can be made smaller and lighter for less harshness, less suspension inertia, and lower unsprung weight.

This is another example of how Mazda spent surprising amounts of money in building the Miata, even though it was making an "affordable" sports car. MacPherson struts are cheaper to build and install than double A-arms, and Mazda already had struts on most of the firm's other cars. It would have been an easy matter to adapt the 323's struts and a trailing-arm rear suspension to the Miata, but the end result would have been a machine that drove much less like a sports car. In fact, Ford built that car—it was called the 1990 Mercury Capri, and it is now out of production.

In any case, there just isn't enough force going into the Miata's upper shock mounts to create a lot of deflection in the engine compartment. That isn't to say that these braces are useless on a Miata, just that they should be the last brace you buy. You'll get much more benefit from the various subframe braces or a style bar.

Suspension Modifications: Shock Absorbers

The Miata's chassis is very sensitive to shock-absorber quality and condition. You can choose from the original equipment shock absorbers as available from your dealer, or standard shock absorbers from the aftermarket. After a tire upgrade, the best way to instantly improve your Miata's handling and ride quality is to upgrade to performance shock absorbers.

In 1994, Mazda added a brace between the shoulder-harness pivots. The change was made to increase side-impact strength, but the chassis benefited as well. Shown is the Brainstorm Products part that does the same job for early cars.

For performance applications, there are a number of choices for a Miata—anything from a fully adjustable Carrera racing shock down to the author's favorite, the height-adjustable Koni. Tokico also sells a performance shock absorber, as does GAB and others. See Chapter 13 for more details on race-preparing a Miata's suspension.

Konis are the most popular among the Miata crowd because they are adjustable for damping while installed on the car, and they offer the ability to lower the car while still using the stock springs. (The Mazda-Bilstein R-Package shocks can also be modified at the spring perch to lower the car, but this requires a fair amount of fabrication.) The Konis are easy enough to adjust (seconds per wheel) that temporary tuning can be done at will. A side advantage for any adjustable shock comes when the damper begins to wear. A turn of the knob and any lost damping force can be dialed back in.

How do you know if you need new shock absorbers? The easiest way is to look at your speedometer. If it says that more than 30,000 miles have gone by since you last replaced your shocks, it's time to get new ones, particularly if you're still on the original units. Some aftermarket shocks last longer than the stock units, and some offer lifetime guarantees. The chart below lists various shock absorber alternatives for the Miata.

Changing Your Shocks or Springs

As we've said, the Miata comes with a fairly sophisticated suspension. The price of this is that it's a bit more complicated to remove and replace the shock absorbers than it might seem it has to be. The shocks and springs are in a combined unit called a "coil-over." To replace the shock, you must remove the entire coil-over as a unit, then disassemble the set

away from the car. You'll need a trick or two to make the job easier, which we will describe. You also will need a spring-compressing tool, since the Miata uses coil-over shock assemblies at all four corners. You can use the simple side-hook style or a professional clamp-style tool and an air wrench to make the job easier. The author used the latter for the demonstration shown in the illustrations. The clamp-style spring compressor costs about $180 at an auto parts store. The air wrench simply reduces the turning time for the clamping bolt.

Start by replacing the front shocks. Here's how: Jack up the front of the car, put jackstands under both sides (never just use a floor jack), and remove both front wheels.

The top of the coil-over is held to the car by two nuts (14 millimeters) accessed from under the hood. Remove these first. The bottom of the coil-over unit is held in by a single eyelet that is secured with a 17-millimeter bolt and nut. Remove this nut next.

To get the coil-over out of the front suspension area, you must first disconnect the hub carrier from either the upper A-arm or the lower A-arm. The safest and best method is to simply unbolt the lower ball-joint tongue from the lower control arm. It is held on by two bolts that are pretty easy to access. (The factory manual says to loosen the lower control arm pivot bolts and press down hard on the brake disc to make enough clearance to remove the coil-over. This works, but it's a bit harder and consigns you to a mandatory front end alignment. Another way is to separate the upper

This is an SCCA SOLO II-approved roll bar with rearward braces that tie into the frame rails. This is as serious as you'll want to go for the street, and it is usually necessary for driver's schools. Note the shoulder harness mounts along the cross tube.

Brand	Adjustability	Comments
Mazda stock	none	good performance good street ride
Mazda R-Package	none	high performance stiffer ride
Tokico standard	none	good performance good street ride
Tokico Illumina	damping	high performance
Carrera	height	high performance
Bilstein	none	high performance good street ride
Koni	damping/height	high performance
GAB	damping	high performance
KYB	none	good performance good street ride

Here's one of the two bolts you want to take out when doing a front shock removal. This will free up the hub carrier from the lower A-arm, allowing the shock to be pulled free.

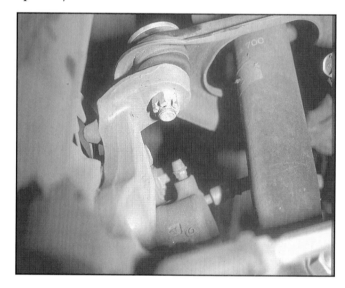

You can open up the front suspension by releasing the upper ball-joint instead of the lower. This requires removing the castle nut and using a special tool.

The shock absorbers (or dampers) on a Miata carry the road springs in an assembly called a "coil-over" (that is, the coil fits over the shock). The main components are the cap, the spring, the boot/bump stop, and the damper itself. A rear coil-over is shown.

ball-joint. this method saves you that $60 for alignment, but you'll have to buy a special tool. That's why the author recommends unbolting the lower ball-joint tongue as the easiest way.) Remove the two bolts from the ball-joint tongue.

After the lower ball-joint tongue is free, turn the steering wheel all the way to one side or the other so that the brake line on the side you're working on is as slack as it can be, and press down on the lower control arm and hub carrier to allow you to get the coil-over out. (When you press the lower control arm and hub carrier downward, the brake line will tighten up and could be broken if enough slack isn't provided.) While this job can be done solo, it's measurably more frustrating that way. Have an assistant use a foot to push down on the brake disc, or use your own, pushing the lower control arm

and hub carrier as low as possible. This will give you enough room to swing the coil-over assembly outward and remove it. Pull the coil-over out through the center of the upper control arm.

When you get the coil-over free from the car, you'll notice a Teflon gasket that sits on top of the upper spring cap. Remove this gasket and clean it on both sides. You'll need to reuse or replace this gasket (it prevents squeaks and chirps as the front suspension works).

Lay the coil-over on the floor, and use your spring compressor to shorten the spring. Take as big a bite as you can on the spring's length—you will need to compress it around 4 inches to relieve the pressure on the cap.

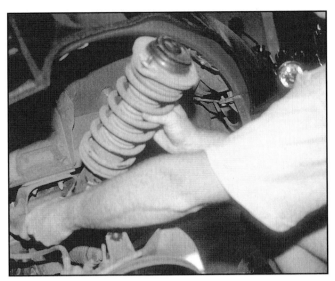

With the lower A-arm free, the coil-over can be pushed down and tilted out of the wheelwell. Be careful so you don't nick the paint!

Once you have the spring compressed enough so that it's not touching the cap or the spring perch, remove the top nut of the shock assembly. This nut is covered with a small plastic lid. Lift off this lid with a knife or small screwdriver. Remove the 14-millimeter nut under the lid. (The spring cap will have to be held from rotating as you loosen the nut.) Once the nut is free, remove the spring cap and the spring.

The shock absorber has a rubber boot covering its shaft. This boot will probably be caught up in your spring compressor. Lifting its lower edge where it attaches over your shock absorber's housing will separate it from the shock, and the old damper can be slid out from the spring. The boot can stay inside the spring if it's caught up.

Insert the new shock absorber into the coil spring and rubber boot. Attach the boot's lower lip over the metal collar of the new shock. Make sure the boot is attached or dirt will intrude into the shock's shaft area.

Put the spring cap back on. The spring cap's hole is D-shaped. Make sure you line up the shaft correctly before you attempt to slide it into the hole. If you have purchased Konis, the spring cap will have to be drilled out to accommodate the new shock's larger shaft diameter. Tighten down the nut that secures the upper spring cap. Some shocks come with their own special nut, since they have a different thread than the stock shaft.

Then, release the spring compressor's tension, paying attention to the alignment of the bottom eyelet to the spring cap's studs: They will have to be 90 degrees out of synch to fit into the car correctly. If you don't get this right, you can

twist the shock's bottom on the car to get it to fit into the lower control arm's receiver, so don't worry. Pay more attention to the spring getting a good seat against its lower perch and the upper cap. It should not be offset or mis-seated.

With the coil-over back together, put the Teflon gasket back in place. Press down again on the brake disc to give you access to put the assembly back into place. Put the bottom in first, then swing the coil-over down and over into place. Keep the lower control arm pressed down as you line up the spring cap's studs with the holes in the inner fender. Put the two 14-millimeter nuts on the spring cap's studs, and torque them to 25 pounds-feet. Then, work the bottom eyelet into the lower control arm's receiver. Get the tongue back into the lower control arm and attach the bolts. Torque them to 65 pounds-feet. Insert the lower eyelet shock bolt and torque it to 60 pounds-feet.

Move to the other side and repeat the procedure. It usually turns out that the first side takes one hour, and the second only takes about 20 minutes.

Then, replace the rear coil-overs. The rears go very quickly if you do them last, having now become an expert at changing Miata coil-over shocks. Be careful that your tired muscles and confident nature don't lure you into a mistake. Take your time to finish the job out right. Since the procedure is essentially the same as for replacing the front coil-overs, it won't be repeated. Keep the following tips in mind, however:

To reach the upper coil-over mounting bolts, remove the spare tire on the passenger's side and the black fuel-filler cover on the driver's side, both in the trunk. Remove the upper nuts with a 14-millimeter socket. The bottom eyelet is secured by a captive nut welded into the lower control arm, so you only have to use a 17-millimeter socket to remove the lower eyelet bolt from the rear side.

After removing the coil-over mounting bolts and nuts, you only have to release the sway bar ends to allow for enough room to lower the control arms out of the way. Again, the shop manual says to loosen the control-arm pivot bolts, but this is unnecessary. As with the front, removing the control-arm bolts would also cause the assembly to go out of alignment. It might be argued that your car should be aligned any time it gets new shock absorbers anyway, and that is largely true. But, if you can't get around to it the week you do these shocks, it's better not to disturb the settings you started with.

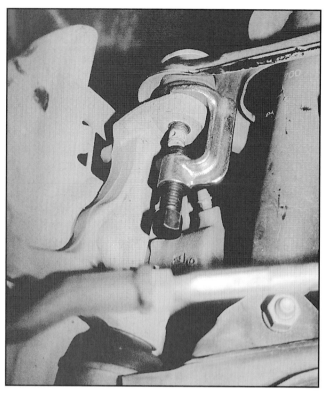

Here is the ball-joint press tool being used to push the joint's shaft out of the hub carrier. A poor man's solution is to use firm strikes upward with a hammer, hitting the A-arm protected by a block of wood (never hit the ball-joint stud). After a few strikes, the ball-joint will release from the hub carrier on most cars (once the castle nut is removed).

A spring compressor is a must. Shown is a very nice tool sold by NAPA stores for under $200. An air wrench really helps here, because you have to turn the pinch bolts many, many revolutions to compress the spring fully.

Alignment

If you start with proper alignment, the suspension will work its magic and even a stock Miata (with good tires) can out-handle most other cars. The Miata comes with one of the most adjustable suspensions out there, which is great for us but may confuse some alignment technicians. If you're having your Miata aligned (we recommend it once a year), copy the adjustment chart from this book and hand it to the technician in a friendly manner. He might appreciate the tips.

Both the front and rear suspensions are fully adjustable for toe-in, caster, and camber. Toe-in is the amount that the tires on an axle point inward or outward toward each other at their forward edges. Most cars run just a bit of toe-in—that is, the tires point a little toward each other when steered straight ahead. This slight amount of toe-in increases stability and makes the car track well down the road. Initial toe-in is necessary because the rubber bushings in any suspension compress a bit when the car is moving, and this compression leads to a slight toe-out in most suspension designs. Braking forces cause the bushings to compress even more, and can create toe-out on its own. Toe-out is a very unstable condition that can cause the car to dart from left to right, even if the toe-out condition is very slight.

As a result, the author recommends a minimum of 1/16 inch of toe-in at the front and rear wheels for road use. For road racing, running 1/8 inch of toe-in on the rear will help out a bit during heavy braking loads. Whether for street or track, these recommendations for toe-in should be used as a general guide, because the proper toe-in for your Miata depends on the total setup of the car and on your driving style. Fortunately, the Miata is so adjustable, an owner can make small adjustments to tune a Miata to his or her liking.

Camber is the tilt of the wheel when viewed head-on, and the Miata is very sensitive to static camber settings. A tire tilted into a corner has more grip than one tilted away from the corner, since the roll of the body will tend to force the inward-tilted tire flatter against the track. Therefore, some amount of negative camber—wherein the tire is tilted inward at the top—is beneficial to handling. Even with the Miata suspension's great camber patterns, the initial settings can get a head start on keeping the tires perpendicular to the pavement. For street use, adjust for at least 1/2 degree of negative camber for the front and rear wheels. In practice, the rear wheels can go to 1 degree of negative camber, but your tire wear will be more rapid. With 1/2 degree you'll still get decent handling and wear on an everyday car.

The racing crowd gets much more aggressive with camber, generally running 1 to 1-1/2 degrees of negative camber in the front and up to 2 1/2 degrees at the rear. The best way

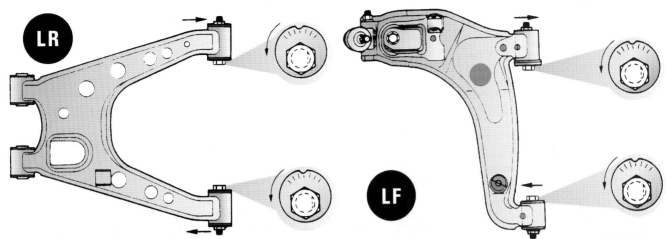

Adjusting the left rear—Rotating the front cam bolt counterclockwise moves the front of the arm in. This produces positive camber and toe-in. Rotating the rear bolt counter clockwise moves the rear of the arm out, producing toe-in and negative camber.

Adjusting the left front—Rotating the front cam bolt counterclockwise moves the front of the control arm in, creating more positive camber and toe-in. Rotating the rear bolt counterclockwise pushes the rear of the arm out, creating toe-in and negative camber. These same adjustments have an opposition effect on the right front wheel. Turning the right front cam bolt clockwise would achieve the same results as turning the left front cam counterclockwise.

to dial the exact setting in is with a tire pyrometer (temperature gauge) and optimized tire pressures. The goal is to have all the temperatures across the tire tread equalized for all four tires on the car. But street drivers don't have to go to this level of detail, and don't get free tires from the manufacturers to replace the ones they burned up in the testing process. Stay between 1/2 and 1 degree negative camber for road use, and you'll be able to generate very high cornering forces and keep the tires on the car for at least 20,000 miles.

When camber is introduced into a tire, camber thrust is created. This is a force coming from the tire's interaction with the road that causes the tire to steer in the direction it is leaning (the way a motorcycle does). If you increase your negative camber much past the 1-1/4 degree mark, you'll be introducing enough camber thrust to affect the dynamic toe settings on your Miata. On cars with a lot of rear negative camber, this results in twitchiness at speed as the outside

wheel moves up and down over bumps. Additionally, as the body leans and the overall negative camber is reduced, the dynamic toe-in will be reduced as well. The suspension bushings relax in the absence of the camber thrust, and the tire will have less self-steering. Granted, this only lasts for a fraction of a second, but think of it happening in a 90-mile-per-hour sweeper and you can see how things might get twitchy. Keep the camber values away from the extremes to preserve a balanced, predictable Miata.

Caster is the angle of a line running from the top ball-joint to the lower ball-joint, as viewed from the side. Think of a chopper-style motorcycle as a motorcycle that has a lot of caster. This affects the self-centering feel of a Miata's steering,

Toe

Toe relates to how the front wheels track down the road— whether they are pigeon-toed or not.

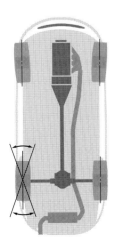

Camber

Camber is the vertical tilt of the wheel as viewed from the front

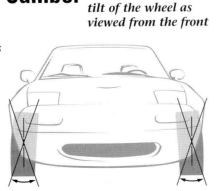

Caster

Caster relates to the "rake" of the front suspension. Think of a chopper motorcycle—that's a lot of caster.

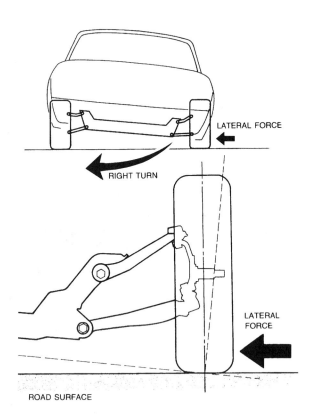

ROAD SURFACE

When a Miata gets into a corner, the lateral force forces the body to roll. This causes the chassis to tilt and the tires to begin to be tilted out of perpendicular alignment with the pavement. It is up to the suspension to counteract this roll-induced positive camber.

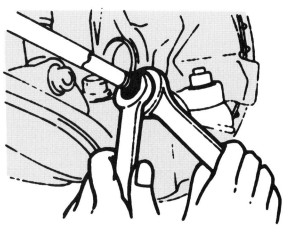

Front toe is adjusted via tie rods. Rotating tie rods clockwise adds toe-in by pulling the front of the hub inward. Because the steering is self-centering, toe adjustment on just one tie rod will leave the steering wheel cockeyed. For quick front-wheel steering geometry changes that are easily corrected, for a day of autocrossing, for example, adjusting one side allows a quick return to the original settings.

The Miata suspension is highly adjustable at all four corners. Mazda made almost any combination possible—the trick is to know how to "tune" the alignment to your driving style.

Rear Toe Adjustment

left wheel	front cam	rear cam
increase	ccw	ccw
decrease	cw	cw

right wheel	front cam	rear cam
increase	cw	cw
decrease	ccw	ccw

Front Camber Adjustment

left wheel	front cam	rear cam
positive	ccw	cw
negative	cw	ccw

right wheel	front cam	rear cam
positive	cw	ccw
negative	ccw	cw

Rear Camber Adjustment

left wheel	front cam	rear cam
positive	ccw	cw
negative	cw	ccw

right wheel	front cam	rear cam
positive	cw	ccw
negative	ccw	cw

particularly if it has manual steering. The Miata has an adjustment for caster, and the recommended setting is to go for maximum caster once the camber has been set. This should come in at somewhere close to 5 degrees.

Do-It-Yourself Alignment

The racing crowd has long relied on portable camber and toe-in gauges to perform quick alignment adjustments at the track. These work well for the casual enthusiast as well. A hand-held camber gauge can be purchased for under $40 and will provide a very accurate measurement of each wheel's camber (see figure). More expensive units are available that will pay for themselves with one alignment. Simple toe-in gauges are available as well that allow you to adjust your front and rear toe settings at home. The accuracy of both of these devices is determined by how conscientious you are. If you go slow and stick to the details, you can do a pretty accurate job all by yourself. However, due to the wide adjustability of the Miata suspension, you can easily make the alignment worse than it was when you started—but nothing so bad that a professional alignment man couldn't fix it. If you like to fiddle with your ride height or camber settings, these are nice tools to have. Remember, changing camber can change toe-in, so you need both tools.

Lowering a Miata

The lower a car sits, in general, the better its handling will be. This is because lowering the body height reduces the torque arm between the roll center of the chassis and the pavement-tire intersection (where the forces come into the

Geometry Counts

During the Miata's development, numerous sports cars were purchased and tested as benchmarks. At the Miyoshi proving grounds, you could find a Porsche 911 Cabriolet, an MGB, an Alfa Romeo 2000, a Fiat X1/9, a Reliant Scimitar, and a Lotus Elan. (Actually, the Miata project had a few Elans, just to make sure one ran when they needed one.)

On one particular day, the test fleet was taken up to a deserted mountain park, and each car was driven up and down by the team engineers. Subjective notes and comments were carefully recorded as the team looked for the right "feel" for the developing Miata. Each of the cars was in good shape, although the Elan had the handicap of very bad shock absorbers on all four wheels. The shocks were shot, in fact, effectively leaving the Elan with no damping to control the suspension's movement.

The cars were thrashed up and down the mountain for eight hours. At the end of the day when comparing notes and making charts in the conference room, the engineers found an amazing discovery. To a man,

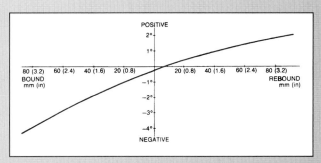

The Miata has one of the industry's best camber patterns. As the suspension is compressed in a corner (bound), the A-arms introduce tilt to the wheel to keep it more perpendicular to the pavement. As the inside wheel of a car has the body roll away from it (rebound), the suspension again introduces tilt to keep the wheel more perpendicular to the pavement for maximized roadholding.

the test group said the Lotus felt like the best-handling car. Even with no shock absorbers to speak of, the excellent suspension geometry and good weight balance of the Elan made it out-handle and out-"feel" all the other cars. Good genes are hard to hide, as the saying goes.

chassis). Study the diagram in this chapter to see how this works.

The force that enters the chassis at the tire is resisted by the suspension and body of the car. The linkages of the suspension cause the car to rotate around a certain point called the "roll center." The vertical distance between the contact patch of the tire and the roll center is a lever, and the cornering forces act on this lever to make the car lean. Lowering the car reduces the lever arm length, thus reducing the amount of body roll. (Astute readers will observe that the roll center moves as the suspensions compress or rebound, but that's a whole other book.)

Mazda chose the Miata's roll centers for a variety of complicated reasons that are beyond the scope of this chapter. Suffice it to say that we can tune it a bit without upsetting the overall balance by lowering the car. Since lowering reduces the lever arm that makes the car lean over, lowering the car performs a sort of "antiroll" function of its own. It is true that the roll centers are lowered as you reduce the body height, and you might think the roll couple would stay the same length. In practice, lowering the body 1 inch only lowers the roll center a fraction of an inch, so the net result is a reduced roll couple.

Recommended Street Suspension Settings

	Front	Rear
Camber	-1/2 to -3/4 degree	-3/4 to -1 degree
Caster	More than 5 degrees	
Toe-in	1/16 inch	1/16 inch

With a do-it-yourself camber gauge, you can accurately measure your camber any time you like. These gauges, under $40, pay for themselves rapidly and are easy to use.

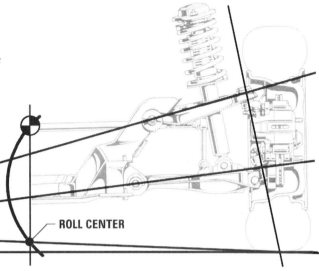

Here is the front suspension diagram of a Miata showing how the roll centers are determined. For a stock Miata, the front roll center is at a point 61 millimeters above the pavement along the centerline of the car. Lowering the chassis also lowers the roll center, but only by a fraction. As the car leans into a corner, the roll centers move as the suspension arms rotate about their bushings.

CENTER OF GRAVITY

ROLL COUPLE

ROLL CENTER

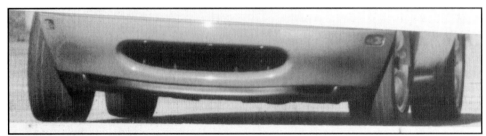

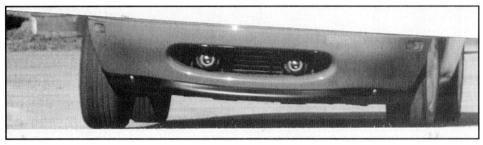

Here is an example of a stock Miata (bottom photo) in a 0.7-G turn. The body rolls 3.4 degrees with the stock sway bars. Note how well the tires are kept perpendicular to the pavement. After installing performance sway bars (24 millimeters at front, 16 millimeters at rear) and lowering springs, 1 degree of roll is taken out for the same 0.7-G turn.

The factory shop manual provides specifications for suspension height, which is measured from the wheel centerline to the fender lip; if you're lowering your Miata, it's important that you end up with even lip heights left to right for the front and rear wheels, respectively. It isn't important that the front and rear heights be exactly the same, although too much disparity can make the car look a little strange. In practice, the rear of a Miata will sit slightly higher than the front.

If you get aggressive and lower your car near the 1-inch mark, you'll also be moving the steering rack downward with respect to the steering knuckle by the same amount. This will introduce what is called "bump steer," in which the geometry works against the rack at each bump. The car will be self-steering, albeit slightly, and your cornering performance will suffer. To counteract this, you'll need to raise your steer-

ing rack the equivalent amount that you lowered your car to reestablish the original geometry. Refer to the fender-lip chart in this chapter and determine how far you are below the shortest recommended height. Space the steering rack upward to counteract the chassis being lowered.

If you decide to lower your Miata, you'll need to decide how to do it. The three most common methods are by fitting shorter aftermarket springs, fitting adjustable-ride-height shock absorbers, and by cutting your stock springs.

Lowering with Springs

For owners looking for the ultimate in performance, stiffer lowering springs and high-performance shock absorber combinations can make the Miata corner as flat as a roller-skate. And the handling can be made more race-car-like than you

Weight Balance

If you're really going to do it right, setting up a car's suspension begins with a balance check. This involves weighing each corner of a Miata to see what weight is being held up by that wheel. In a perfect world, each tire would carry the same weight, front to rear and right to left. Since your Miata has been designed to be pretty near perfect, it should make in interesting exercise to weigh each corner and see what it's really doing.

To weigh our car, the technicians pulled out a simple but expensive set of electronic scales, one for each wheel. We lifted the Miata up and slid one of the transducer pads under each corner and took the weights. Pretty simple if you have the right tools.

We had arrived with the hardtop on, half a tank of gas, and all of this car's assorted aftermarket parts in place (sport-style bar, supercharger, Panasport wheels, and so on). This would give us a real-world view of what a road-going Miata weighs wet (with all fluids on board). We even threw the driver into place to get the total balance (a 50th-percentile American male: 5 feet, 8 inches and 160 pounds). The weights came out as follows, in pounds.

	Left	Right	Totals	Percent
Front	647	596	1,243	50.1
Rear	620	619	1,239	49.9
Totals	1,267	1,215	2,482	
Percent	51.0	49.0		

We were amazed at the result of this study. To end up so close to a 50/50 weight distribution in all planes is a true testament to the Miata's design. Even the driver, who represented 7 percent of the car's total weight, did not upset the balance.

The Miata comes with near-perfect weight balance front to rear and left to right. Checking the balance after suspension modifications is a good way to keep each tire doing its job.

For reference, the car itself weighed in at 2,320 pounds. If we were to eliminate the fuel, the hardtop, the supercharger, and the sport-style bar, we would have come at 2,167 pounds—very close to the published weight of 2,160 for our 1990 model. Those extra pounds are certainly in the wheels and tires. The 15-inch Panasports are slightly heavier than the featherweight stock alloys, and the larger tires are heavier than stock as well.

If we had found the weights were not equal front to rear, we could have considered juggling some small parts. The left to right balance can be adjusted by spring rates, moving parts around, or by using adjustable spring perches on the shocks.

The conclusion is that you really don't need to worry about your Miata's weight balance unless you have added some heavy accessories or have made significant suspension or spring changes. If you're setting up your Miata for racing, you should perform this type of test to see how your car weighs in.

ever imagined—for better or for worse, but usually for the worse. Back when the Miata was introduced, tuners rushed to make shorter and shorter springs with stiffer and stiffer rates. What resulted were a lot of low Miatas with unhappy owners. The basic problem with these springs is that they reduce the available wheel travel, which means that the spring rate must be heavier to keep the suspension from bottoming.

Loss of wheel travel is a bad thing, and not just because the ride suffers from the heavier springs; handling suffers, too. If you stiffen the suspension up so much that the chassis is being vertically accelerated by road bumps rather than isolated from them by the suspension, things get ugly fast. Imagine the car becoming an unsprung mass of 2,200 pounds instead of just the 200 or so pounds divided among the four unsprung corners. Too stiff a spring or sway bar will prevent the Miata's suspension from doing its job, and your tire will be skipping across bumps rather than tracking over them. Remember, a tire in midair has zero traction.

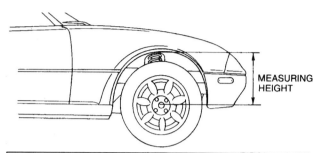

HEIGHT FROM CENTER OF mm WHEEL TO FENDER BRIM (in)	CAMBER	CASTER
328—337 (12.9—13.3)	−0°20' ± 30'	5°16' ± 45'
338—347 (13.3—13.7)	0°03' ± 30'	5°02' ± 45'
348—357 (13.7—14.1)	0°24' ± 30'	4°49' ± 45'
358—367 (14.1—14.4)	0°44' ± 30'	4°35' ± 45'
368—377 (14.4—14.8)	1°02' ± 30'	4°21' ± 45'

The factory service manual shows how to measure the heights of a stock Miata. As you lower the car, the camber naturally goes negative—just where you want it to go for performance.

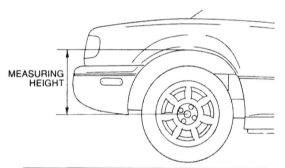

HEIGHT FROM CENTER OF mm WHEEL TO FENDER BRIM (in)	CAMBER CAMBER
345—355 (13.6—14.0)	−1°08' ± 30'
356—365 (14.0—14.4)	−0°54' ± 30'
366—375 (14.4—14.8)	−0°43' ± 30'
376—385 (14.8—15.2)	−0°35' ± 30'
386—395 (15.2—15.6)	−0°30' ± 30'

The rear suspension responds to lower heights in the same way as the front—negative camber is introduced as the body drops.

If you're going to go for a lowered look, there are numerous companies offering short springs that are stiffer for the Miata. You can go as much as 2 inches lower with performance springs, but the ride will suffer markedly in street use. Remember, you'll also be changing the roll centers and sway bar function, so tread carefully when you go to modify a Miata's height. Some's good, but too much is just that.

So how low is too low? Each shock absorber has what's called a bump stop. This is a hard-rubber doughnut inside the rubber boot on each shock. When the outside case of the shock approaches the end of the rod, it would collide steel-to-steel against the shock mount if it weren't for the bump stop. A Miata handles pretty terribly when it's on the bump stops. If you lower your car too much, you'll be on these bump stops in most hard corners with any irregularities. Getting bounced off a corner because your car hit the bump stops at 100 miles per hour is a rude awakening indeed. Beyond that, if the forces of this internal collision become too large, you can crack a suspension mount. The stock bump stops will start to get active if you lower your car more than 1 1/4 inches all around. If you want to go lower, you need to trim your bump stops.

As for tires and lowering, with the car lowered 3/4 of an inch all the way around, in general a 215/50x16-inch tire will scrape in the wheel wells when driving over driveway entrances and the like. Not damaging, but annoying. A 205/50x15 tire will not scrape under any normal circumstance.

Some performance spring manufacturers claim that they have variable-rate springs available for the Miata, but don't be too impressed by this. Your Miata has variable-rate geometry as it comes from the factory. Due to the lever motion of the suspension arms as the stock spring is compressed, the effective ratio increases all by itself. Progressive rates in an aftermarket spring aren't an important feature unto themselves—you already have it.

While fitting shorter, stiffer springs is a popular way to lower a Miata, it is not a wise choice for a street car. If you're racing on a regular basis you may find a benefit from stiffer, lower springs. Even for the racer, however, the disadvantages of these springs often outweigh their advantages, because the Miata was designed with good wheel travel and aggressive camber patterns from the factory.

"Camber patterns" is a term that relates to how the camber of the wheel increases or decreases as the wheel moves relative to the chassis. This is different than the static camber setting made when a car is on the alignment rack. When you go into a corner, the body of the Miata will lean. As it leans, the outer front and rear suspensions are compressed just as if they'd hit a bump. As this happens, the geometry is designed so that the tilt (or camber) of the wheel-tire assembly increases to counteract the lean of the body.

If the wheel-tire assembly stayed perfectly perpendicular to the floor pan of the car, then the tires would roll hopelessly over into positive camber during a turn. For years, the suspension-tuning industry has aggressively fed the market heavy sway bars and stiff springs to counteract body roll, but these are largely aimed at

The well-liked Koni shock absorber has adjustable spring perches that allow a Miata to be lowered while keeping the stock spring rate.

Since the Koni shocks have a larger piston rod, you will need to drill out your cap's center hole (stock setup shown). This is easily done with a hand drill.

cars on which the suspension has poor camber patterns to begin with. In these cases, any effort to reduce body roll results in better perpendicularity of the wheel-tire assembly during cornering. That's why tuners work to keep some cars from leaning at all costs; the ride may suffer, but it's the only way to compensate for the untoward motions of the suspension relative to the body during cornering.

Thanks to the careful design of the Miata suspension, as the outer suspension is compressed during hard cornering, the wheels automatically tilt in to compensate for the lean of the body. This keeps the wheel-tire assemblies pretty much perpendicular to the pavement under any angle of body roll, essentially eliminating the need to keep the body level. The point is simply that body lean is not the enemy in a Miata, but only part of the big equation. While taming body roll may indeed make the car feel more racy and stable—which is not without value—it will do little to improve its actual cornering ability. Stiff springs and heavy sway bars just aren't that necessary in tuning the Miata's suspension.

Lowering with Adjustable Shock Absorbers

Fortunately, there's a better way to lower your Miata than by substituting shorter, heavier springs: shock absorbers that have adjustment for ride height. The Miata's springs are physically mounted to its shock absorbers, held in place with caps at the top and bottom. On some shocks, the lower cap (or "spring perch") can be moved up or down to easily change the ride height.

Currently, two brands of shocks are available with adjustable perches. Carrera Shocks makes a competition damper that has a threaded base for the Miata's lower spring

These are Mazda Competition Department threaded spring perch adapters that allow a wide range of adjustment for ride height. Racers use these at each corner to lower the car and to balance the weight on each wheel, left to right and front to back.

perches, which allows fine adjustment of ride-height at each corner of the car. Koni makes a Miata shock absorber with a C-clip that fits into one of three groves on the shock case; this allows the spring perches to be moved higher or lower, as desired. The center groove matches the stock perch position and thus the stock ride height, while the lowest setting will lower your Miata about 1/2 inch all the way around. This is a nice compromise for daily driving use; you won't be crashing against the bump stops all the time, but you'll also be lowering the car enough to get an attractive stance and a subtle

Is the Miata's Power Steering Too Good?

A few owners complain about the power steering in the Miata. They feel that it provides too much assist. Here's a simple solution: Convert your car to a manual steering for a few dollars and an hour's time.

What does a manual-steering Miata feel like? Run by your dealer and ask for a test drive in a base-model car. At highway speeds, the on-center feel is superb. It's only in the parking lot that you'll be working a little harder. Around corners and at high speed, the manual unit has a finely balanced feel, just enough resistance, and a good ratio for control.

Many owners prefer to change out the power-assisted steering with a manual rack from a base-model Miata. The steering effort is not too difficult to live with, and the on-center feel and road response is greatly improved over the power steering system.

For around $300 you can do the job right and get the feel the Miata designers tried to match with the power steering.

If you have air conditioning on your car, you'll need to install the base-model idler pulley to keep the air conditioning compressor belt in tension after you take off your power-steering pump. The part number for the pulley is BP01-15-940, and it retails for about $31. You'll also need to buy the bracket for this pulley, part number BP01-15-951, which retails for about $57. With a Miata Club discount, the pair come in close to $70. You'll also need a dif-

While the Miata's manual steering effort isn't as high as on some front-wheel-drive compacts, the real test is your opinion in the dealer's parking lot. One tip: Get into the habit of getting the car rolling before you turn the steering wheel. Power steering has lulled us all into the habit of cranking the steering wheel while parked dead. In the nonpower-assisted world, this just isn't done. A little speed will make up for a lot of power-steering fluid.

The replacement procedure from power to manual steering is quite simple. Unfortunately, you can't simply take the pump off a power-steering car and run the rack without assist. The internal gear ratio is too low, so the effort would be far too high.

ferent belt, due to the shorter run. Of course, if you don't have air conditioning, you can simply remove your power-steering pump without a concern about belts and pulleys.

The other obvious part to buy is the manual steering rack. The part number is NA01-32-110 and the retail price is $254.50, but again, a Miata Club discount will get that closer to $200. Remanufactured racks go for around $150.

The whole operation begins with the removal of your power-steering pump and hoses. This is a very straightforward under-hood procedure, but take care to collect any fluid in an appropriate container.

To remove the original steering rack, jack up the front of your Miata and support it with jackstands. Put the wheels in the straight-ahead position and tie off the steering wheel so that it doesn't turn while you have the rack off the car. Then simply follow the numbered sequence in the diagram.

To remove the tie-rod ends from the steering hubs, loosen the boots and unscrew the tie-rods from the rack. You can also use a ball-joint splitter to pop the tie-rod ends. Splitters are available for a few dollars at a local auto parts store. Never use a hammer to beat the tie-rod bolt out of the steering arm or you'll weaken the bolt, even if you don't ruin its shape. A few bolts and hoses later, the rack will come off in your hands.

The new manual-steering rack that you'll get from Mazda will not have the tie-rod ends on it. Measure the position of each tie-rod end on each side of the original rack. Unscrew and transfer both tie-rod ends to the new rack, putting them in the same relative positions so that you don't ruin your tires on the way to the alignment shop when you're finished.

Bolt up the new rack following the reverse of your removal procedure. Use the following torque values: tie-rod end bolts 29 pounds-feet, rack mounting bolts 43 pounds-feet, and steering-shaft pinch bolt 20 pounds-feet. Since you should never reuse a cotter pin, send an assistant out for a new pair for the tie-rod ends. Recheck all your work and let your car off the stands.

As anxious as you might be to go for a spin, your first task is to get your car aligned. Since you've moved things all around, you'll be taking rubber off your front tires with each mile you go. Get to your dealer or an alignment shop and get a full four-wheel alignment to factory specifications.

All of this may sound like a major change, but it's a relatively simple task to perform. The big change comes in the way your Miata will drive. If you've ever considered your Miata's power steering to be too light, spend a few minutes in a base-model car and see if this procedure is for you.

reduction in body roll. Recall that the Konis are also adjustable for damping values, so they can be stiffened up for the occasional autocross or to compensate for wear.

Mazda Motorsports has also come to the rescue of racers with threaded sleeves that create a finely adjustable lower spring perch. Made to fit either the Bilstein or Koni shocks, this complete lowering kit comes with four threaded sleeves, spring perches, rubber top spring pads, and shock adapters.

Lowering by Cutting Coils

The least expensive method of lowering your Miata is to cut the stock springs. Shade-tree mechanics have been cutting springs to lower cars for years. The purists and spring manufacturers hate this practice, but you can get away with it, if you must.

You'll need a die grinder or an acetylene torch to cut the springs. If you have a choice, use a die grinder because it creates less heat, so it doesn't anneal as much of the spring. The torch method trashes about one-half of the remaining coil, making your spring less useful. Wear safety glasses.

With the spring out of the car and off of the shock absorber, you can have good access to cut the spring at the right spot. The choice of how many coils to cut is one of diminishing returns. If you cut too many coils off, you actually change nothing except the spring rate. Take off too few, and you haven't made any difference either.

To lower your Miata about 1/2 inch all around, cut 1 1/8 coils off of the front springs and 1 1/2 coils off the rear springs. This is as far as you can go without buying new springs or shock absorbers. Your ride quality will not suffer noticeably, and you won't spend too much more time on the bump stops. Home-chopped springs and a new set of new shocks make for a pretty good suspension setup at a bargain-basement price.

Sway Bar Installation

Front or rear sway bars are easy to install, and require simply the use of jackstands and the removal of the main

SUSPENSION TUNING

ADJUSTMENT	To Add Understeer	To Add Oversteer
Tire pressure, front	Lower pressure	Raise pressure
Tire pressure, rear	Raise pressure	Lower pressure
Front tire width	Reduce width	Increase width
Rear tire width	Increase width	Reduce width
Front wheel width	Reduce width	Increase width
Rear wheel width	Increase width	Reduce width
Camber, front wheel	Add positive camber	Add negative camber
Camber, rear wheel	Add negative camber	Add positive camber
Front springs	Stiffer	Softer
Rear springs	Softer	Stiffer
Front sway bar	Larger, stiffer	Smaller, softer
Rear sway bar	Smaller, softer	Larger, stiffer
Weight front/rear	Move forward	Move rearward

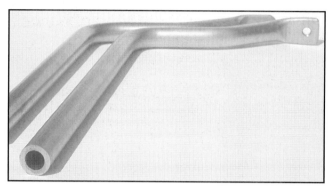

New to the market are tubular sway bars that work just like the solid units but save weight. Since a sway bar is a torsion spring, the material in the middle never does any work. Taking it out does not harm the function of the bar.

Unlike the front sway bar mounts, the rear mounts can take as large a bar as you want to put in without failing. Urethane bushings work great, but will make a lot of noise if antiseize lubricant is not liberally used to coat the bar where it goes through the bushing.

In one Saturday, you can transform your Miata with new shocks, springs, sway bars, wheels, and tires. The trick is to tune your parts to your driving style. You can also mess up a good thing in one Saturday with the wrong recipe.

mounting bracket bolts and control-link bolts. The front and rear sway bar removal and installation procedure is fairly obvious as long as you pay attention to the anti-seize note for urethane bushing installations as mentioned earlier.

Most sway-bar sets sold for Miatas come with an adjustable rear sway bar. If you get this kind, set the rear bar in the middle position first. You can then adjust the bar to suit your driving style per the instructions given here.

Oversteer is when your rear wheels swing outside your turning arc; in other words, the rotation you get is "over" the rotation you expected. Understeer is when the front of the car pushes to the outside of your turning arc~you get "under" the rotation you expected. By making various adjustments, you can tune your car to be perfectly neutral (usually best) or to have a slight amount of understeer at high speeds (usually safest). Below is a very general matrix of how to tune your suspension. Remember that a Miata responds to very slight changes and comes from the factory very neutral in its handling–your goal.

Bushings

The author asked one of Mazda's top suspension engineers what would be the first thing he'd improve on a Miata with 60,000 miles. His answer was quick and short: Replace all the suspension bushings.

This was a surprising answer, but one that bodes well for the serious enthusiast. The rubber bushings in any car's suspension are compliant to reduce noise and vibration. But a necessary evil that comes along with compliant bushings is that the critical alignment the designers put into the car doesn't stay constant. The Miata engineers did a commendable job of using high-tech bushings to maximize the accuracy of the suspension movement while minimizing road harshness, but over time, these rubber bushings become less able to hold up under heavy loads. If you have over 40,000 miles of hard driving on the car, it's time to replace the bushings.

Mazda Motorsports sells complete upper or lower control arms if you want to go the easy way. This eliminates the hassle of pressing bushings in and out of the stock control arms (a procedure covered in the racing chapter). It also sells replacement control-arm bushings that are 40 percent stiffer than the stock parts, a good step in the right direction. If you want to go stiffer, Mazda Motorsports also carries a urethane bushing set for the control arms and sway bars. To take it a step further, you can get a coil-over top mount that has 40 percent stiffer rubber bushings in it as well. The urethane bushings are more for the serious racer, because they make suspension action noticeably harsher, but a street car could benefit from the rubber units without making the car too noisy or harsh.

Brakes

The Miata is graced with good brakes on the 1990 to 1993 models and very good brakes on the 1994 and later models. In 1994, Mazda increased the size of the rotors on the front and rear of the Miata to compensate for the larger engine, the slightly heavier chassis, and the increased horsepower of that model. All Miatas have four-wheel disc brakes, the fronts being vented for added heat dissipation. Since the front brakes do 60-70 percent of all braking, Mazda ensured that larger-diameter rotors and higher-performance calipers were used on the front wheels.

The system has very good balance as set up from the factory, and showroom-stock racers have campaigned well on the stock hardware with nothing but a change of pad material. The 180-horsepower SCCA E Production cars run with the stock setup and racing pads, and E Production champ Pratt Cole ran two seasons on his first set of factory brakes—testament enough to Mazda's design work.

Replacing Brake Fluid

The easiest, cheapest, and most important way to keep your brakes working their best, or even to improve older brakes, is to periodically change the brake fluid.

The Miata uses Department of Transportation (DOT) 3 (alcohol-based) brake fluid that you should change every two years. Since brake fluid absorbs water, after about 24 months of use the fluid will become contaminated. This water can corrode your brake-system components (and your clutch's hydraulic-system components as well). Worse still, water-contaminated brake fluid boils at a much lower temperature than fresh brake fluid, so if you drive hard on old fluid, you might find yourself without effective brakes.

Silicone-based brake fluids (DOT 5) are not recommended for use in a Miata. There are reports that they create a spongy pedal feel, and in general it has not turned out to be the "improved performance" brake fluid that everyone had hoped it would be. Another problem is that if you change to silicone brake fluid, you will likely contaminate the new fluid with the old type because it's difficult to remove all traces of your stock fluid when making the change. Never mix alcohol-based brake fluid with silicone-based fluid.

Installing Stainless-Steel Brake Lines

One replacement fix that works very well is replacing the stock brake lines with braided stainless-steel lines. The standard brake lines running from the chassis to the calipers are made of rubber and have a certain amount of flex; they balloon ever so slightly as you apply the brake pedal. Replacing these with stainless-steel lines greatly reduces the flex and will increase the accuracy of your pedal feel for greater braking control. Stainless brake line sets are available throughout the aftermarket and from Mazda Motorsports at fair prices. The rear brake lines require a special junction block, so make sure that any set you order is specific to the Miata.

The brake lines are simple to replace, but make sure you have the right tools. High-quality metric open-end wrenches will be needed to break loose the brake lines. Adjustable wrenches and locking pliers are a definite no-no. Since you'll be spilling most of your brake fluid, have enough on hand to flush and replace the entire system's worth (32 ounces will cover everything including the air-bleeding process).

Drilled Rotors

There are vented cross-drilled rotors available that have even greater heat dissipation than Mazda's stock rotors. Some argue that these have less surface area because of the metal

Keeping your brake system up to par involves cleaning out the old fluid once every two years. Using a Mighty-Vac tool makes the job a one-man pleasure. Old fluid is sucked out the bleed nipple on each caliper. New fluid is occasionally added to the master cylinder to keep the system full. After bleeding all four corners, you're done.

that's missing where the lightening holes have been drilled. Testing has shown that cross-drilled rotors are less susceptible to fade than stock Miata rotors, as would be expected. It's a matter of driving style. Go for high-performance brake pads first, and if you're brakes still fade, try cross-drilled rotors.

Drilled rotors cost under $200 for a pair from Moss Motors, Dealer Alternative, Brainstorm, and many other common sources.

An alternative to drilled rotors is slotted rotors. While these do not have the cooling capabilities of rotors with air-flow holes cut into them, the slots cut into the disc surface greatly assist the expulsion of water and brake dust debris, which does improve braking performance to a certain degree. Slotted rotors are available from Moss Motors for $99 a set.

Brake Pads

Many performance pads are available to improve your Miata's brakes. For normal or even aggressive street use, the stock Mazda pads from your dealer give good performance. They don't dust too badly and perform well in fade tests for all but racing applications. Fortunately, the Miata is not prone to brake squeal, regardless of which type of pad a customer uses, so for normal street use, even the cheapest $11 pads from the local Pep Boys will work well on a Miata.

If you want even higher performance than the stock pads offer, it is available from the aftermarket. Hawk, Porterfield, and others sell pads made of carbon-metallic material that work well on the Miata. As you move higher and higher into the performance realm of brake pads that include a higher carbon-fiber content, take notice that these pads take longer to warm up than stock pads. Particularly in cold climates, you'll notice vastly reduced braking performance for the first two or three stops of the day. If you live at the top of a tall hill, this may be important to you.

When you go to replace the pads, pay attention to your master-cylinder reservoir level. If you've topped off your fluid level as your pads have worn down, retracting the caliper pistons to replace the worn-out pads with new ones will push brake fluid back upstream and your reservoir may overflow. Since brake fluid makes a great paint remover, you can quickly ruin the looks of your engine compartment by making this mistake. Before you

The Miata master cylinder (shown here with way too little brake fluid in it) and proportioning valve. The latter equalizes the braking pressure between the front and rear wheels, keeping either from premature lock-up.

The Miata comes with vented front brakes. One way to improve the cooling, and the resistance to fading, is to drill holes through the rotors, allowing air to circulate to the inside vents. The reduction in brake surface area is minimal, but the cooling effect is substantial.

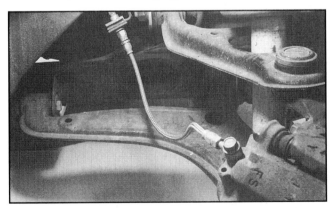

When you are changing your brake fluid, it might be a good time to consider stainless-steel brake lines. These firm up your brake pedal's "feel" and give you more precise control over your brakes.

start, use a paper towel or rag to soak up at least a quarter of the fluid in the reservoir.

Bigger is Better

Changing to bigger brakes is generally only necessary for the most aggressive drivers and racers. Even a 200-horsepower early Miata will do quite well with stainless-steel brake lines and high-performance brake pads on the stock rotors. Nevertheless, if you want to upgrade to bigger brakes, there are two ways to do it for 1990-1993 models and one for the 1994-on models.

The easiest way to get larger brakes on 1990-1993 Miatas is to fit the components used on the 1994-on models. There's a common misconception that this is a difficult job to do, but in reality you only need a few hand tools, the larger rotors, and the caliper brackets from the larger brakes. You can buy the complete assembly, backing plate and all, from a wrecking yard, or buy new parts from a dealer. New brackets will run about $200 for all four from a mail-order Mazda dealer with a Miata Club member discount. You'll also need to order new late-model brake pads from your favorite supplier.

An interesting aspect of the later brackets, as shown in the illustration in this chapter, is that the pivot socket for the calipers (highlighted in red) is on opposite ends of the bracket, compared to the early brackets. Thus, the need for swapping sides when the brackets are installed. Read that again: The part number listed for the left side is used on the right, and vice versa.

Mazda part numbers for the brackets:
Front left: NA75-33-291 (used on the right front)
Front right: NA75-33-281 (used on the left front)
Rear left: NA75-26-29X (used on the right rear)
Rear right: NA76-26-28X (used on the left rear)

The backing plate will require a bit of judicious Vise-Grip application. The new rotors are too big to clear the bent backing-plate lip, so it has to be straightened out. You don't want to remove the plate entirely, because it also acts as an air duct to help cool the brakes and diverts rain water away from the rotor to help keep them dry. Spin the rotor to make sure that it doesn't bind up any place before installing the brackets.

To install the brackets, bolt them to the spindles with the supplied 14-millimeter bolts. Standard torque for these is 58 pounds-feet. The 12-millimeter bolt that holds the caliper in the lower pivot should just be tightened to 35-45 pounds-feet. Use thread-locking compound on all bolts.

Aside from retrofitting the 1994-on brakes to an early car, there are suppliers offering big brake kits for the Miata for even greater braking performance. Some tuners have been successful in mounting second-generation RX-7 brake rotors to the Miata. Dealer Alternative sells the ultimate front-brake setup for the Miata: four-piston Wildwood calipers and cross-drilled 11.3-inch rotors (you'll need 15x7-inch wheels to clear the calipers).

Antilock Braking Systems (ABS)

Antilock brakes became an available option on Miatas beginning in the 1992 model year. While ABS is generally not considered a performance feature, it is a desirable feature for street driving, especially during panic stops or in inclement weather. Although there are no high-performance modifications available for the Miata ABS system, the parts and modifications listed in this chapter will work just as well on ABS-equipped Miatas. One caution though: Do not try to install the larger brakes from a 1994 or later car to a 1992 or 1993 ABS-equipped Miata.

One way to improve a 1.6-liter car's braking performance is to install the 1994 and later brake system. The easy way to do this is to order the complete package from a wrecking yard such as Mazmart.

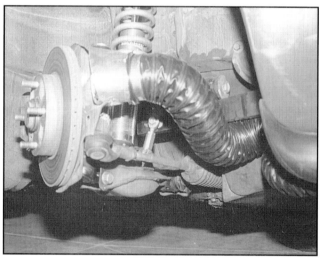

How the racers keep their brakes cool: Routing fresh air from the front air dam right to the rotor brings in lots of cooling air to the front brakes.

Miatas are known for having finicky rear calipers: The pistons have a tendency to freeze up in harsh environments. The only cure for now is replacement, because rebuild kits are not available to fix the problem.

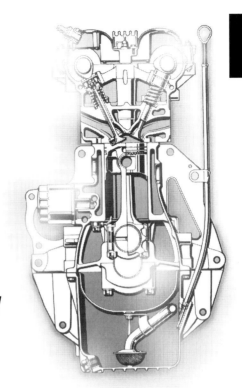

Engine Overview

Everybody wants to go faster. The No. 1 question the Miata Club gets daily is how to make members' cars more powerful. You can never be too rich or too fast—or something like that.

Though some owners have always clamored for more power from Mazda, the mother company has been clever in its decision to keep the Miata at its 116-133 standard horsepower ratings. The reason behind this might surprise you. Mazda was very keen on watching the insurance ratings of the original Honda CRX, which shot skyward in the later years of its life and made the car unaffordable for its target market. Mazda has therefore made a wise decision to create a very stout and strong, highly sophisticated engine that nevertheless offers reasonable horsepower numbers so that its insurance ratings stay low.

Mazda has left it up to the performance aftermarket to develop items that would increase the engine output, and thankfully these suppliers have aggressively answered the call, with a wide variety of choices and products available for the powerplant. Your job is to make the right choices, and this book's purpose is to guide you along that decision path. This chapter's job is to give a broad overview of the Miata's complex engine systems. After all, you can't select the best engine modifications until you understand how the engine works in stock form.

The Easiest Way to Get More Power

The first thing to realize is that the stock Miata engine has a lot more power than most drivers ever take advantage of.

The general response the Club gives to members seeking more power is to ask them at what rpm they shift their car. You might be surprised to learn that about 70 percent of Miata owners shift out of each gear at no higher than 4,000 rpm. The best advice for these people is to go out and buy a roll of masking tape: They should use it to cover up their tachometer and to start shifting their car when they feel the engine losing power, which is going to happen around 7,000 rpm. These people would be going much, much faster, and driving a car that had 50 percent more power than the one they drove when they shifted at 4,000 rpm.

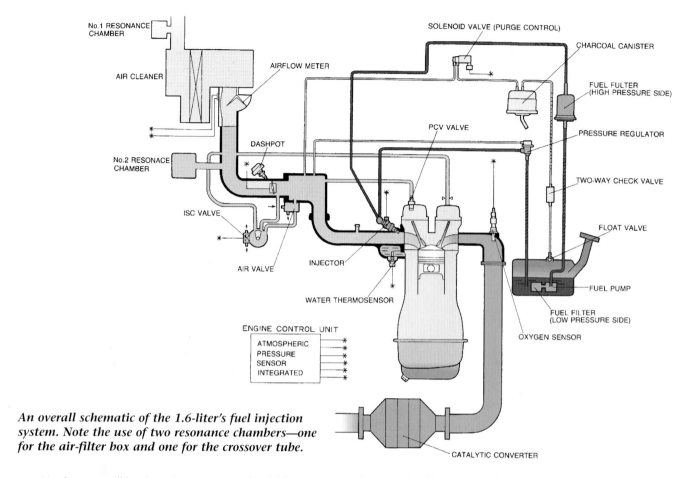

An overall schematic of the 1.6-liter's fuel injection system. Note the use of two resonance chambers—one for the air-filter box and one for the crossover tube.

No damage will be done to your engine by driving up to 7,000 rpm regularly. Now, if you drive across the country at 7,000 rpm in second gear, certainly your engine would wear faster, but going near the redline at every shift on a well-maintained engine that has had its oil changed regularly will no more wear it out prematurely than swinging a door all the way open will wear out the hinges prematurely. The engine is designed to safely go to 7,500 rpm without damage. The noise it makes up there is wonderful as well. For those scared of blowing up an engine, the Powertrain Control Module (PCM) that controls the fuel management actually has a safety cutout feature at 7,250 rpm to prevent overrevving. Autocrossers and racers know this well; they generally bang up against the rev limiter on every shift, maximizing the rpm and the horsepower available for maximum acceleration. So before you buy anything to make your Miata faster, invest in a little daring when it comes to shift points; go for the redline.

After you've mastered that, then you can start talking about throwing parts and money at the engine.

Finding More Power

So let's move to the business of making power. It all gets down to breathing when you come to the nub of it. Here's a primer on the big picture when it comes to burning gasoline in your engine:

The internal-combustion engine is basically an air pump. It sucks in air, throws in some gas (the ideal recipe is 14.7 parts air to one part gasoline), puts the mixture under pressure (to compound the explosion), and then blows it up. The explosion pushes the piston down, and that turns the crankshaft to capture that power. In a four-stroke engine like the Miata's, it takes three strokes to prepare for that one power stroke, so it's important to optimize those three as best we can.

In formal terms, each stroke is as follows: intake (piston moving down the cylinder, sucking in the air-fuel mixture), compression (piston moves back up the cylinder, compressing the mixture), power (spark plug fires and the explosion pushes the piston down, creating power), and exhaust (the piston moves back up the cylinder, pushing out the exhaust gases left over from combustion).

Getting air into an engine and getting exhaust out centers around the concept of volumetric efficiency. Simply stated, this is the percentage of air an engine actually sucks in, compared to a theoretically perfect engine. In reality, two main problems arise when an engine tries to bring in air: restrictions and inertia.

No matter how smooth or large the intake tract is, there will be some restrictions as air flows through it. The air has to travel through the following components in order: air filter, airflow meter, throttle body, intake manifold, cylinder head ports, and intake valves, finally arriving at the combustion chamber where it can do some good.

You might suggest simply making these components extra-large to offset any restrictions, and you'd be partly right. If you only want maximum airflow when the engine is at maximum speed, bigger is better. This is the tactic the race crowd uses. But what about torque in the mid-rpm range, where most of us drive every day? Making the intact tract as big as all outdoors will kill airflow at part-throttle conditions. We need our friend inertia to help us out, and inertia likes smaller ports.

Think of a door to a subway car that's only wide enough for five people abreast. Let's say that 25 people can enter the car at a normal walking pace in 10 seconds. Each person is walking relatively slowly. If we begin to force the doors closed before everyone is in, the flow of people walking slowly will be stopped easily. Now consider a subway car with a door only large enough for a single person to enter at a time. For the same 10-second stop, the 25 commuters will have to be running pretty fast to get through the door in time. As we try to close the door, the speed of the last few in line will probably squeeze them through the doorway. The inertia of each person—plus the pushing of the guy behind them—will shove more passengers in during the door-closing stage.

The intake valve of your engine is that subway door; only a certain amount of time is available for the fuel-air mixture to get in. If you make the passages narrow, the intake charge will be moving faster and more molecules will cram their way past the valve as it's closing. This may sound inconsequential, but this "ram" effect is worth a lot of power at low engine speeds. But at high engine speeds the smaller port just becomes restrictive, and that's the problem that engine designers face: What works well at one engine speed is less efficient at others.

This all belies the benefit of multivalve engines. Two smaller intake valves are theoretically better than one large valve, since the two smaller valves can flow the same volume as a single large one, but they also enjoy a noticeable ram effect. Your Miata engine has two intake valves and two exhaust valves per cylinder to take full advantage of this phenomenon. Each smaller valve also has less inertia than a larger, heavier valve, meaning the engine should be able to

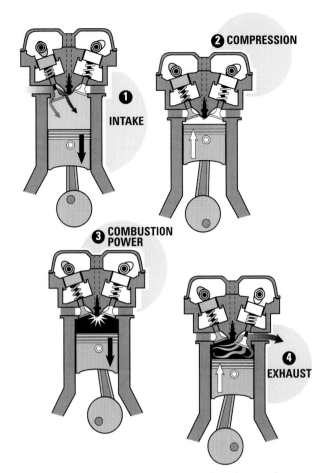

The four strokes of an internal combustion engine. The two most important ones for making power are the intake and exhaust. The more air and fuel you get in, the bigger the explosion. After combustion, getting the waste gas out of the cylinder makes room for more fresh charge.

spin to higher rpm without valve float.

To increase volumetric efficiency even more, complicated tuned ports that combine acoustic and pressure waves can add a bit more efficiency. The Miata engine has a volumetric efficiency of around 88 percent; this is very good, and puts it right at the forefront of modern mass-production engines. The efficiency comes from a combination of long intake runners (for inertial ram effect and pressure-wave tuning), a large intake tract, the multivalve cylinder head, and a header-style exhaust manifold. For comparison, an old-style pushrod American V-8 with a two-barrel carburetor has a volumetric efficiency of around 77 percent.

The formula for air capacity (in cubic feet per minute, or cfm) of an engine comes from its displacement: cubic feet per minute = maximum rpm x displacement (in cubic inches).

For a 1.6-liter Miata running at the rev limiter, the value is (7,200 x 97) (3,456 = 202 cubic feet per minute. Now, that's how much air the engine could ingest if its volumetric efficiency were 100 percent. In reality, the Miata can only flow around 88 percent of that amount, yielding a real-world air capacity of 178 cubic feet per minute. The newer 1.8-liter engine has a real-world air capacity of around 206 cubic feet per minute (cfm).

One key to more power is to increase that volumetric efficiency above 88 percent. Super-tuned race engines can have higher numbers at specific rpm ranges. With enough ram effect and inertial dumping, engine builders can approach 100 percent volumetric efficiency at certain speeds. As for forced induction, the volumetric efficiency easily exceeds 100 percent, thanks to the extra push the air gets on its way into the cylinders.

ITEM		SPECIFICATION
idle speed	rpm	800-900 (850±50) [MT]*
		750-850 (800±50)[AT]*
ignition timing	BTDC	9°-11° (10°±1°)*
Throttle Body		
throat diameter	mm (in)	55 {2.2}
Fuel Pump		
type		impeller (in-tank)
output pressure	kPa (kgf/cm2, psi)	480-657 {4.9-6.7, 69-95}
Fuel filter		
type	low-pressure side	nylon element
	high-pressure side	paper element
Pressure Regulator		
type		diaphram
regulating pressure	kPa (kgf/cm2, psi)	265-314 {2.7-3.2, 38-46}
Fuel Injector		
type		high-ohmic
type of drive		voltage
resistance	Ω	12-16 (at 20°C {68°F})
Idle Air Control Valve		
solenoid resistance	Ω	10.7-12.3 (at 20°C {68°F})
Air Valve		
opening temperature		below 40°C {104°F}
Purge Solenoid Valve		
solenoid resistance	Ω	23-27 (20°C {68°F})
Crankshaft Position Sensor		
type		hall effect
Engine Coolant Temperature Sensor		
resistance	kΩ　20°C (68°F)	2.21-2.69
	80°C (179°F)	0.287-0.349
Fuel Tank		
capacity	L (US gal, Imp gal)	48 {12.7, 10.5}
Air Cleaner Housing		
element type		oil permeated
Accelerator Cable		
free play	mm (in)	1-3 {0.039-0.118}
Fuel		unleaded regular
specification		(RON 87 or higher)

* With System Selector (49 B019 9AO) test switch at "SELF TEST".

The specifications for the 1.8-liter's fuel injection system. It is also programmed with "limp home" values.

How Your Fuel Injection Works

One of the main reasons for the Miata's excellent performance and drivability is the sophisticated fuel injection system Mazda designed for it. Of course this sophistication came at the price of complexity. Fortunately, the basic concepts of the system are easily understood when looked at piece-by-piece, and once you understand it, you'll probably have a better idea of how to modify it for better performance.

Thanks to the market pressures for better fuel economy and drivability as well as strict emissions standards, automakers have adopted a superior way to mete gasoline into engines: fuel injection. Instead of a bowl of fuel from which the engine pulls gasoline according to airflow (our old friend, the carburetor), now the whole process is controlled by a computer (the PCM) that takes readings from the engine, determines exactly how much fuel it needs, and then squirts just that amount right at the intake valve, where the air is rushing into the combustion chamber.

An airflow meter in the intake tract generates a signal based on how much air is passing through it. Inside the airflow meter is a flap that works just like a weather vane; a variable resistor (rheostat) connected to the flap sends a signal to the PCM based on the flap's angle.

The airflow meter and the PCM are carefully calibrated to work together. As the airflow meter sends out a signal showing a certain amount of airflow, the PCM sends a signal to the injectors, telling them to stay open the precise amount of time required to deliver the proper amount of fuel.

Downstream in the exhaust manifold is an oxygen sensor that takes a reading of how much leftover oxygen remains in the exhaust gases. If it sees that the fuel mixture is a little lean, it will tell the PCM to leave the injectors open a bit longer to let some more fuel in; if it sees the exhaust gases being rich, it tells the PCM to deliver less fuel.

Each of four injectors is fed by a pipe called the fuel rail. Gasoline comes in one end from the fuel pump (at high pressure), fills the rail, then goes through the regulator and returns to the tank. The regulator holds the pressure to a maximum of 43 psi.

PCM Self-Diagnostic Feature

The first step to making more power is to make sure that your engine is working as it was designed to. If you have a failed component or sensor, there's power being lost right off the bat. One of the greatest things about the Miata's fuel injection system is that it will tell you when something goes wrong. For the average tinkerer, this can save hundreds of dollars in repairs by telling you which item is malfunctioning.

This system is on both the 1.6- and 1.8-liter cars and uses the Check Engine light in the instrument panel to flash a code that tells which system has failed or is out of specification.

To read the codes, first open the diagnostic connector that is positioned just on top of the driver's-side shock absorber, under the hood. Raise the lid on the small black box to reveal the legend for the connector.

To test your engine, first start it up and let it reach normal operating temperature. Then shut the engine off and proceed with work at the diagnostic connector. Using an unfolded paper clip, connect the GND (ground) and the TEN (test engine) pins together. Return to the driver's seat and turn your ignition key to "ON," but do not start the engine.

Observe the Check Engine light in your instrument panel. It will flash a certain number of times; count the number of flashes to indicate the malfunction code.

If the code is a two-digit number, the "tens" digit will be displayed first, then for 1.6 seconds the light will be dark; after this pause, the indicator will flash the "ones" digit. Don't worry if you don't catch it the first time: The cycle will repeat after a four-second dark pause. Additionally, if there are multiple codes, they each will be separated by a four-second dark pause and may include two-digit codes. You may have to pay attention pretty carefully before understanding what the flashes are trying to tell you.

Take as long as you need to record the codes, and then refer to the chart that follows or Section F of your factory service manual.

After you've fixed the offending part, you'll need to clear your codes. To do this, locate your BTN fuse in your underhood fuse box, which is on the fender well by the wiper motor (passenger's side). Pull the cover off and remove the BTN fuse for 5 seconds, and then reinsert it in its spot. You might need to activate your

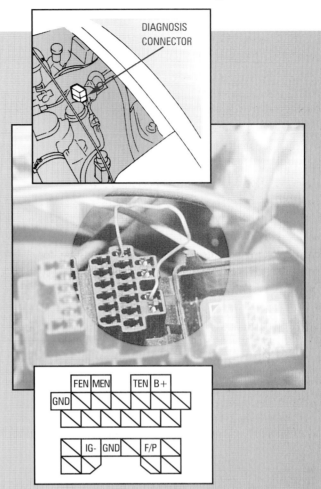

Over by the left-side shock tower is the diagnostic connector—your window into the engine computer and how your system is functioning.

brake lights on and off a few times with the BTN fuse out (the car's harness has enough capacitance to hold the memory in the PCM; activating the brake lights or performing a similar function will drain the PCM harness). With your jumper wire still in place on the diagnostic connector, turn your key to the "ON" position and see that the Check Engine light does not flash a code (don't start the engine before checking for cleared codes). Take your jumper wire out and restart your engine, rev it up a few times, and then recheck for trouble codes. All should be clear.

Unfortunately, this fine system went away with the introduction of the OBDII system in 1996. However, there is relatively inexpensive software available that will decode the OBDII signals and display the results on your laptop computer. If you have a later Miata and a laptop, this software can be a pretty good investment.

ITEM				SPECIFICATION
idle speed	rpm			850 ± 50*
Ignition timing	BTDC			10° ± 1°*
Throttle body				
Type				Horizontal draft
Throat Diameter	mm (in)			55 (2.2)
Fuel Pump				
Type				Impeller (in-tank)
Output pressure	kPa (kg/cm², psi)			441-589 (4.5-6.0, 64-85)
Fuel filter				
Type	Low pressure side			Nylon element
	High pressure side			Paper element
Pressure regulator				
Type				Diaphram
Regulating pressure	kPa (kg/cm2, psi)			265-314 (2.7-3.2, 38-46)
Injector				
Type				High-ohmic
Type of drive				Voltage
Resistance	Ω			12-16 (at 20°C, 68°F)
ISC valve (solenoid valve [idle speed control])				
Solenoid resistance				11-13 (at 20°C, 68°F)
Solenoid valve (Purge Control)				
Solenoid resistance				23-27 (at 20°C, 68°F)
Crank angle sensor				
Type				Optical pick-up
Airflow meter				
	E_2 - - Vs	Fully closed		200 — 600
	E_2 - - Vs	Fully open		20 — 1,200
	E_2 - - Vc			200 — 400
Resistance Ω	E_2 - - THAA	-20°C (-4°F)		13,600 — 18,400
	(intake air	20°C (68°F)		2,210 — 26,900
	thermistor)	60°C (140°F)		493 — 667
	E_1 - - Fc	Fully closed		∞
	E_1 - - Fc	Fully open		0
Water thermosensor				
		-20°C (-4°F)		14.6—17.8
Resistance kΩ		20°C (68°F)		2.2—2.7
		60°C (140°F)		0.29—0.35
Circuit opening relay				
	STA—E_1			21—43
Resistance Ω	B—Fc			109—226
	B—Fp			∞
Fuel tank				
Capacity	liters (US gal, Imp gal)			45 (11.9, 9.9)
Air cleaner				
Element type				oil permeated
Accelerator cable				
Free play	mm (in.)			1—3 (0.039—0.118)
Fuel				
Specification				Unleaded regular (RON 87 or higher)

* With System Selector (49 B019 9AO) test switch at "SELF TEST".

The specifications for the 1.6-liter's system. Before modifying anything, it is a good idea to know what the sensors in the fuel injection system are doing. For most of the devices, a "limp home" mode is saved in the PCM for when a device fails. The PCM reads a default value for the defective sensor and gets you home. The Check Engine light on the dash will illuminate in the instrument panel.

This might seem unremarkable until you realize that the oxygen sensor sends out its status report thousands of time per second. Using high-speed calculations, the PCM can instantaneously adjust the balance to keep the engine power at a maximum and emissions at a minimum.

As you travel down the road at 60 miles per hour at 3,000 rpm, each cylinder is exploding fuel at a rate of 25 times per second. It takes a fast computer to stay on top of how fuel delivery is going, but even the fast PCM in the Miata couldn't keep up if it had to solely rely on continual updates from the airflow sensor and oxygen sensor to keep things in line. In practice, each car's PCM is programmed with several "maps" of the engine's fuel needs at combinations of rpm, airflow rate, coolant temperature, outside air temperature, altitude, and so on. These maps were developed by the engineers at the factory, who test engines in all conditions at all loads. If the engineers have done their jobs right, the car will have a perfect-running engine in all conditions, from autocrossing in winter to grocery-getting in summer. Starting in model-year 1996 with the federal government's OBDII (On-Board Diagnostics II) requirement, all PCMs are reprogrammable at the dealership, allowing for updates and service changes to be done with no parts being changed.

When you start your Miata's engine from cold, the PCM "looks up" the correct fuel injection amount from its cold-running map to run the injectors until the engine warms up. This cold-running map includes a richer fuel mixture to help the engine compensate for condensation in the intake tract, an increased air delivery rate to raise the idle speed, and retarded timing to heat up the catalytic converter faster. Once the oxygen sensor wakes up and the coolant temperature gets to a certain point, the PCM goes to its normal closed-loop map and starts listening to the oxygen sensor's

You can clear trouble codes by pulling the BTN fuse located in your underhood fuse box, over by the wiper motor. It is the third fuse from the firewall along the row closest to the engine.

	Malfunction display			
Code No.	Pattern of output signal (Self-Diagnosis System Checker)	Sensor or subsystem	On-board diagnosis system	Fail-safe
01	ON / OFF	IGF signal	No IGF-signal	—
03	ON / OFF	SGT signal	No SGT signal	Cancels fuel injection
04	ON / OFF	SGC signal	No SGC signal	Cancels fuel injection and electronic spark distribution
08	ON / OFF	Mass airflow sensor	Open or short circuit	Basic fuel injection amount fixed as for two driving modes (1) Idle switch: ON (2) Idle switch: OFF
09	ON / OFF	Engine coolant temperature sensor	Open or short circuit	Maintains constant 35°C {95°F} command
10	ON / OFF	Intake air temperature sensor (Mass airflow sensor)	Open or short circuit	Maintains constant 20°C {68°F} command
12	ON / OFF	Throttle position sensor	Open or short circuit	Maintains constant command of throttle valve wide open throttle
14	ON / OFF	Barometric absolute pressure sensor	Open or short circuit	Maintains constant command of sea level pressure
15	ON / OFF	Heated oxygen sensor (Inactivation)	Sensor output continues less than 0.55V 180 sec. after engine exceeds 1,500 rpm	Cancels engine closed loop operation
16	ON / OFF	EGR function sensor	Open or short circuit	Maintains constant command of EGR valve
17	ON / OFF	Heated oxygen sensor (Inversion)	Sensor output continues unchanged 20 sec. after engine exceeds 1,500 rpm	Cancels engine closed loop operation
25	ON / OFF	PRC solenoid valve	Open or short circuit	—
26	ON / OFF	Purge solenoid valve	Open or short circuit	—
28	ON / OFF	EGR solenoid valve (vacuum)	Open or short circuit	—
29	ON / OFF	EGR solenoid valve (vent)	Open or short circuit	—
34	ON / OFF	Idle air control valve	Open or short circuit	—

If any particular system fails for even one split second, the PCM records a code that you can retrieve for later diagnosis. If you have more than one fault code at one time, the engine light in the instrument panel will flash one code, then wait four seconds and show another.

RELATIONSHIP CHART

Input Devices \ Output Devices	Fuel injector — Fuel Injection Amount	Fuel injector — Fuel Injection Timing	Idle Air Control Valve	Purge Solenoid Valve	A/C Relay (A/C Cut-Off)	Igniter (Ignition Timing Control)	EGR Solenoid Valve (Vacuum)	EGR Solenoid Valve (Vent)	PRC Solenoid Valve	Powertrain Control Module (Transmission)	Coolant fan relay	Condenser fan relay
TEN Terminal (Data link connector)	×	×	○	×	×	○	×	×	○	×	○	○
Ignition Switch (Start Position)	○	○	○	×	○	○	×	×	○	×	○	○
Steering Pressure Sensor	×	×	○	×	○	×	×	×	×	×	×	×
Blower Switch	×	×	○	×	×	×	×	×	×	×	×	×
Headlight Switch	×	×	○	×	×	×	×	×	×	×	×	×
Stoplight Switch	○	×	○	×	×	×	×	×	×	×	×	×
Neutral and Clutch Switches (MT)	○	×	○	○	○	○	×	×	×	×	×	×
Park/neutral switch (AT)	○	×	○	○	○	○	×	×	×	×	×	×
Air Conditioning Sensor	×	×	○	×	○	×	×	×	×	×	○	○
Throttle Position Sensor — Idle Switch (IDL)	○	×	○	○	○	○	○	○	×	×	○	○
Throttle Position Sensor — Sensor (TVO)	○	×	○	○	○	○	○	○	○	×	×	○
Barometric Absolute Pressure Sensor	○	×	○	○	×	×	×	×	×	×	×	×
IGF Signal	○	×	×	×	×	○	×	×	×	×	×	×
Heated Oxygen Sensor	○	×	×	○	×	×	×	×	×	×	×	×
Engine Coolant Temperature Sensor	○	×	○	○	○	○	C	○	○	○	○	○
Mass Airflow Sensor — Sensor	○	×	×	○	×	○	○	×	○	×	×	×
Mass Airflow Sensor — Intake Air Temperature Sensor	○	×	○	○	×	○	○	○	○	×	×	×
Crankshaft Position Sensor — SGT-Signal	○	○	○	○	○	○	○	○	○	×	×	×
Crankshaft Position Sensor — SGC-Signal	×	○	×	×	×	○	×	×	×	×	×	×

35U0FX–007

All of the sensors on the Miata engine have a job to do. This chart shows which sensors affect which functions, as calculated by the PCM. This chart is for the 1.8-liter, but the 1.6-liter's chart is similar, except for not having an EGR function.

OUTPUT DEVICE \ ENGINE CONDITION		CRANKING (COLD ENGINE)	WARMING UP (DURING IDLE)	MEDIUM LOAD		ACCELERATION	HEAVY LOAD	DECELERATION	IDLE	IG: ON (ENGINE NOT RUNNING)
				COLD	WARM					
FUEL INJECTOR	FUEL INJECTION AMOUNT	Rich	Rich	Rich	Normal	Rich	Rich	Fuel cut	Normal	No Injection
FUEL PUMP RELAY		ON	ON	ON	ON	ON	ON	ON	ON	OFF
IGNITER		Fixed at BTDC 7°	Depends on engine condition							
PURGE SOLENOID VALVE		OFF	OFF	OFF	OFF	ON (Purge)	ON (Purge)	OFF	OFF	OFF
BAC VALVE	IDLE AIR CONTROL VALVE	ON (Fixed duty)	ON (Closed loop duty)	ON (Fixed duty)	ON (Fixed duty)	ON (Fixed duty)	ON (Fixed duty)	ON (Fixed duty)	ON (Closed loop duty)	OFF
	AIR VALVE	OPEN	OPEN	OPEN	CLOSED	CLOSED	CLOSED	CLOSED	CLOSED	—
A/C RELAY		OFF (A/C cut)	ON	ON	ON	OFF (A/C cut)	ON	ON	ON	OFF
PRC SOLENOID VALVE		OFF	OFF	OFF	OFF (Vacuum to pressure regulator)	OFF	OFF	OFF	ON (During hot start only)	OFF
EGR SOLENOID VALVE	VENT / VACUUM	OFF	OFF	OFF	OFF	ON (System operates: amount of EGR changes)	ON	ON	OFF	OFF

During different parts of any driving cycle, the PCM is controlling the engine according to a predetermined plan. Warm-up and idle are modes of operation where emissions are carefully controlled.

MIATA ENGINE HOP-UP OPTIONS:

PHASE I: BRIGHTENED COMMUTER
Ten extra horsepower for under $300
- Ignition timing to 14 degrees BTDC
- Cooler thermostat
  (NAPA Standard part #42 with gasket)
- Free flow panel air filter for stock box
- Performance muffler and exhaust pipe
  (cat-back system)

PHASE II: STRONG STREET PERFORMER
Eighteen extra horsepower for under $800
- Ignition timing to 14 degrees BTDC
- Cooler thermostat
  (NAPA Standard part #42 with gasket)
- Free flow panel air filter for stock box
- High performance header
- Performance muffler and exhaust pipe
  (cat-back system)
- Cold air intake system
  (i.e. Jackson Racing, Racing Beat, or Brianstorm)

PHASE III: STREET DOMINATOR
Sixty extra horsepower for around $2900
- Ignition timing to 14 degrees BTDC
- J&S Safeguard ignition retarder
- Sebring Supercharger
- Performance muffler

PHASE IV: DRAG RACER
One hundred extra horsepower for around $5000
- J&S Safeguard ignition retarder
- BEGI 12 psi turbocharger kit with intercooler
- High capacity fuel injectors
- High capacity fuel pump
- Performance clutch
- Free flow catalytic convertor
- Performance muffler and exhaust pipe
  (cat-back system)

output. In practice, the oxygen sensor is more of a downwind scout that allows for minute adjustments above or below the map's instruction than it is a major officer in the campaign.

Some PCMs are set up to learn from the oxygen sensor's reports and permanently reprogram their maps according to how the engine is being used and how it's responding to the current mapping program. This works well in taking into account engine wear, or if you move from the beach to the mountains. The Miata's PCM doesn't have this feature, but that's no great loss because, in general, the Miata's engine performance is so consistent that it doesn't need it.

One more interesting feature is the idle-speed control. There's a small idle-speed control valve that can bleed air past the throttle, automatically raising rpm to compensate for additional loads placed on the engine, such as when you engage your heater fan or turn on your headlights. The PCM monitors the engine speed and the electrical load to make sure it doesn't speed up the engine too much. For even finer control of the idle speed, the PCM will advance or retard the ignition timing as needed, often multiple times per second.

Ignition timing settings are also programmed into the PCM maps. And some systems have a knock sensor that senses if your engine is pinging from poor fuel quality and

retards the timing accordingly. Series One Miatas (through 1997) are sufficiently knock-resistant not to need this last feature, but the increased compression ratio inaugurated inthe 1999 model requires a knock sensor, so one is standard on these powerplants.

There are more duties for the PCM: exhaust gas recirculation (on 1.8-liter Miatas), evaporative canister purging, hot-restart protocols, and so on. All in all, it is a wonderful system for making each combustion cycle effective and efficient. For us, it means solid power to the ground at every moment and a smooth-running engine for well past 100,000 miles.

The point of all this is to show you that Mazda worked very hard to optimize the Miata engine. An excellent fuel injection system (especially on the 1.8-liter cars), a high compression ratio, a cylinder head with four valves per cylinder, a highly tuned intake manifold, and a tubular exhaust header all add up to a well-tuned engine. In the old days, cars could benefit from a few easy hot-rod tips, but in the Miata, the performance work has largely been done already. Think of it this way: Mazda engineers took a pretty good engine (the short block from the 323) and did everything they could think of to get more power and keep it reliable. That doesn't leave a lot left undone for the rest of us. Nevertheless, some of the following chapters will describe ways to take the Miata engine a bit further.

Ignition

When the Miata was being designed, one problem that arose was where to put the distributor. Driving the distributor off of the camshaft was typical practice, but we wanted to get the engine as far back in the chassis as possible for better weight distribution and handling. In the case of the 323 engine, the distributor was too big and would have run into the Miata's firewall. To solve this problem, we incorporated a crank-angle sensor into the cylinder head and let the PCM work out the spark plug firing details. By using a short crank-angle sensor and two ignition coils, a compact system was developed that had the right physical size and better performance than a traditional distributor. This arrangement allowed the engine to be pushed farther back in the chassis for the optimal front/rear weight bias.

The PCM sends dynamic signals to either ignition coil and fires off the appropriate spark plug at the right time. Since there are two coils and four cylinders, two spark plugs are firing at one time. The electrical current from one coil travels down one spark plug, through the cylinder head, and up the other; for example, down the No. 4 plug and up the No. 1 plug. While you might think that this is a long way for the spark current to travel, remember that electricity moves at 186,000 miles per second, the speed of light. The spark current runs down the wire, through the cylinder head, and back up its opposite plug's wire in less than 0.000000005 second. Interestingly, this is why platinum spark plugs aren't of any benefit for the Miata. Since most manufacturers only plate one of the electrodes (either the side wire or the center electrode), the platinum benefit only occurs on two plugs. Coating a spark plug electrode with platinum only affects the plug's durability, so you're not missing any horsepower by using conventional plugs.

The Miata Club has run dyno tests on just about every modification available for the Miata's ignition system, from PCM chips to fancy plugs and wire systems. Another short discussion: None of them works any better than the stock system. Even so, basic ignition-system maintenance and a few simple modifications will result in long-lasting performance from and subtle but important improvements to your ignition.

Ignition Advance and Low-End Power

Given that Mazda controls the Miata's ignition timing with the PCM, there's no mechanical limit to the advance curve chosen for maximum power. The stock timing advance curve follows standard engine practice for a modern powerplant, running relatively linearly from 10 degrees at idle to 28 degrees at 5,000 rpm. No further timing advance is added from 5,000 rpm to the fuel cutout at 7,200 rpm. The only anomaly is a slight "hump" of retardation around 4,000 rpm. This retardation is used to reduce detonation possibilities, working around a particular characteristic of the engine. Both the 1.6- and 1.8-liter have this hump; it doesn't affect peak horsepower.

The 1990-1997 Miatas don't have an active knock sensor, but rather rely on accurate engine maps and sensor signals to control detonation. Experience has shown the Miata engine to be very resistant to detonation, with stock engines easily running up to 14 degrees before top dead center (BTDC) of base timing on regular 87-octane fuel. For more power, Mazda did add an active knock sensor to the 1999 model Miatas.

You can get 20 percent more torque at 1,000 rpm by increasing your base ignition timing from the stock 10 degrees BTDC to 18 degrees BTDC. The extra low-end torque is particularly useful for drivers who like to shift under 5,000 rpm. This 18-degree advance setting will, however, require the use of high-octane fuel, meaning 92 octane or greater. Even accounting for the added fuel cost (under $100 for a 12,000-mile-per-year car), this is the cheapest and best horsepower you can add to a Miata. It comes in at exactly the right spot, too—in the low-rev range, where the Miata is weakest.

If you shift most of the time at 6,500 rpm or greater and are looking for more top-end power, advance your base timing to only 14 degrees BTDC. This is the optimal setting for maximum peak horsepower at top rpm, and it still offers a noticeable boost in low and midrange power and torque. At 14 degrees of timing, you also won't necessarily need high-octane fuel. After the timing is altered, listen for detonation to determine the octane rating your particular engine will require.

The oxygenated fuels now used in some areas have less knock resistance than standard gasoline of the same octane rating, so listen for the sound of small marbles rattling around in your engine; detonation in a Miata will mostly occur above 3,500 rpm going up a slight grade in fourth or fifth gear. As you press down on the throttle, the marble-sound will come in if you're running too much timing or marginal fuel.

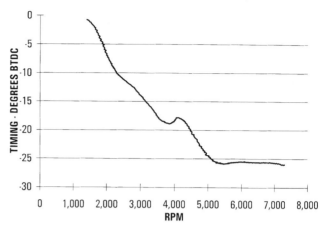

The ignition timing curve for a stock 1.6-liter Miata (the 1.8-liter engine has a similar curve). Note the retardation around 4,000 rpm. This is built in to maximize power at this particular rpm range. This normally happens as an engine nears its peak volumetric efficiency in the rpm range.

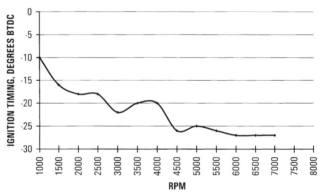

Using an engine dynamometer and checking for maximum power at each rpm, the following data comes out. This is for a 1.8-liter engine. The smaller engine responds similarly.

Changing Your Engine's Timing

It's necessary to follow several critical steps to set any Miata's timing. First, locate the blue connector in the engine compartment just behind the driver's-side headlamp door. It has a blue dummy connector clipped into place that, when removed, will expose a male electrical junction. This junction provides under-the-hood battery voltage to power a timing light or any other testers that need 12 volts DC. (This is useful since the battery is located in the trunk.) Hook your timing light's power lead in here and use the engine block for the ground.

IGNITION TIMING POWER INCREASE

	STOCK	14 DBTDC	18 DBTDC
MAX HP	90.7	99.5	98.0
MAX TORQUE	82.6	89.7	87.9

If you live at high rpm, 14 degrees of base timing advance will make you sing. If you spend more of your time under 4,500 rpm, 18 degrees of timing (and high-octane fuel) will serve you better.

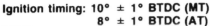

Ignition timing: 10° ± 1° BTDC (MT)
8° ± 1° BTDC (AT)

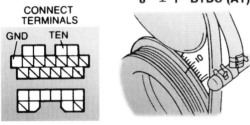

CONNECT
TERMINALS

GND   TEN

The stock timing specification for manual-transmission cars is 10 degrees BTDC. Each mark on the timing pointer equals 2 degrees of timing. Since the Miata engine rotates clockwise, the marks increase in value to the left of the "10" mark. Top dead center is five marks to the right of the "10" mark.

Every throttle body has an idle-speed screw. Make sure to adjust the idle speed to 850 rpm before checking timing. Idle speed should be adjusted with the jumper wire between the GND (ground) and TEN (test engine) terminals of the diagnostic connector. When you remove the jumper, the idle speed should just rise slightly (25 rpm) to show that the idle-speed control valve is taking up the slack in the system.

Next, locate the diagnostic connector atop the driver's-side inner fender. It's a little black box on a pedestal. Open the cover and study the legend on the inside of the cover.

To check your ignition timing, run a jumper wire between the GND (ground) and the TEN (test engine) terminals. If you're good with a straightened paper clip, you can use this as your jumper wire. This connection puts the ignition system into the test mode and allows you to measure ignition timing and engine speed without any input from the PCM.

The best sort of timing light to use has an inductive spark-plug-wire pickup. Hook this up to the plug wire for cylinder No. 1 (the cylinder closest to the radiator). Make sure all your leads are clear of the fan and other moving parts and are not near any hot manifolds. Start the engine, allow it to warm, and read your dash tachometer; idle speed should be between 800 and 900 rpm. If not, locate the throttle body (see diagram) and remove the small black round plug that covers the idle-speed adjustment screw. Slowly turn the screw until idle speed is 800-900 rpm.

Locate the yellow timing mark on the crank pulley and the timing scale located on the front engine cover (it might be necessary to clean both of these areas when the engine is off). Make sure that the 10-degree mark is visible on the tab extending from the engine cover. On 1.8-liter engines, Mazda has put two marks on the crank pulley. Use the yellow one.

With the engine idling at the correct rpm, check ignition timing by aiming the timing light at the front crank pulley. The yellow timing mark on the crank pulley should line up with the 10-degree mark plus or minus 1 degree. Each mark designates 2 degrees of timing.

To adjust the timing, locate the crank-angle sensor at the rear of the cam cover (passenger's side for the 1.6, driver's side for the 1.8). Loosen the 12-millimeter lock bolt just enough to be able to move the crank-angle sensor slightly. Slowly rotate the sensor in one direction or the other to get the ignition timing you want. Clockwise rotation (while facing the radiator) retards the timing. Tighten the lock bolt and recheck the timing marks (tightening the lock bolt sometimes throws the timing off). Rev the engine and make sure that the ignition timing advances.

The lock bolt on the 1.8-liter engine is a pain to get to, but Mazda put a very tall head on it to help things a little. A 1/4-inch socket drive and 12-millimeter socket can just slip in behind the crank-angle sensor. This is a real knuckle scraper, so be careful.

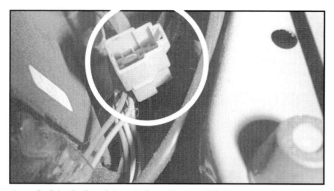

Just behind the driver's headlamp lid (on U.S. market cars) is a blue connector that supplies 12 volts for underhood operations. Tie your timing light's positive lead to this connector. If you blow the fuse protecting this connector, you'll find it on the wiper circuit in the fuse box.

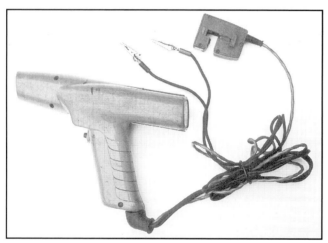

A Miata owner's best friend. Make sure to use an inductive timing light with alligator clips on the power leads. This is an old Snap-On unit that is indestructible.

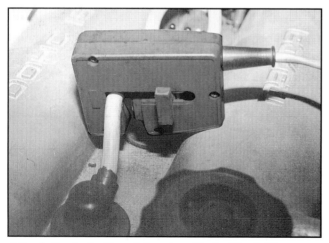

Attach the inductive pickup to cylinder No. 1 (the one closest to the radiator) to set the timing.

Any changes in timing will affect idle speed. Check the tachometer again and make any necessary adjustments to bring the idle speed back to 800-900 rpm.

Spark Plugs and Wires

The stock Miata plug wires go belly-up after around 30,000 miles—that's pretty much a given. Use an ohmmeter periodically to check the wires. Each plug wire should have 16,000 ohms of resistance for each 3 feet of length. This means that the short little No. 4 wire will have a lower resistance reading than its longer siblings.

But even this test isn't a reliable way to determine if a set is faulty; suspect the wires first if you have any sort of engine misfire. When you route your new wires, keep them as far apart from each other as you can, using the clips Mazda put in the cam cover. Wire-to-wire crossfire makes for terrible

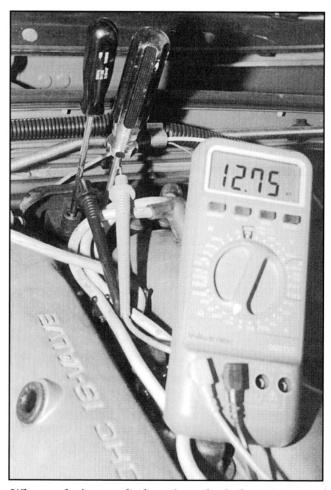

When replacing spark plug wires, check the resistance of the secondary circuits of your ignition coils. Due to the shape of the posts, you'll have to insert a screwdriver down each coil tower to get a connection. The resistance of an individual coil should not exceed 13,000 or be less than 9,000 ohms. If it outside this range, replace it.

detonation. Keeping the wires from each other will prevent this from happening.

Beyond replacing the wires, there's not much more than fresh spark plugs needed to help a Miata along. Naturally aspirated Miatas will never overtax the stock system. On turbocharged or supercharged cars, however, the added heat of a blown engine will put you at risk for preignition on the standard spark plugs, so you should run a spark plug that's one step cooler than the standard plug. This means you need one of the following spark plugs for a forced-induction engine: Bosch FR7DCX, Champion RC9YC4, NGK BKR7E-11, or Nippon-Denso K16PR-U11.

The Miata's spark plugs come out and go in just like any other engine's, with two special caveats that follow. Spark plugs are best removed before you warm up the engine; this avoids burnt fingers and dropped plugs. To start with you'll need a spark-plug wrench with a rubber boot inside. Since the Miata's plugs are deep down in a hole and you'll be pulling vertically to remove them, the rubber boot in the socket is the only way to pull the plug up out of the hole.

Carefully remove the plug wire from the spark plug by pulling straight up on the boot; never pull on the wire. Remove the spark plugs, and keep them in the order they were installed so that you can tell which cylinders they came from. Now, examine each plug. Differences in spark-plug appearance might indicate unusual cylinder conditions. The perfect plug looks toasty-tan in color and has clean edges to the side wire and center electrode. Since the Miata has such

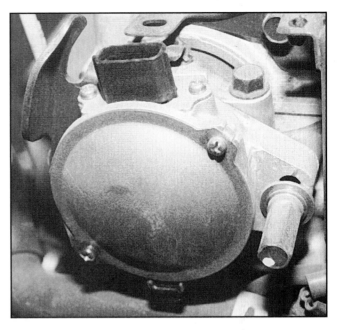

To adjust the timing, you'll need to loosen the pinch bolt that holds the crank angle sensor in place. On 1.6-liter cars, it can be reached from the intake side of the engine with a 12-millimeter box wrench. For the 1.8-liter engines, you'll need a 1/4-inch drive socket wrench with a 12-millimeter socket in place to reach the tall-headed bolt from the exhaust side.

The coils are not interchangeable from 1.8-liter to 1.6-liter, but both perform similar functions, firing two spark plugs at once. These coils are sufficient for even the most modified of engines.

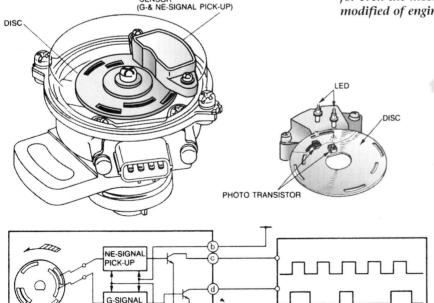

In lieu of a distributor, the Miata uses a crank angle sensor. This sensor delivers two low-voltage signals to the PCM, which determines fuel injection amount and ignition events.

a good fuel injection system, you'll rarely see a plug that's fouled from too rich a mixture. You might see some oil fouling (black, wet deposits on the center insulator and base), and this indicates a problem with the piston rings or valve guides in that cylinder.

If you are going to reuse the spark plugs, examine the threads carefully and replace the gaskets. Better yet, replace the plugs. At under $8 for a full set, it just doesn't make much sense to cheap out here. Before installing the plugs, gap them with a wire-type gauge to 0.039-0.043 inch. The ideal setting is 0.040 inch.

Here's another requirement: Use antiseize compound on your spark plugs before you put them in. Countless careless owners have forgotten this step and ruined their cylinder heads. Remember that the Miata has an aluminum alloy head and that spark plugs are made of steel. Corrosion often sets in due to the dissimilar metals and locks the plug into the head. When forced out, the corroded plug can pull the threads right out of the head or break off and leave parts stuck in the spark plug hole. Either way, it is a messy deal that costs much more than the $3 you'd have spent for a tube of antiseize compound.

Once you're set to reinstall everything, thread the plugs by hand and tighten with the spark-plug socket. The torque spec is 15 pounds-feet, which you can measure with a torque wrench or just do by eye; 15 pounds-feet is about a quarter turn past finger tight. Be very careful not to overtighten the plugs, as the aluminum cylinder head's threads may strip.

Always use antiseize on your spark plug threads when reinserting a spark plug. Standard plug gap is 0.040 inch. It is recommended that you use duct tape to tie your socket extensions together (not shown) so they don't get stuck down in the engine.

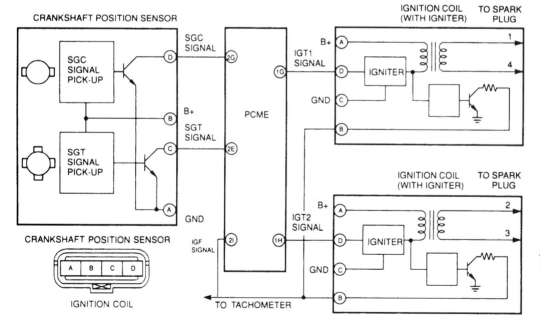

How the PCM and the ignition coils hook together on the 1.8-liter engine. The 1.6-liter's system is similar except the igniter is outside the coil. Since the electrical path is opposite than normal on cylinders No. 2 and No. 4, some timing lights won't trigger themselves from these two cylinders, just in case you're checking for spark at those wires with a timing light.

Induction System Improvements

The factory engineers who massaged the Miata's engine for maximum power were also determined to guarantee a broad range of power across the rev band. Some peak power was given away in favor of making some good low-end torque, so one of the best ways to increase the maximum top-end power is to modify the intake tract. The standard Miata intake tract is relatively long, which takes advantage of natural pulse doubling to boost low-end power and drivability. Long tracts are less efficient for high-end output, however.

Virtually all of the aftermarket intake-tract devices out there create higher horsepower at higher rpm at a sacrifice in low-rpm grunt. This isn't to say you can't improve on the stock intake tract, but a lot of aftermarket modifications may actually hurt your everyday performance, or even the performance at all engine speeds. As with everything else on a Miata, you have to identify a realistic goal and proceed carefully to make sure you wind up with an improvement, rather than going backward.

A crude but simple way to check to see if your intake system is restrictive is to mount a sensitive vacuum gauge on your windshield and plumb it to a nipple somewhere between the throttle and the airflow meter. Run the car at 7,200 rpm in second gear down the highway and have an observer look at the gauge. If any vacuum is registered, something is restrictive. Remove the air filter element and run the same test. If the vacuum reading goes down (closer to 0), the air filter was restrictive. If it stays at the same reading, your restriction is in the airflow meter or in the plumbing. You can also test the throttle body by measuring for vacuum in the intake manifold at wide open throttle (WOT). If the reading in the intake manifold at WOT is the same as in the crossover pipe (before the throttle body), then your throttle bore is not restrictive.

Make sure to note the difference between restriction and length tuning. The system should never be restrictive, but when you shorten the overall length of the intake track, high-rpm performance will be enhanced by tuning factors. Some devices affect the dynamic tuning on a system that has no restrictions and make greater power. Don't think of a hot intake system as being less restrictive, it is only changing the dynamic tuning. The stock system is not restrictive, per se.

Air Filters and Airboxes

Let's start where the air comes in first—at the air box. Probably the most popular modification for Miatas over the years has been to change the air filter. The stock panel-type filter is a pretty good piece for the money, but some horsepower gains can be found by replacing it with a higher-flow unit.

One of the more popular aftermarket filters is the cotton-mesh panel type. Dyno testing has shown these to offer only a slight advantage in flow over the stock unit, but they are reusable and could be the last filter you'll have to buy for your car. Recently, Jackson Racing has created another type of infinitely reusable air filter that produces measurably more power than any other unit on the dyno—around three to four horses at peak rpm. Since it delivers cheap horsepower and may ultimately pay for itself by eliminating the need to buy new stock filters, it's a good investment at under $50.

The next step in increasing performance along the intake track is to replace the stock air-filter box with a tuned induction piece. As oversized as the Mazda unit is, some power can be gained by routing the air along smoother routes. Various manufacturers make these units, such as Racing Beat, HKS, Millen, and others. There's horsepower to be gained here, but some of it comes from simply moving power around the rpm range rather than increasing it across the range.

Moving the power up the rev range isn't necessarily a bad thing. Your 0-60 times will be lower, provided you continue to shift at high rpm. Since the Miata comes with a

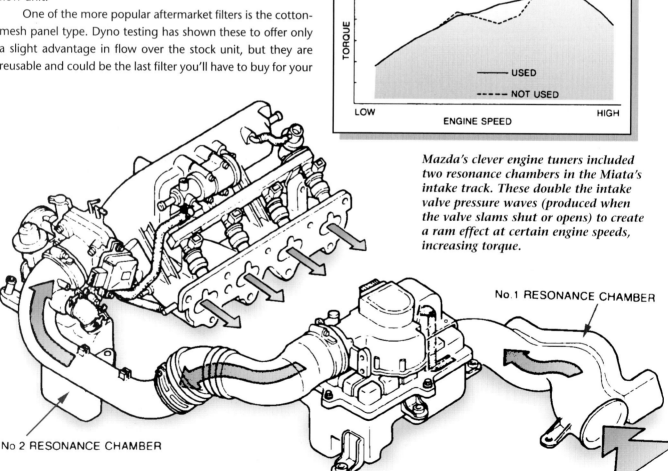

Mazda's clever engine tuners included two resonance chambers in the Miata's intake track. These double the intake valve pressure waves (produced when the valve slams shut or opens) to create a ram effect at certain engine speeds, increasing torque.

No.1 RESONANCE CHAMBER

No 2 RESONANCE CHAMBER

close-ratio gearbox, you can keep the engine in the peak torque and horsepower range easily. None of these devices make the engine feel too peaky for daily use, and they're the first steps to take toward improving flat-out performance, if not necessarily toward improving throttle response in real-world driving. Most tuned intake-tract devices run $150-$300.

If you want to step up a little higher, the industry leader is the Jackson Racing Cold-Air Induction Kit. This replaces the stock intake tract up to the throttle body. It incorporates a high-performance panel-type air filter and directs cold air from directly ahead of the radiator into a tuned airbox, through the airflow meter, and then into the throttle body. In general, a Miata will gain around 12-14 horses with one of these kits. Currently, Jackson Racing's Cold-Air kit delivers the maximum performance gain you can get from an off-the-shelf intake-tract modification.

The secrets to the Jackson Racing system are twofold. First, it shortens the total length of the intake tract, thus reducing the effective restriction. Second—and more importantly—it introduces cold air directly into the system. The general rule is that you can get a 1 percent power increase for every 7 degrees Fahrenheit you lower the intake air temperature. Since summer underhood temperatures in a Miata can exceed 150 degrees, bringing in the air from the front of the car is worth a significant amount of power. Dropping the intake charge 60 degrees Fahrenheit can yield around 9 percent more peak horsepower; on a Miata, that's about 10 ponies just for routing the air from a better source.

Due to the success of the Jackson system, a few other cold-air intakes have been developed by competitors. Racing Beat has a nice unit that bolts to the stock air box.

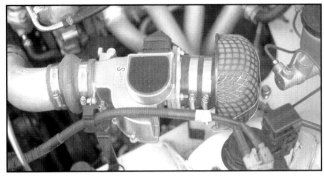

One of the first performance intake systems for the Miata was developed by Japanese tuner HKS. Its POWERFLOW product increases airflow at high rpm for increased horsepower.

Racing Beat, a long-time tuner of Mazdas, has developed this nicely built intake system that offers higher flow rates at high rpm. It also picks up cooler air from behind the headlamp lid.

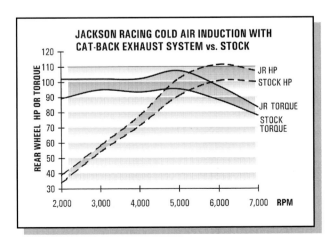

Dynojet chassis dynamometer curve for a stock 1.8-liter engine versus 1.8-liter with a cold air induction system.

The popular Jackson Racing cold air induction system. It started as an MFM system for the 1.6-liter cars that incorporated a hot-wire airflow meter. The core of the power increase came from the cold air, so it was adapted for the stock airflow meter. At around $400, it is a very solid step toward opening a Miata engine up.

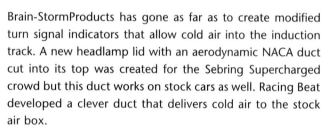

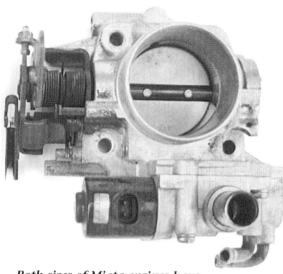

Both sizes of Miata engines have a 55-millimeter throttle body. The idle-speed control valve changes with the 1.8 liter. It is more adaptable and is controlled completely by the PCM.

Brain-StormProducts has gone as far as to create modified turn signal indicators that allow cold air into the induction track. A new headlamp lid with an aerodynamic NACA duct cut into its top was created for the Sebring Supercharged crowd but this duct works on stock cars as well. Racing Beat developed a clever duct that delivers cold air to the stock air box.

When evaluating a design, pay attention to total intake tract length. Shorter runs mean less time for underhood temperature to soak back into the intake stream. And don't get too excited about how much of an effect you're having—the intake manifold holds the air for a significant portion of the intake cycle, and the manifold is water-heated to 187 degrees no matter what. Every little bit helps, though, so getting the air from a colder source is a great way to start. Most cold-air intakes come in at the $30 per horsepower range-retailing from $300 to $500.

Throttle Bodies

Moving down the intake stream, the next item is the throttle body. Many other vehicles such as Volkswagens and Mustang 5-liter V-8s benefit from having larger throttle bodies installed on their intake manifolds. Miatas come with a 55-millimeter throttle body, on both the 1.6- and 1.8-liter engines.

This is another short discussion: The stock throttle body flows sufficient air even for supercharged and turbocharged engines. The author's advice is not to invest in larger throttle bodies for the Miata. As evidence of the lack of benefit, no company is known to offer such a device.

The stock throttle body can get gummed up with oil deposits (thanks to the cam cover vent to the intake tube). Check your throttle body bore for cleanliness. If there are black deposits, gently remove them with mineral spirits or carburetor cleaner. Do not clean off the coating that Mazda put in the bore to assist in throttle blade seating. If you take off the coating, the throttle will leak worse. If the throttle leaks, rough idling and poor drivability will occur.

Intake Manifold

Next down the tract is the intake manifold. The stock intake manifold has a generous plenum set on long runners designed to increase the ram effect at low revs for greater cylinder filling. Mazda designed this manifold using skills acquired during the rotary-engine program. Rotary engines operate as two-stroke motors, so the pressure pulses that run up and down their intake tracts become very important to engine tuning.

For daily driving, the stock Miata manifold is quite sufficient, and the only improvement that can be done is offered by a company called 'Extrudehone.' Their process is one in which an abrasive sludge is pumped through the intake manifold in such a way that the inside surfaces are polished smooth. This increases the airflow capacity of the intake manifold by reducing the turbulence and drag along the walls of the plenum and runners. The story goes that Smoky Yunick invented this process when trying to get around the NASCAR rule book which stated that no "mechanical" means could be used to port a cylinder head. Abrasive sludge is not mechanical, per se.

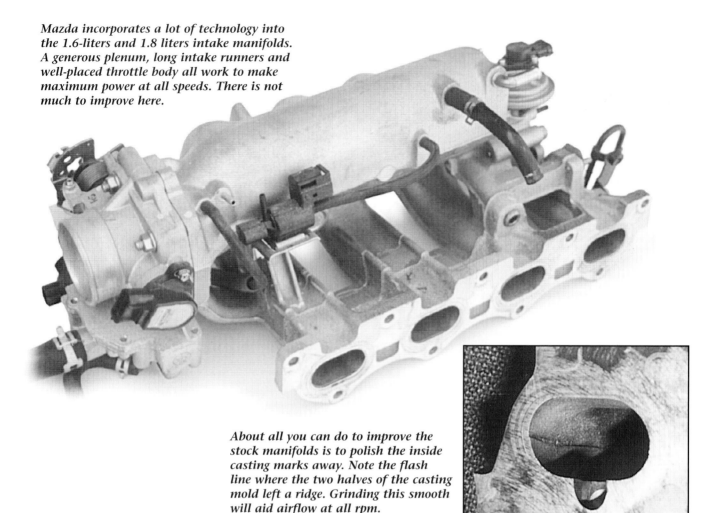

Mazda incorporates a lot of technology into the 1.6-liters and 1.8 liters intake manifolds. A generous plenum, long intake runners and well-placed throttle body all work to make maximum power at all speeds. There is not much to improve here.

About all you can do to improve the stock manifolds is to polish the inside casting marks away. Note the flash line where the two halves of the casting mold left a ridge. Grinding this smooth will aid airflow at all rpm.

The Extrudehone modification is not an inexpensive process, costing about $300-$400 for a Miata manifold. The horsepower gains are largely at the mid- to high-rpm range. Dyno tests show this modification to be worth just over 10 horses, or around $35 per horsepower. For the purist, it's the best way to optimize a Miata intake manifold.

Beyond porting the manifold itself, one way to optimize the intake airflow is to match the intake manifold to the cylinder head. Mazda did a pretty good job casting the intake manifold, but slight variations in the casting process can create offsets where the ports mate to the manifold. The only practical way to match ports is to have both the cylinder head and intake manifold machined while they're off of the car. Removing these pieces is a major pain, but never grind any material off of the cylinder head with it still on the engine—you'll never capture all of the grinding particles, and they'll make a mess of your rings and cylinder walls.

If you have a Saturday to kill and just are itching to do something, take off your intake manifold and inspect how it

For the new 1999 Miata, Mazda found a few more horsepower by changing to a variable-length intake manifold. At low rpm, the intake tubes are kept long for good ram effect. At high rpm, the tubes are routed along a shorter path to get the air in the cylinder faster. The engine now makes 140 peak horsepower (some of that due to an increased compression ratio).

An experimental system using a short manifold and individual throttle bodies mounted directly to the cylinder head. The stock PCM drives the injectors for maximum top-rpm power.

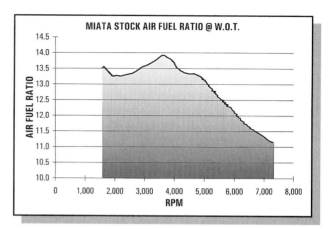

Contrary to what you may think, stock Miatas do not run lean. At WOT, the fuel injection system runs off memory (no oxygen sensor input) and runs more than rich enough to make maximum power. The trick is getting more air in and getting the exhaust gases out.

matches up to the cylinder head. One way to do this is with a homemade cardboard template. Cut its outer shape and bolt holes using the stock steel gasket as a template. Then, hold the cardboard gasket up against the manifold and cut the port shapes out using the manifold ports as a guide. Move the gasket over to the cylinder head next, and see if the manifold has any mismatched portions with respect to the head's ports.

If the manifold doesn't quite match up in a few areas, you can safely grind away any obvious flashing or casting flaws in the intake ports on the manifold with a hand file. Since the manifold is made of aluminum, you can make progress pretty readily. If you have a Dremel or similar power grinder, it can be used if you're careful not to grind away too much material at once. Recheck your work frequently and fine-tune it as necessary. Once you're finished, flush the manifold with hot water and soap to clear out all grinding debris, and then reinstall it on the engine. You can reuse the stock steel gasket about three times.

No matter how much porting or polishing you do, the stock manifold is only going to flow so much air because the inside length is fixed, and its length limits high-rpm breathing. The author has been playing around with the adaptation of a shorter manifold and racing throttle bodies to make the shortest possible intake tract. On the car, this system looks a lot like a pair of 45 DCOE Webers, but in fact they're not

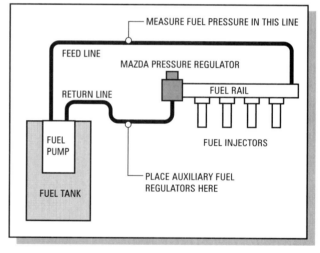

To measure your fuel pressure, tap into the fuel system at the point shown. While stock fuel pressure is not adjustable, a low pressure can explain a loss of top-rpm power.

1.6 INJECTION

Fuel Pressure	Fuel Flow
43	20.0 lbs/hr
50	22.4
60	24.5
70	26.5
80	28.3

For the 1.8-liter motor, Mazda incorporated some needed improvements and some required ones. The airflow meter was changed to a hot-wire system superior for mid-range drivability. Emission regulations brought in an EGR system to reduce NOx emissions.

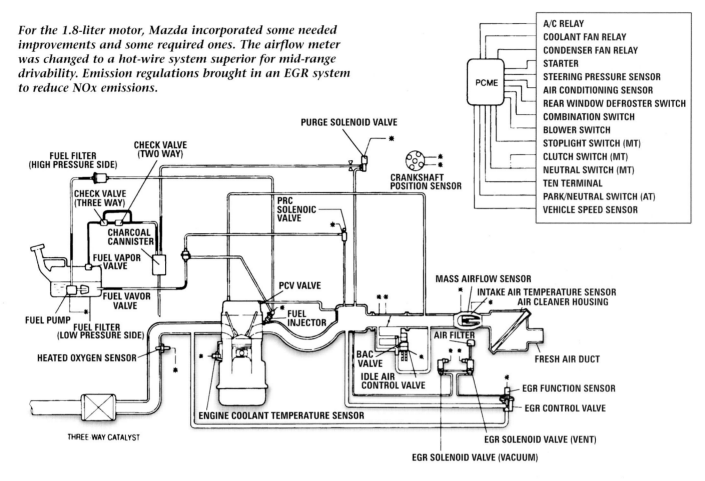

carburetors but throttle bodies housing fuel injectors. This is a sophisticated system that uses four single butterflies and velocity stacks in combination with a short-runner manifold to create the maximum possible airflow. High-rpm power is greatly increased with a proportional reduction in low-speed torque. The injectors are run by the stock PCM with a dedicated fuel pressure regulator. This is an example of how far you can take the optimization of the intake system.

Fuel Delivery

The fuel pump is mounted in the fuel tank (hung from the tank's top under the rear package shelf) and runs "wet" in the fuel itself. The fuel flows out a delivery line coming out of the fuel pump, up to the fuel rail, through a pressure regulator that limits fuel-system pressure to 43 psi, down the rail to each injector, then through a regulator, and finally into a "dump" line returning to the fuel tank.

For reference, the stock 1.6-liter Miata's fuel injectors are rated to run at 43 psi of fuel pressure in the fuel rail. At this pressure they can deliver 20 pounds of fuel per hour. The 1.8-liter's injectors are rated at 22 pounds per hour at the same 43 psi.

The fuel injectors are initially calibrated on the assumption that air at the injector tip will be at atmospheric pressure, while fuel coming into the injectors will be at 43 psi. However, when the throttle is partly closed or at idle, there's actually a vacuum in the intake manifold, and this will suck more fuel out of the injectors than atmospheric pressure would. To counteract this, Mazda could have shortened the duty cycle of the injectors—the time they stay open—but this would have created poor atomization of fuel at the injector tip, to the detriment of emissions and drivability. A better solution was to reduce the rail pressure under these conditions, effectively rebalancing the ratio of fuel pressure to air pressure. For this reason the stock regulator reduces pressure at the rail to 35 psi at idle.

The 1.8-liter cars close the vacuum line to the regulator during hot restart to provide a bit more fuel to overcome the fuel vaporization that occurs in a hot engine. By momentarily killing the vacuum to the regulator, the rail pressure can briefly go to a full 43 psi.

Some aftermarket tuners sell a static regulator that creates an adjustable restriction in the fuel-return line. This raises the pressure at all times so that the injectors are continually flowing additional fuel. These are advertised as a way to improve performance, but almost all fuel-injected engines today already have plenty of fuel capacity. Getting more gasoline into an engine is never very hard; the trick is getting in more air with which to help burn the gasoline.

Tests with sophisticated air-fuel ratio measurement devices show that the fuel-management system for either size Miata engine is excellent, and, if anything, already a touch too rich. No improvement can be gained by installing larger injectors or increasing the fuel pressure in the rail on an otherwise stock engine. You have to make significant changes to the displacement or breathing capacity of the Miata engine before you'll outstrip the stock injection system's ability to deliver fuel.

As just mentioned, you can easily increase the fuel-flow rate from the stock injectors simply by raising the fuel rail pressure. Miata injectors can take up to 85 psi of fuel pressure and still flow (this is not the case with all injector types). See the accompanying chart to see various flow rates at various pressures.

This method of increasing fuel injector flow has been regularly used by the turbocharging and supercharging industry using a boost-sensitive pressure regulator. The rail pressure stays at the stock setting until boost is seen, at which point a restriction is introduced into the fuel-return line. As the pump pushes against the restriction, the rail pressure is increased and more fuel is sent to the cylinders. This works well up to around 80 psi on the stock pump, at which point it runs out of steam and can't flow any more fuel. Higher-capacity fuel pumps are available for even greater pressures and flow rates, but the Miata injectors don't like more than about 85 psi.

Fuel Pumps

The stock Miata fuel pump's flow rate and delivery pressure are more than adequate for a stock engine, but these pumps do lose flow rate over time. Booster pumps are available to compensate for a tired main pump, but the most effective solution is simply to replace your tired stock pump with a new one.

To check the pump's health, buy an accurate fuel-pressure gauge and rig it up to the fuel line between the fuel tank and the fuel rail inlet. The stock fuel regulator is on the downstream end of the fuel rail, so you want to measure the pressure upstream of the regulator. With a few hardware-store plumbing items you can make a simple T-junction to tie the gauge into the system and measure the pressure. Use high-pressure fuel hoses and Teflon tape on your fittings to ensure that nothing leaks—this is gasoline you're working with, so a leaky pressure system is potentially very dangerous.

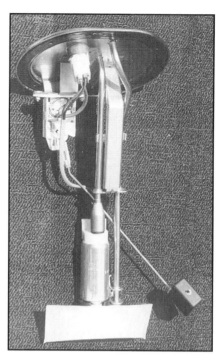

The stock fuel pump is hung in the gas tank from above and runs "wet" all the time. The gasoline actually serves to cool the electric motor. Shown is a high-performance pump sold by Moss Motors and others, necessary for forced induction engines running over 7 psi of boost.

The best place to tap into the fuel-feed line is at the metal tube-to-rubber hose junction along the passenger-side frame rail. You'll see two tubes coming up from under the car, the pressurized fuel line from the pump and the dump line that returns excess fuel to the tank. Most Miatas have a white paint mark on the return line, which carries very little pressure. Make sure you're testing the high-pressure fuel feed line when measuring fuel pressure.

After all the plumbing is connected and safe, start your engine and remove the vacuum line to the stock regulator. Your pressure should read over 40 psi at the least. Now reconnect the vacuum line to the regulator to confirm that the pressure drops by at least 6 psi. If it doesn't drop, you have a bad regulator. Replace it before you go on. When testing fuel pressures, you need to do it with the engine running. If you simply use the diagnostic connector jump wire trick to get the fuel pump going, it'll be seeing only 12 volts. The fuel pump normally runs at 13.5 volts and has measurably more output at this voltage. If you must, you can connect a battery charger to the battery and get the system voltage up closer to 13.5 volts and use the jumper-wire method.

To road-test your fuel pump, duct-tape your pressure-testing gauge to the outside of your windshield (never route

To trick the PCM into thinking an airflow meter was still active, a plunger rheostat was put in place with an actuating cam on the throttle shaft. This made the PCM advance the timing in the correct fashion as engine rpm rose.

Just for fun, the author put a pair of MGB carburetors on a 1.6-liter Miata. The SU carbs looked and ran great, but the fuel injection still made more power.

fuel into the cockpit, even on a new gauge) and go for a drive. Have an assistant observe the pressure gauge while you drive. If the pressure drops at high-rpm, WOT conditions, the fuel pump isn't up to snuff.

The stock pump works well as a replacement for naturally aspirated engines, but not if you're going to forced induction with more than 8 psi of boost. Moss selsl a direct replacement in-tank pump that flows enough fuel to support 250 horsepower. It will work well in an otherwise stock system for owners wanting an extra margin of capacity, and costs less than the Mazda pump as well. Since replacing the existing pump does require removing it from the fuel tank, another route is to install a booster pump along the inlet fuel line. BEGI sells a good example of this type, which comes with all the related wiring and relays to operate it safely.

Still another way to get more fuel into a highly modified Miata engine is to simply put in larger injectors. In practice it's cheaper and easier to raise the fuel pressure than to replace all four injectors, unless your injectors are defective to begin with, but as mentioned above, only boosted engines really need more fuel in any case. This will be covered in more detail in the Forced Induction chapter.

Adding a Carburetor
Just for fun, the author once put two SU carburetors from an old MGB onto a 1.6-liter Miata. A custom intake manifold was

fabricated and some electronic trickery was performed to fool the PCM into letting the engine start. (The PCM was still looking for an airflow meter and throttle-position sensor, both of which were jettisoned, but this didn't keep it from running the engine.) The SUs really worked, though they would, of course, never be "smoggable." In the end, the SU package was surprisingly elegant, and it certainly warmed the cockles of the author's classic-sports car heart. Midrange performance was actually improved over the stock Miata, and it was great not having a rev-limiter at 7,250 rpm. Probably the most fun was pulling the manual choke knob out every morning (conveniently located in place of the cigarette lighter). Emissions were dismal, however, which is why we don't see SU carbs on new vehicles any more.

Miata racers competing in SCCA E Production racing will be allowed to install a single 45 DCOE Weber carburetor, and just to outline how to do this, here's a short description of how to maintain the PCM functions without an airflow meter and throttle-position sensor. But first, let's talk about the airflow meter and throttle-position sensor.

Airflow Meters
All 1.6-liter Miatas are equipped with a vane-type airflow meter. This is essentially a flapper valve that's pushed open with increased airflow through the flow meter. As the vane opens, a wiper resister changes the resistance of the circuit inside the meter, and this sends a signal to the PCM. At idle, the airflow meter has an output of around 4.5 volts; at WOT and high rpm, the airflow meter signal reads about 0.4 volts.

INTAKE AIR TEMPERATURE SENSOR

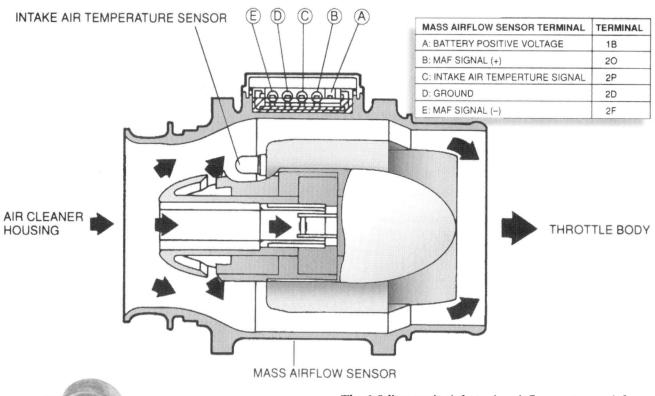

MASS AIRFLOW SENSOR TERMINAL	TERMINAL
A: BATTERY POSITIVE VOLTAGE	1B
B: MAF SIGNAL (+)	2O
C: INTAKE AIR TEMPERTURE SIGNAL	2P
D: GROUND	2D
E: MAF SIGNAL (−)	2F

AIR CLEANER HOUSING

THROTTLE BODY

MASS AIRFLOW SENSOR

The 1.6-liter's airflow meter (left) is a vane-type, in which the inrushing air pushes a hinged door open. A variable resistor attached to the door tells the PCM how much air is coming in. The small post in the opening contains the intake air temperature sensor. You can adapt a larger airflow meter from a larger Mazda engine. Both the RX-7 and the 626 units (shown) will electrically fit the Miata's fuel injection system. These are necessary only when drastic changes have been made to the breathing capacity of the engine.On the right is the 1.8 liter's hot-wire airflow meter. Voltage is sent to a wire suspended inside the unit. Inrushing air cools the hot wire. The current needed to keep the wire isothermal is used by the PCM to calculate airflow. It is much more rapid in its response than the vane-type airflow meter.

The 1.8-liter engine's hot wire airflow meter can't be improved upon just yet. Transient response is terrific and restriction is low

The 1.6-liter's airflow meter has a switch to prevent the fuel pump from staying on if the meter doesn't see airflow. This is a safety device in case the engine stops running in an accident—fuel flow will be stopped as well. If your engine starts and then stops immediately, it might be that your airflow meter's connector isn't hooked up correctly.

In the case of 1.8-liter Miatas, Mazda uses a more sophisticated hot-wire airflow meter. In this device, a thin wire is heated to a preset temperature, and as the airflow increases its cooling effect forces the wire to draw more current to maintain a constant temperature. This increase in amperage is read by the PCM, giving it a very accurate figure for calculating airflow. The resulting signal is similar to the vane type's but reversed, being around 1.5 volts at idle and around 4.5 volts at WOT and maximum rpm.

Testing has shown that neither of these devices is particularly restrictive, even on forced-induction motors. The 1.8's hot-wire airflow meter is more adaptable to modification and gives superior drivability due to its faster response time, greater sensitivity, and better transient response. In addition, response at throttle tip-in (when the throttle first begins to open) is crisper with the hot-wire meter.

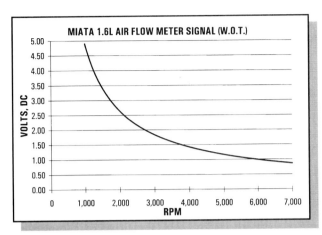

At WOT, the vane type airflow meter returns the voltages shown to the PCM at various rpm. At idle the voltage is around 4.5 volts.

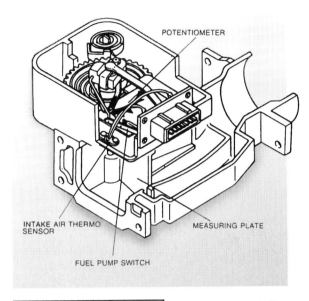

Many people think that increasing the size of the 1.6's vane-type meter or reducing the tension on its return spring can improve performance, either by enhancing airflow or by providing a better air-fuel mixture at throttle tip-in. After much testing, it was concluded that neither is true. Mazda chose an oversized airflow meter that even forced-induction engines can't swamp. On a flow bench, the 1.6-liter's airflow meter will test out at approximately 170 cubic feet per minute; the 1.8-liter unit flows up to around 200 cubic feet per minute. Unless you have done something serious to the breathing of your Miata, the stock unit works fine for naturally aspirated engines. If you want to, however, the larger airflow meters from the Mazda 626 or second-generation RX-7 will adapt easily to the stock system. This would be of benefit only to aggressively overbored engines with ported heads and wild induction systems. It should be remembered that the airflow meter does most of its work in midrange drivability. At WOT, the throttle-position sensor signal and the PCM map determine the majority of the fuel injection amount.

Even the forced-induction crowd generally sticks with the stock airflow meter for both sizes of Miata engines. Upstream measurements show no pressure drop upstream of the throttle even during maximum power operation, indicating that flow rates of over 300 cubic feet per minute are possible. However, with naturally-aspirated engines, many racers use the RX-7 air flow meters to eliminate any hint of restriction on their 1.6L motors.

Throttle-Position Sensor

On 1.6-liter Miatas, the throttle-position sensor is a simple switch that tells the PCM when the throttle is completely closed or completely open. Using three wires to the

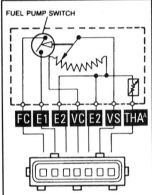

The 1.6-liter's airflow meter has a fuel pump switch that cuts off the power to the fuel pump if airflow stops. This is a safety device in case an engine dies during a wreck.

FE ....Fuel pump lead
E1 ....Fuel pump ground
E2 ....Ground
VE........+5 volts
VS ....Air flow signal
THAA...Air temp signal

throttle-position sensor, the PCM can tell the position of the throttle plate.

On 1.8-liter cars, the throttle-position sensor is a continuously variable resistor fed by four wires. A voltage signal is returned to the PCM at any given throttle position, so the PCM always knows where the throttle blade is. This is part of the more sophisticated fuel injection system on the 1.8-liter cars. In general, both the 1.6- and 1.8-liter motors have excellent fuel injections systems.

Getting Around the System

When stand-alone injection systems or carburetors are put on a Miata engine, something has to be done with the airflow-meter and throttle-position-sensor signals. Without the proper information, the PCM won't know how to set the ignition timing. In practice, however, the throttle-position-sensor signal can be ignored if the airflow-meter signal is properly handled.

For the SU-carburetor setup, a plunger-type potentiometer was mounted to the side of the carb. This switch was

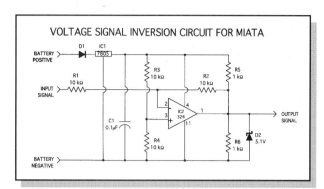

If you want to use a mass air pressure (MAP) sensor instead of a airflow meter on a 1.6-liter, you'll need to invert its output signal. The Miata airflow meter runs from 4.5 volts at idle to 0.4 volts at WOT, pretty much the opposite of a MAP sensor. Build this circuit from parts found at Radio Shack (around $7) to invert the signal and protect the PCM.

actually a throttle-position sensor from a mid-1980s Mazda B2000 truck. It received a voltage signal and returned a decreasing voltage as the plunger was depressed. A small cam was made that clamped onto the throttle shaft and depressed the plunger as the throttle was opened.

The PCM uses a 5-volt reference signal for most of its sensors, including the airflow meter. For our project car, a 5-volt signal was fed to the plunger throttle-position sensor, while a 5- to 1.5-volt signal was returned while the throttle moved from idle to full throttle. In this way, the PCM was tricked into thinking that airflow meter was operating, so the ignition timing was advanced appropriately.

Since the PCM uses the airflow-meter signal in conjunction with the engine-speed signal, when the modified system returned a full airflow signal once the throttle was depressed (even if the engine was at low rpm), the PCM would make the right calculation by referencing the engine-speed data. Thus, a proper ignition advance curve was manipulated. By changing the profile of the throttle-shaft cam that rode on the plunger throttle-position sensor, a more or less aggressive ignition curve could be tuned for optimum performance.

An alternative method for recreating the airflow meter's signal is to use a MAP (Mass Air Pressure) sensor commonly available from auto parts stores. In the same way, a 5-volt signal can be fed into a MAP sensor and a decreasing voltage signal returned to the PCM. While throttle position and manifold vacuum are closely related, the MAP sensor scheme will give a slightly different ignition advance curve. The benefit of the MAP sensor setup is its ease of construction. Since most MAP sensors put out 0 volts at high vacuum and 5 volts at zero vacuum, you need a voltage inverter to get the signal going the right way for the PCM.

For maximum top-end power, you can go to very short manifolds (available from Mazdaspeed) and put on some traditional Weber carburetors. While low rpm torque will suffer, the top-rpm range will benefit from the short intake path.

If you're running without the airflow meter on a 1.6-liter car, you'll need to bypass the fuel-pump safety device in the airflow meter. Otherwise the pump will cut off just after startup because it isn't seeing the correct signal. To bypass this, run a jumper from pin E1 to pin Fc in the connector. Note: You will be bypassing a safety device on the Miata if you do this.

Back to Webers. Dual Weber carburetors can be installed using the Mazdaspeed manifold. It is recommend to use 40 DCOE Webers to keep the intake velocities high and improve mid-range throttle response. You should use 32-millimeter chokes as well.

Webers allow almost infinite mixture adjustment. As a starting point, the following setup will get a Miata close to ideal; road-testing will allow you to optimize each component:

Main jets: 135	Air bleeds: 160
Emulsion tubes: F15	Pump jets: 40
Pump bleed: 40	Idle jet: 45
Idle bleed: F8	Auxiliary venturi: 4.5 millimeter

Conclusion

The easiest way to make power in this department is to focus on work upstream of the throttle body. Air filters, intake-tract changes, and cold-air intakes work well on the Miata. But from the throttle body downstream, Mazda did its homework, so improvements are harder to find. As for fuel mixture, even the most modified naturally aspirated engines don't run lean on the stock injection system. If however, you find yourself needing more fuel, review the tips in Chapter 13 for feeding a force-induction engine.

Exhaust System

Just as some great power gains are available in the Miata's intake tract, its exhaust system has some room for improvement as well. The stock Miata is held to a strict federal drive-by noise rating, which is why the stock muffler has a rather restricted nature. Aftermarket companies aren't held to these noise requirements, so they can build exhaust systems for increased flow. Most of these systems also offer a meatier exhaust tone in the bargain, which some customers deem reason enough to switch. Keep in mind, however, that if the noise gets too far out of hand, the customer may have to deal with unwanted attention from the local authorities.

The stock Miata exhaust system is made of high-quality stainless steel and guaranteed for five years or 50,000 miles. When buying a replacement system, the author recommends choosing stainless steel as well. Mild-steel units are available at a cheaper price, and if you're looking to change exhaust systems every two years or if your Miata only gets occasional use, these will be fine. However, even Miatas that only see occasional use will have an appreciable amount of condensation inside the tailpipe, which will rust out a mild-steel unit over time.

"Cat-Back" Systems

One of the first things anyone looking for more power on a Miata should consider is changing the final exhaust. The catalytic converter is mounted near the transmission housing, and going to an aftermarket "cat-back" system—meaning swapping out everything behind the catalytic converter—can increase top-end performance. Across the board, a basic aftermarket cat-back exhaust may be worth about 3 to 4 horsepower. The very best of them, such as Jackson Racing's system, can add up to 7 horsepower.

It's difficult to describe exhaust tones in a book, but suffice it to say that a Miata with a performance exhaust generally makes a very nice sound. There is, however, a booming

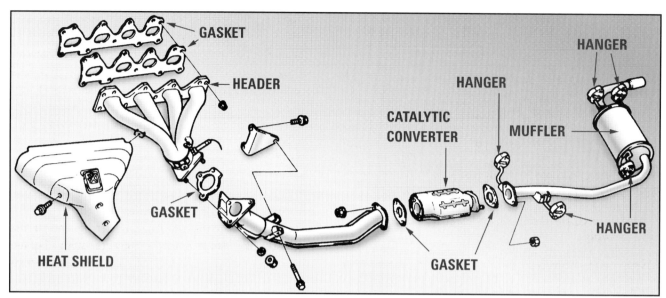

resonance natural to the Miata engine that starts around 3,000 rpm, and some of the less-expensive cat-back systems don't do a good-enough job of attenuating this boom. If you drive your car regularly on the highway (where 60 miles per hour equals 3,000 rpm in fifth gear), be careful to purchase a system that doesn't suffer this weakness. This is a bad place to save a few extra bucks.

Changing the rear muffler and intermediate pipe on a Miata is pretty simple. It can be done in about a half an hour by an experienced enthusiast. The recommended procedure is as follows:

1. The night before you want to remove your old system, spray the catalytic converter studs and nuts generously with WD-40. These have a tendency to shear off on dis-assembly, and are difficult to replace. If you lube them in advance, you can often avoid thee problem.
2. Back the car onto ramps, secure the handbrake, and chock the front wheels.
3. Allow the exhaust system to become cool to the touch.
4. Lubricate with WD-40 the two nuts on the catalytic con-verter that hold the rear mid-pipe in place, and then remove them. Move slowly as you remove these bolts; if you meet any abnormal resistance or sense that the nuts are binding on the threads, run the nut back down tight again, reapply more WD-40, and begin the process over. We can't emphasize this enough: A ham-fisted approach will shear the studs off in short order.
5. If you do shear off a stud, secure the old exhaust system with wire or plumbing straps, toss your new unit in the passenger's seat, and drive to a muffler shop. The 30-odd dollars you'll pay them to finish the installation will be

Mazda didn't skimp on quality in designing the stock exhaust system. Well-engineered and made of stainless steel, it might outlive the car. However, a few more horses can be found with an aftermarket system.

Go to any Miata Club event and you will see just about every combination of header and muffler imaginable. These engines brighten right up at the hint of a better breathing exhaust, so almost any system will help you gain power. Caveats include material quality, fitment, and noise levels.

The stock header is not terribly restrictive. The 1.6-liter's header shown uses a single-wire oxygen sensor in the collector. The 1.8-liter unit has a heated three-wire oxygen sensor that responds more quickly and more reliably.

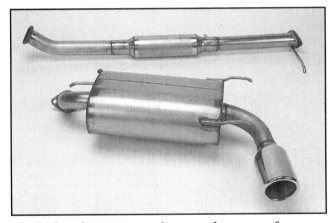

The highest horsepower gains on a dyno came from this "cat-back" system from Jackson Racing. Since Jackson has a dyno, experimentation allowed a fully optimized unit to be developed.

Brainstorm Products has a well-made equal-length-tubing header that not only looks good, but ekes out a few more high-rpm horsepower. Things to consider when buying a header include oxygen sensor location, proximity to the heater hoses coming out of the fire-wall, closeness to frame rails, and special coatings for longer life.

better than having to deal with the aftermath of the stud failure in your driveway.

6. Assuming you haven't sheared the studs and both catalytic converter nuts are now removed, follow the exhaust pipe backwards and look for the rubber hangers that secure the exhaust system. The two nuts are the only permanent fasteners in the system, so once the rubber hangers are loose, you're ready to drop the muffler and pipe. (Actually, they'll drop on their own at this point!)

7. Position the new system up under the car and install the rearmost hanger on the muffler end.

8. Then move up to the catalytic converter end and put the exhaust-pipe flange onto the converter studs. Tighten down the nuts (slowly). Put antiseize on the studs to minimize the chance of them corroding in place.

9. Install the remaining rubber hangers.

10. Start the car, check for audible leaks (little chirping sounds), and let the engine idle while the packing oil smokes off.

Aftermarket Headers

Mazda didn't scrimp when it came to creating a stock performance exhaust header for the Miata. The factory's four-into-one stainless-steel tube header has surprisingly good performance. Still, slight improvements in high-rpm power can be had from some of the aftermarket's four-into-two-into-one offerings. According to the dyno data, headers should be one of the last things you buy; the improvement only adds up to 2 or 3 horsepower, mostly at the top end. Good units are available from Racing Beat, Brainstorm Products, Jackson Racing and others.

Since the greater exhaust gas flow capacity of a performance header will only be realized if the rest of the system is less restrictive, it is advisable to opt for a high-flow catalytic converter and a performance muffler before you change out headers.

For owners of 1994 and later cars, make sure the header suppliers have done their homework in getting the EGR pipe in the right place. Ask them directly how difficult it will be to hook up the EGR pipe. A poorly placed EGR port on a header, or some jerry-built custom pipe can lead to hours of frustration under the hood.

Contrary to what you might think, the aftermarket headers designed for the Miata are generally easy to install. Back in the early days, quite a few headers just wouldn't fit on the car; now, enough have been sold so that the mainstream manufacturers have sorted out most of the problems. If you order an aftermarket header, for longevity's sake make sure

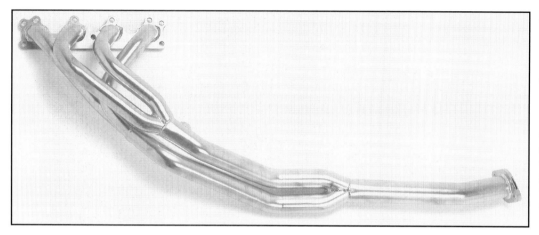

A performance header will have very long tubes that help to draw the exhaust gases out of the cylinders by using the gases' inertia to "pull" more exhaust out. This header shows the classic 4-2-1 design where four tubes lead to two tubes then into one tube.

it's either stainless steel or has an aluminized or ceramic coating. Also inquire about the location of its oxygen sensor; it should be near the same spot as the stock unit's. And don't forget the exhaust-gas recirculation (EGR) line on 1.8-liter cars—if this is poorly placed, your installation will be a bear.

So the formula goes like this: Change your final muffler first, then upgrade the catalytic converter, and if that isn't enough, go for the high-performance header. Use antiseize compound on all your connections and make sure that there is at least 1 inch of clearance between the exhaust system and the chassis/body at any given point, from the header to the muffler.

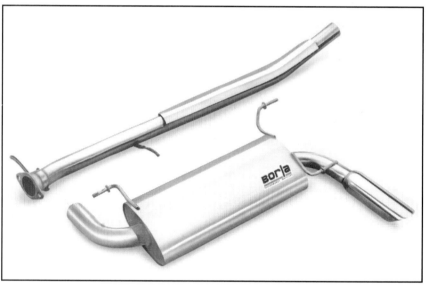

One of the first stainless steel performance systems came from Borla. These "cat-back" systems fit well, have a pleasant exhaust tone, and last indefinitely.

Many owners change out the mufflers just for the good sounds a performance muffler makes. In the author's opinion, based on the systems heard so far, the Borla and the Jackson Racing cat-back setups have better sound quality without being too loud. The systems from Trust/Greddy and Racing Beat also sound nice. No system really sounds bad, but some have a more pleasant tone from inside and outside the car.

Mazda carefully tuned the sound quality, something the engineering team took upon itself to do, a little "finesse" for the final product. As any Alfa enthusiast will tell you, a DOHC four-cylinder (with four valves per cylinder, no less) and a high-compression ratio is going to have a pretty good singing voice to start with. As an interesting side note, since the induction and exhaust events are closely tied, changing the intake system will affect your overall engine tone, albeit to a lesser extent than a muffler change. One of the cold-air intake systems and a performance muffler make quite a symphony from the front and the rear of a Miata. As the old hot rodders' axiom goes: If it's louder, it must be faster!

Internal Engine Modifications

As mentioned earlier, the Miata engine's short block began life in the econocar 323. This was Mazda's bread-and-butter engine, being produced at the rate of some 40,000 units per month in Japan. The Miata team got a leg up on hot-rodding this engine when it looked at the 323 GTX turbo engine that was developed on the same block. Lighter rotating components, a windage tray for the oil sump, a higher compression ratios, and other modifications had all been developed for the all-wheel-drive GTX pocket-rocket, and their durability was already proven.

While there are many ways to make a Miata faster without tearing the engine down, after some point the owner will have to freshen up the mechanical innards. Once you have the engine apart, some tricks can be applied.

When to Break It Open

A Miata engine with 100,000-plus miles is probably up for at least a cylinder-head freshening. This is the area that takes the most abuse and is largely responsible for the compression loss that shows up at this age. This is when most engines are showing around 175 psi or less in compression, down from the stock spec of 192. With nearly a 10 percent loss in compression, that's a substantial amount of horsepower escaping in a motor that produces just over 100 ponies to begin with.

You can pick up a compression tester at the local auto parts store for under $40. Make

Check each cylinder with a compression gauge to see if you are making all the power Mazda put into the engine. If you have a cylinder under 175 psi, it may be time for a rebuild.

Used engines are available from various wrecking yards. Look for a low-mileage engine (under 30,000 miles) that has no damage from an accident. Ask for a dressed engine (ignition coils, fuel injectors, alternator, and so on) to make sure you're not getting just a bare long block.

sure to get one that has a check valve that holds the gauge reading until you release it, because this feature makes one-person tests possible. You'll also want to get one with an extension hose, because the Miata spark plug holes are deep in the head.

To check the compression, warm up the engine, remove all the spark plugs, screw the tester into each cylinder one at a time, and crank the engine over for five seconds on each cylinder test. Read the compression gauge and write the compression figure on a pad. Read the other cylinders and compare the numbers when finished. No one cylinder should be 10 percent below the other cylinders' readings, and they all should be above 175 psi. If a cylinder reads low, put about two tablespoons of oil down the spark plug hole of the cylinder in question and take another compression reading. If the pressure goes up, your rings are bad in that cylinder (the oil temporarily improves the piston ring seal).

To be more sophisticated about it, you can do what is called a leak-down test. You'll use the same compression gauge and a T-block from the hardware store. Using an air

compressor with a pressure regulator and gauge on it, set the compressor line for 100 psi. Feed that line into the "T-block, and connect your compression gauge to a second port in the T-block. Temporarily plug the third hole in the T-block. Turn on the compressor (still set at 100 psi output) and confirm that your compression gauge shows 100 psi. If it doesn't, make a note of the correction factor between the two gauges. Then run the spark plug hole fitting line to the cylinder to be tested and connect its other end to the T- block. Now air will be coming from the compressor at 100 psi, go through the T-block, and into the cylinder. The compression gauge will measure whether the cylinder is holding the 100 psi or not.

If the compression gauge shows a lower pressure than is being fed, the difference (amount less than 100 psi) is your leak-down percentage. If your compression gauge reads 90 psi, you have 10 percent leakage. Generally, 10 percent leakage is acceptable, over 20 percent is bad.

To find the source of your leak, listen to the exhaust pipe.

If you hear a hiss there, the air is leaking past a bad exhaust valve. Take the snorkel off the throttle body and listen to the intake manifold. A hiss there indicates a bad intake valve. If these are quiet, take out the oil dipstick and listen for a hiss coming from the crankcase—a sure sign of worn rings or pistons. From this test, you can decide which part (or that all parts) of your engine need rebuilding.

If you decide it's time to do a rebuild, there are several things you can do while building the motor to produce more power. Some require additional expertise, which means sending parts out to machine shops, but some you can do on your own. If you decide to take this project on yourself, it might be wise to seek out a high-mileage used powerplant. They can be had for around $300 with a little searching. This purchase will allow you to prepare a fresh engine while still keeping the original in your Miata until you're finished. It helps to keep your Miata going so you can go and get parts.

Of course, you can also avoid having to do any rebuilding at all by simply buying a good, low-mileage used powerplant. These go for less than $1,000 and are the cheapest way to revive a tired Miata. Any year 1.6-liter will fit any other year; 1994 and 1995 1.8-liters are interchangeable, as are 1996 and later engines, but they can't cross over from one range to the other. The later cars have OBDII control systems and a different set of sensors that would be hard to update or retrofit. In either case, stay away from the automatic-transmission engines—they have lower compression ratios and milder cam timing—unless you're looking to boost the engine with a forced-induction system or other serious mods.

Let's look at doing a rebuild, top to bottom. Before tearing down the motor, start your parts list. You'll absolutely need some items to rebuild the engine, and others make sense to do while the machinery is out and accessible. Necessities include the following: a Mazda workshop manual, engine rebuild gasket kit, valve guides, freeze plugs, cylinder-head studs, timing belt and tensioner (don't risk it), and connecting-rod hardware. Optional items that are recommended for replacement include the following: motor mounts (not necessary, but oh what a difference), water pump, heater and radiator hoses (do them while they're easy), and a clutch, pressure plate, and lightened flywheel. The rest of the stuff will be added to the list as it's checked for spec.

If you go into this on your own, get the Mazda shop manual and take things apart by the book. The factory shop manual has very specific instructions on engine disassembly, the reasons for which may not be apparent at first. Their logic

The stock camshafts already have a pretty aggressive lift and overlap specification. Even the hydraulic lifters have served the racers well for those using the stock fuel cut at 7,250 rpm.

Mazda made lighter cam sprockets for the Miata to reduce rotational mass. Experiments with adjustable cam sprockets (to date) have not unlocked any power improvements, unlike for other import engines.

will undoubtedly arise during assembly, however, or worse still, when the engine is running again! During the teardown process, keep track of which parts belong together and from which cylinder they came. Since they've spent tens of thousands of miles getting accustomed to each other, you don't want to mix them up or you might have problems later.

Each part in the engine can either be replaced with a better part, or it can be modified to enhance its performance. It's usually a simple question of whether the economics or time are worth the effort. We won't list everything here, only the common tricks that apply to the Miata. Most of these rest in the balancing and blueprinting of the engine. This simply means that each part of the same type weighs the same so that all rotational mass is evenly weighted and each part is to an exact spec.

Cylinder Head Work

If you only have 70,000 or so miles on your car, you might consider doing a valve job to freshen things up and calling it a day. Whether you do a complete engine rebuild or not, the following notes apply to optimizing the Miata's cylinder head.

The cylinder head is responsible for creating most of the power the Miata engine produces. Therefore, it also has the most room for improvement with some individual attention it just doesn't get from the factory. Most of this is done with porting, but first you'll need to check everything for proper function and spec.

The Miata comes with a very well-designed cylinder head that incorporates two intake valves and two exhaust valves per cylinder. Two intakes valves are used, for the inertia-effect reasons discussed earlier and also to aid in packaging the intake hardware within the Miata's tight cylinder-head confines. These inertia (or ram) effects are not insignificant, by the way. Some tuners opt for the supersonic speed threshold at max flow velocities—that's over 700 local miles per hour, depending on the pressures involved. The same arguments apply to the exhaust valves.

The Miata has two 1.30-inch diameter intake valves and two 1.10-inch exhaust valves per cylinder. The exhaust valves are smaller due to the fact that exhaust gases leave the combustion chamber under pressure—peak combustion pressure is over 600 psi. Intake valves have to deal with a maximum pressure differential of 10 psi of vacuum, so they need to be larger to allow more air-fuel mixture into the cylinder.

If you want to optimize the intake and exhaust ports in your cylinder head, send the assembly out to a machine shop that specializes in porting heads. You can try porting it yourself, but for maximum results this is a job that's better left to a pro with the right equipment. Find a shop that specializes in multivalve heads and has a flow bench. This is a good place to put your money, and will provide the best return in power for cash. Talk to the technician and let him know just what you're after.

If you're not looking to spend money, then take a conservative approach and simply clean up any obvious marks in the head and smooth out the rough surfaces. Have the valves triple-cut to smooth the airflow into and out of the cylinder. A five-angle cut is even "trickier," if your shop can do the work. The idea is to make the transition from combustion chamber to port as smooth as possible, mimicking a smooth radius. Make sure the area where the valve seats is not too narrow—some porters get too aggressive here. For a street engine, an intake landing should be no less than 0.060-inch wide. For the exhaust valves, go for a 0.075-inch seat width

The famed HLA or lifter that has been the one weak point of the Miata engine. If you don't choose your oil correctly, these will not pump up at cold start and make a loud ticking noise. Thinner oils such as 5W-20 weights appear to solve the problem for most owners. Synthetics work well too, but can cause oil leaks on engines not run on synthetics since new.

Four valves—no waiting. Mazda uses two intake and two exhaust valves for a couple of reasons. The individual port velocities are higher, contributing to the ram effect at low speeds. It also gives a smaller column of air to accelerate into motion at high speeds. Two valves can be packaged to deliver more airflow than one large valve in the combustion chamber.

(this seat is important in transferring heat; the added surface area will be beneficial in this regard). Racers can reduce these numbers by half if they only need a 30-hour engine life before rebuild.

Once the valve seats have been cut, lap the valves with a lapping compound, pressing the valve into the seat and removing any material that's preventing a good seal. Check valve springs for square and spring rate and replace any units that are out of spec. You may add heavy-duty valve springs, but you'll need to upgrade the lifters if you do so. In general, heavier springs in a Miata will only serve to increase your frictional losses due to drag at the cam-lobe surface. If you don't have valve float, you don't need stiffer springs.

Engine Removal

There may come a day when you want to either rebuild or replace your engine. Getting an engine out of a Miata isn't all that difficult if you're a methodical worker and have the right tools. To walk through it step by step, here are a few pieces of advice:

Before you start:

Try to recruit some help before getting into the swap. If you're ambitious enough to try this yourself, then you probably associate with the same type of people—so give them a call. The assistance of a parental unit and fellow racer, both mechanically inclined, were enlisted for this project. It made guiding the engine in and out much easier and sped up the entire process.

Wear appropriate attire, not your favorite auto-oriented T-shirt or jeans. In fact, wear clothes that you wouldn't mind turning into rags; it might happen. A long- sleeve shirt isn't a bad idea, since everything in the engine bay seems to have a sharp edge. And don't forget your eye protection—you'll be handling some nasty fluids and working underneath the car, where everything you've ever run over is waiting to fall in your face.

This job will also provide a good opportunity to administer some maintenance on the car. Fresh coolant hoses and belts are a must; they'll never be this easy to get at again.

If the new engine has been sitting, inspect any seals and gaskets that might have dried up. If you're not on an ultra-tight budget, replace them anyway. Using the existing gaskets may lead to leaks.

Confidence

Follow the removal process more or less by the book, taking the occasional shortcut only if you really can't justify Mazda's recommended approach. The factory manual also provides a good backup when you can't

The easiest way to get the powerplant out of a Miata is to bring the transmission along with it. A cherry picker is a must, as are protective covers for the fenders and front bumper.

figure something out yourself, so keep it handy. Also, a video camera boosts the confidence level if there's concern about the reassembly; shoot the removal process carefully, and you can answer any questions that might crop up during the installation phase.

The Operation

Open the hood and mark the outlines of the hinges. This is a nice trick that virtually guarantees good hood alignment when you're through.

Cover the fenders, bumper cover, and headlight covers, because they will inevitably sustain the knock of a tool or the scrape of an engine. With the car up on jackstands and the battery disconnected, you're ready to begin the disassembly.

Remove the air box and its plumbing to the throttle body. Next, pull the radiator and its hoses. You'll also need to disconnect the heater hoses. If you opt to disconnect them at the firewall, be careful not to bend the heater-core connections, which are made of very thin metal. While you're tugging on hoses, pull any vacuum lines to the throttle body and label where they go.

The last hoses to be disconnected are the fuel lines. Take note that the hose toward the front of the car goes to the lower fuel pipe. Depressurize the lines by removing the gas cap. If the job will take more than a day, leave the gas cap off to avoid repressurizing, which may cause the fuel lines to drip. With your eye protection on, wrap the hoses with a rag and disconnect them. Plug the ends with a bolt that fits snugly inside the line.

On to the wiring harnesses: Mark all the harnesses so they can be reconnected properly. Because all the harnesses fall into place and use different connectors, they're pretty simple to reconnect, but marking them will save you time in reassembly.

Unplug the leads at the top of the power-steering

pump and the thermostat. The oxygen-sensor line starts at the header and ends at the rear of the cam cover, where you disconnect it. On the passenger side of the bellhousing are some harnesses that run down the top of the transmission. These need to be unclamped. While you're at the rear of the engine, unplug the crank-angle sensor and ignition coil. In the same area are a couple of ground wires that need to be unbolted from the intake plenum.

Halfway toward the front of the intake is the fuel injection connector that should be unhooked. Continue moving forward to the throttle body, where you'll unplug the idle-speed control valve and throttle sensor. Next disconnect the alternator, oil pressure gauge, and starter, which all reside underneath the intake. The power-steering pump and air-conditioning compressor should now be unbolted and tied up to the sides of the engine bay. Take care when bending the hoses to avoid any damage.

If you're tired of bending over, relief is in sight. You can sit down for this next task, the shifter removal. Start by taking out the center console. Unwind the shift knob and disconnect one or two wire harnesses to get the console out of the way. Next, unscrew the rubber shift boot and then the bolts holding the shifter in place.

Now for a more comfortable position—laying down under the car! Soak the junction of the header and exhaust pipe with some hardware loosener and remove the bolts. While you're at it, unbolt the exhaust bracket from the bellhousing. Move over to the passenger side of the transmission after that and unbolt the clutch slave cylinder. Hang the cylinder by a wire to avoid harming the hydraulic line.

Now move toward the back of the car. As you reach over the top of the transmission near the shifter,

Once out, the transmission is separated from the engine and the serious work begins.

you'll find two wiring harnesses. Mark the harnesses and disconnect them. In this same area are two bolts that connect the powerplant frame (PPF) to the transmission. Place a floor jack under the transmission and jack it up enough to relieve the weight from the PPF. If you don't do this, the unit will drop in the rear. From a safe position—not directly underneath the transmission—remove the bolts.

At this point, everything that needs to be disconnected, unhooked, or removed has been taken care of except for the motor mounts. Before attacking these, hook up the engine to a hoist. If the unit doesn't still have factory hooks, bolt the hoist chain directly to the engine as indicated in the manual, with equal lengths of chain. Crank up the hoist so the chain is taut before removing the motor-mount bolts.

Position one person at the lift and the other under the car, within reach of the transmission. Place some rags under the junction of the transmission and driveshaft, as the next steps will spill a few ounces of transmission oil. As the tranny man carefully lowers the jack, pull the hoist away from the car so the propeller shaft will disengage from the transmission. The tranny man should also be prepared to secure the driveshaft as it drops out; remember, there will be fluid coming out of the end of the gearbox, so plan accordingly.

As you move the hoist forward from the car, crank up the hoist to raise the engine above the front of the car, while keeping an eye on the clearance between the powerplant's bellhousing and the body's firewall and transmission tunnel.

Once the engine is clear of the car, rest the entire powerplant on some soft wooden blocks, taking care not to point-load the oil pan too badly. Unbolt the transmission from the block, and you're done.

Have the cylinder head milled if you're looking to increase the compression ratio. The minimum cylinder-head height specification from Mazda is 133.8 millimeters, which is as low as you can go if you're in a racing class. Street tuners can take it lower, since the cam belt has a tensioner that can take up the slack of a lower cam-pulley-to-crankshaft dimension. Given the shape of the Miata's combustion chambers, every 0.065 inch you mill off the head removes about 0.15 cubic inches from the chamber and increases the compression ratio approximately half a compression-ratio point.

If you're building a forced-induction engine, simply have the head cleaned up with the lightest of cuts. You'll want to keep the combustion-chamber volume the same—decreased volume will hurt you in the detonation department.

The final step in the head freshening can be done when the engine is back together. It's called "port matching" and is essentially matching up the holes on the head with the holes on the intake manifold and exhaust header. The process of doing this at home was outlined earlier; just remember that you're trying to make these two areas as seamless as possible, but erring on the side of removing too little material, rather than too much. The smoother the transition to and from the head, the less disturbance there is in the transfer of fuel and exhaust.

Camshaft Issues

The stock 1.6-liter intake camshaft opens at 5 degrees BTDC and closes at 51 degrees after bottom dead center (ABDC). The exhaust cam opens at 53 degrees BTDC and closes at 15 degrees ABDC. The 1.8 has similar cam timing. This equates to 236 degrees of intake duration and 248 degrees of exhaust duration. These are pretty aggressive values, which is why the Miata creates its peak horsepower at 6,500 rpm, just 700 rpm shy of the fuel cutoff. Camshafts with different timing and profiles for intake and exhaust generally show no appreciable improvements in otherwise-stock Miata engines, so the author recommends keeping the stock camshaft, unless significant work has been done to the cylinder heads and you are willing to live with a shift in the power band to the high-rpm range.

That's not to say that minuscule gains can't be made here. HKS currently sells aftermarket cams for the Miata that have increased lift. The stock lift for the intake valve is 0.256 inch, and the exhaust lift is 0.255 inch. The HKS cam has an intake lift of 0.264 inch and an exhaust lift of 0.268 inch. Increasing the lift by 0.013 inch may not sound like much, but it does slightly improve flow. On a 1.30-inch intake valve, the HKS cam increases the valves' "open area" by 0.011 square inches per valve. The total intake open area is

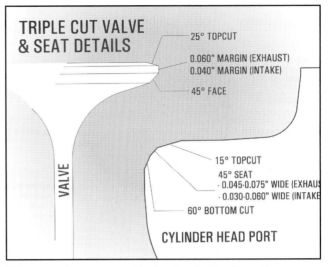

When you have your cylinder head rebuilt, go for a triple-cut seat on all valves. This smoothes the transition from port wall to seat and on into the combustion chamber. A straight 45-degree cut leaves an abrupt change. In a perfect engine, the outside cuts would actually be gentle radii that keep the airflow smooth and nonturbulent.

Use a Plastigage to measure bearing clearances at the crank main and rod journals as well as at the camshaft journals. These are easy to use and available at any auto parts store.

therefore increased by 3 percent. Intake velocities are lowered ever so slightly, so these cams do shift the power band upward a touch. These aren't great changes, but would serve to optimize the ultimate naturally aspirated engine.

Racers will benefit from having the cam-bearing bores align-honed or align-bored. This will reduce the friction required to rotate the cams. After the work, don't forget to

If you've been using additives, you'll find out their benefit when you tear an engine down. There is not one that has been proven to extend engine life beyond what a good oil changed out every 3,000 miles will do.

This Miata engine has seen 200,000 miles of hard use. The scoring in the cylinder means the machinist will have to rebore the cylinder, making it 0.010 inch larger than it was in diameter. If the scoring is deeper than that, he can go up to 0.040 inch.

The crank's main bearings fit into the block and are held by small tangs at their ends. Never force a bearing into place. It is also a good idea to wear gloves when handling bearings—your hand oils will start corrosion once the engine is sealed up.

double-check the cam bearing journals' oil clearance with a Plastigage; maximum clearance is 0.006 inch (0.15 mm).

The stock hydraulic lifter actuators ("HLA"s in Mazdaspeak) have been a source of trouble for Mazda for some time. They don't break or wear out, but in some engines they also don't pump up correctly, even if thinner or synthetic oil is used. If necessary, the dealership's parts counter can sell you new HLAs with larger oil holes that allow the lifter to pump up more easily. This is the best solution for a street engine that has a chronic lifter noise problem, but don't change the HLAs out until you've experimented with other brands or grades of oil; some simply work better than others on a particular engine. Otherwise, unless you're revving past 7,200 rpm, the stock lifters work fine and require no adjustment. Mazda uses them for this reason. Adjusting valves on a DOHC engine with shims is not a fun task (ask any Alfa mechanic).

The stock Miata HLAs are the limiting factor to the maximum rpm that a Miata can achieve. They tend to "pump down" at very high rotational speeds. The oil doesn't have time to refill the lifter reservoirs between valve actuations, so the overall lifts get shorter and shorter. If you do regularly rev past 7,200 rpm (this applies to competitors in E Production SCCA racing who use the Weber carburetor or to street enthusiasts running carbs or aftermarket PCMs), the stock HLAs should be replaced with solid lifters from Mazda's competition-parts line. For tuners wishing to raise the rev limit, these solid lifters can provide additional performance at higher rpm and will shift a particular engine's rotational limitations to its next-weakest link, the valve (spring) float.

Solid lifters require adjustment shims, which Mazda sells

as well. If you stick with HLAs, check to make sure they're pumping up properly and replace any units that are bad. To test an HLA, hold it in your hand and compress it; if it moves when you squeeze it, it's bad.

As long as we're on this subject, a quick note about aesthetics. Some owners have made their engines look hotter by removing the top plastic cover that hides the cam pulleys and timing belt. Others have machined the cam cover to fully expose the belt drive. This is done in some racing circles to allow quick access to adjustable cam sprockets, but since the standard Miata engine doesn't respond to cam-timing changes—and considering that the belt life will be greatly

Making sure your crankshaft is within specification is critical to a good engine build. If you don't have the equipment, your machinist can do the job. Make sure to copy the specs out of the factory service manual for reference.

Serious engine builders test out their work on an engine dyno. Here the Miata Club engineers put a 1.6-liter through the paces, optimizing fuel delivery for maximum power. Note the complete wiring harness that has to be pulled from a Miata to run the complicated engine control system.

reduced if it's exposed to the dirt and grime of the engine bay—this is a bad idea for street cars.

The Bottom End

If you're going for a full rebuild, do the head work as mentioned above and then continue disassembling the engine per the shop manual procedures. Use top-quality zip-type plastic bags to keep assemblies together, and label everything you take off. Make sure that you have a clean and organized workspace that will not be disturbed during the entire process.

Send the block to a machine shop for cleaning to remove all interior corrosion. You should also have the block decked to provided a level surface for the head to mate on to. You can have the block and head decked to minimum height for more compression, but this process is usually reserved for competition purposes, since any warpage renders the head or block useless and raised compression can cause detonation with standard pump gas.

It turns out that the deck heights of the Miata blocks (both 1.6-liter and 1.8-liter) have a certain amount of tolerance shift from engine to engine. Deck height is the measurement from the top of the cylinder block to the crankshaft centerline. The minimum specification for this value is 221.5 millimeters, but racers have found that there's a wide variation in the deck heights on Miata blocks. A too-tall block will result in lower compression ratios and reduced power across the board. When reworking a Miata engine block, have your machine shop dress the top of the block to match your

installed piston heights (crank, bearings, rods, pistons all in the block). You don't want the pistons sitting down in the bores (at top dead center for any given cylinder) more than 0.004 inch if you can help it.

If you have the budget and your machine shop knows what it's doing, have your block align-honed or align-bored. This is a process wherein the crankshaft's main bearing caps are torqued in place and the holes, bearing to bearing, are cut to perfect alignment. It's a finesse point, but 0.003 inch of misalignment will create drag on the crankshaft as it tries to spin.

Raising Displacement

It's been said a million times: There's no substitute for cubic inches. (Make that a million and one times.) It's true, but boring out an engine is a very intrusive and expensive way to increase power and is largely reserved for the all-out racing crowd, who are limited by rules as to what means they can use to increase output. For street applications, it's much easier to go to intake and exhaust mods or a forced-induction system to get even greater gains for considerably less effort and expense per horsepower.

Nevertheless, truly serious engine builders will probably increase displacement anyway. One way to do so is to order a set of J&E 0.040-inch-overbore pistons. The block gladly accepts this overbore and instantly rewards its owner with increased compression and power. Each piston should be carefully weighed, and material should be removed from the underside of each piston as necessary to lighten them into

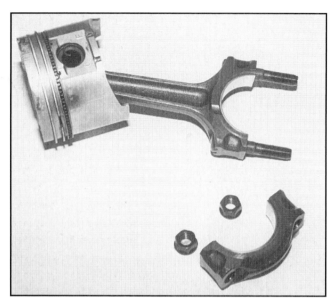

Balance each of your pistons and rods to match the lightest one in your set. This will help reduce power-robbing vibration in the crankshaft. For a race engine, make sure to replace the rod bolts (available from Mazda Competition Department).

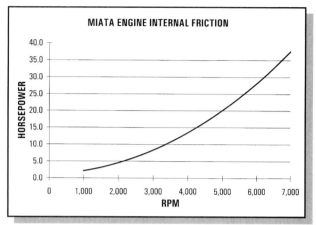

All the work that goes into bearing and piston-to-wall clearances pays off when you can reduce the internal friction inherent to any engine. A 5-horsepower reduction in friction is 5 more horsepower at the flywheel and on the back straight.

balance. Be very careful not to remove too much in one area, however, but rather a thin layer across the entire surface area.

To calculate a cylinder's swept volume (displacement), use the following formula: $V_s = \left(\frac{\pi}{4}\right)(\text{BORE})^2(\text{STROKE})$ Total engine displacement is calculated by simply multiplying the cylinder swept volume by the number of cylinders—obviously four in the case of the Miata.

The stock 1.6-liter engine has a swept volume of 24.354 cubic inches per cylinder (not accounting for the cylinder-head combustion chamber volume), for a total of 97.416 cubic inches. Boring this engine out by 0.040 inch will give you 24.992 cubic inches per cylinder, for a total engine displacement of 99.969 cubic inches. This is 2.549 more cubic inches than the stock engine, which is worth about three horsepower in practice. On a 1.8-liter engine, the 0.040-inch overbore will give you 2.770 more cubic inches, for about 3.3 more horsepower. Not a bunch, but everything counts for the serious engine builder. The actual power increase will also be higher as a function of increased compression ratio, so take this into account before you mill your cylinder head too far down. The 1.6-liter Miata has a calculated cylinder-head combustion chamber volume of 2.89 cubic inches (11.8 cc). Use that to calculate the new compression ratio with this formula:

$$\text{COMPRESSION RATIO} = \frac{\text{CYLINDER VOLUME} + \text{CHAMBER VOLUME}}{\text{CHAMBER VOLUME}}$$

For an 0.040-inch-overbored 1.6-liter engine, the new compression ratio is 9.6:1, up 2 percent. Not a big deal, but compression ratio is key to making more power. A 1.8-liter engine comes in at 9.2:1 compression ratio after a 0.040-inch overbore, the same 2 percent increase.

Tell your machinist to fit the pistons with no more than 0.002 inch of clearance for a street engine, piston skirt to cylinder wall. For a race engine running on synthetic oil, you can loosen this up a bit to no more than 0.004 inch to reduce friction a bit. Making this request of the machinist requires that you have the pistons before you bring the block in, so don't show up empty-handed. Tell the machinist that you're building a race engine and maybe he'll warm up to your project instead of giving it the usual taxi rebuild. Machine work is only as good as the attention span of the machinist, so get on his or her good side from the start.

When you get your block back from the machinist, make sure that he hot-tanked it after the machine work to clean out all the shavings. Spray the cylinders with penetrating oil (WD-40) immediately, and repeat this once again before assembly to prevent corrosion during the rebuild process.

If you use the standard-gapped piston rings, make sure to file the ends to a ring gap of 0.006 inch for the top two rings and 0.008 inch for the oil ring. Do this with the ring shoved squarely 3.25 inches down each bore by using an upside-down piston to push it into place. Measure the end gap with a feeler gauge and file to fit. Too big of a gap means lost compression and power; too small means a bound or broken ring. Match the rings to each cylinder and mark them; cylinder to cylinder variances will change the end gaps.

Incidentally, Total Seal makes gapless rings for these pistons that will reduce normal compression loss at the ring gap—an inexpensive way to pick up some power. If you use gapped rings, space the end gaps of the three rings per the diagram shown.

Crankshaft and Connecting Rods

At the core of the engine is the crank. Miata cranks are great as is, though they can be nitrided to increase longevity. This won't give you any horsepower, but it will strengthen the one item that everything else is based upon. Next, micropolish the crank with ultra-fine emery paper to reduce surface friction with bearings.

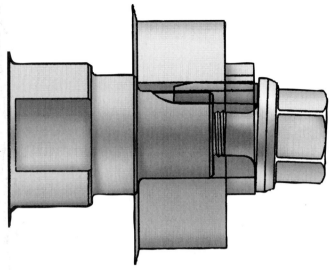

On reassembly, make sure you get the crank nose keyway in the right way, especially on early cars (pre-1992). Shown here is the wrong way (key is upside down), which leaves a bit of the key protruding forward of the pulley. The crank bolt is cocked by the protrusion and will fail soon after fire-up.

If you plan to install a blower or turbo, you may want to consider some heavy-duty connecting rods and hardware for your motor. The 323 GTX rods are stronger than the Miata units, but with the price of an increase in weight. If your wallet (or your reciprocating mass) can't handle that, try a set of Carrillo rods, but order them in advance, since it's at least a two-month wait.

If you stick with the stock or 323 rods, then you'll need to do some work on them with a die grinder. Remove any rough casting marks and weigh each rod, removing material to get them all to weigh the same. Make up a hanger to weigh each end of the rod so you can balance the small ends and large ends, respectively, across all four rods. Start with the lightest rod and lighten the rest to match.

Once the rods are balanced and cleaned up, send them out to get shot-peened. This is a process where the rods are bombarded with a stream of BBs. They pound the outer layer of metal and create a stronger surface, like the hard-candy shell that protects the chocolate.

When the rods and crank are ready, fit the crank to the block and check the main-bearing clearances using a Plastigage and a torque wrench. You should have no more than 0.004 inch of oil clearance on an old crank. If it's more, have it ground down to the next undersize. Mazda

sells 0.010-inch undersize main and big-end rod bearings. On a newly machined crank, the Plastigage oil clearance measurement should be no more than 0.0014 inch. The rod big-ends should have a Plastigage oil clearance of no more than 0.004 inch with respect to the crank when torqued properly. If they're looser than this, have the crank rod journals turned down and use appropriately matched bearings. These should fit with a tighter clearance of no more than 0.002 inch.

The final measurement for the crank is the end play as it sits in the block. Use a large screwdriver and a feeler gauge to see if the crank can move more than 0.012 inch. If it can, thrust washers are available from Mazda in 0.010-inch increments to fit a machined crankshaft.

In light of these clearances and measurements, you might want to have your machinist do the final assembly to these specs if you've never done a short-block buildup before. It's not that hard, but make sure you have the time to do it right. You will pay a bit more to farm it out, but if you trust your machinist, he has a much shorter learning curve to building a short block than you do. Racers do it themselves, in general, because they want it done perfectly and have a greater motivation than shop rates—they want to win.

At this point, the bottom end work is pretty much finished. Assemble the lightweight flywheel, clutch disk, pressure plate, rods, pistons, and crank, and have the entire group spin-balanced. Not only does this ensure that all the parts will work together harmonically, but a balanced engine will last much longer by not working the block and reciprocating masses against each other.

On reassembly of the bottom end, be sure to check all clearances and torque on hardware. With tolerances measured in thousandths of inches, there isn't any room to guess. The gasket set you ordered will have new seals and gaskets—use every one. You have now created the perfect foundation for your rebuilt cylinder head.

Conclusion

Even if you don't spend a bundle on a rebuild, a well-prepared motor, built with OEM parts, will outperform an assembly-line motor. Time spent ensuring exacting torques and clearances, balancing and blueprinting, and cleaning up casting marks will produce a powerful engine with great endurance. There isn't one secret part in the Miata's engine that will make that magic horsepower gain. If you try to dramatically strengthen one part, you'll inevitably find a weak link one more item away.

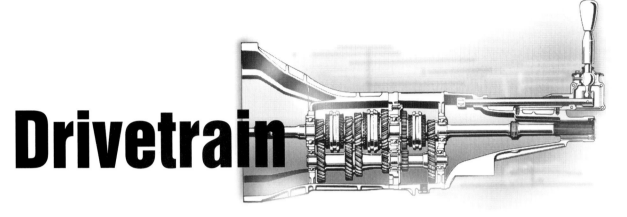

Drivetrain

Downstream of the engine, Mazda made the Miata pretty stout. The transmission came from the second-generation RX-7 family, a larger and more powerful car. The rear differential has its roots in the RX-7 and 929 sedan parts bin, so it has sufficient strength for anything short of a V-8 engined car. There are a few components worth improving once you've made the engine stronger, however.

Clutch

The stock Miata clutch is a very sturdy device, able to handle up to 190 horsepower without modification. Normally aspirated Miatas see their clutches last far beyond the 50,000-mark, unless abused.

The 1.6-liter cars come with a 200-millimeter-diameter disc. For the 1.8-liter, the clutch diameter was increased to 215 millimeters. The smaller size of the 1.6-liter's clutch reduces inertial force and provides quicker shifts, compared to the 1.8-liter's clutch.

A number of aftermarket high-performance clutch discs and pressure plates are available for the Miata. The two most popular are from Centerforce and Jackson Racing. These stronger clutches become important particularly for turbocharged or supercharged engines that are driven hard. However, it should be noted that many forced-induction Miatas do just fine on the stock components.

The stock Mazda clutch parts are comparable in price to high-performance replacements, so when it comes time for a clutch job you might want to upgrade the hardware as a matter of course. When replacing a clutch, make sure that the flywheel is inspected (especially the pilot bearing). Replace the following parts each time, regardless of how serviceable they might appear to be: clutch disc, pressure plate, throwout bearing, and clutch-system hydraulic fluid.

Replacing a clutch can be done by the owner if he or she has a set of car ramps and a very good helper. The PPF (Powerplant Frame) has to be disconnected from the transmission, and the catalytic converter has to come off, making this a bit of an involved process. The transmission comes off as well, so this is a muscle job. Most shops charge five hours' labor for a Miata clutch job—not a bad deal when you consider the grunting involved.

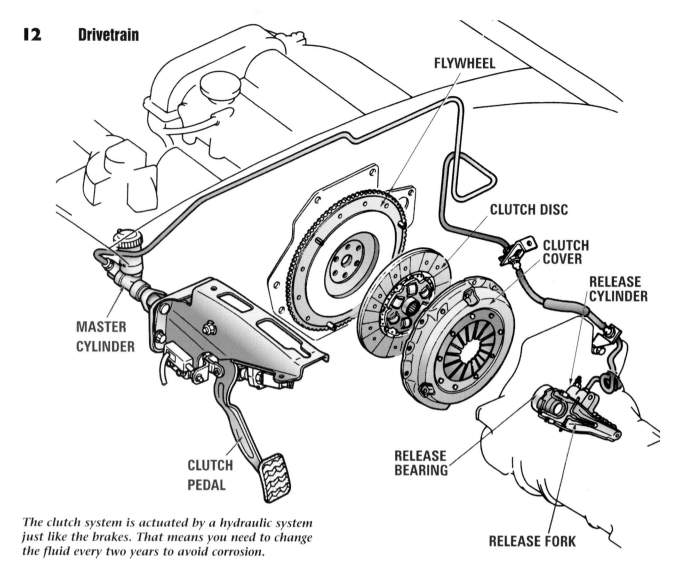

FLYWHEEL

CLUTCH DISC

CLUTCH COVER

RELEASE CYLINDER

MASTER CYLINDER

CLUTCH PEDAL

RELEASE BEARING

RELEASE FORK

The clutch system is actuated by a hydraulic system just like the brakes. That means you need to change the fluid every two years to avoid corrosion.

The clutch effort for a stock Miata is excellent with good feel and predictable engagement. Still, there's no danger in creating a stiff pedal with the performance clutches—the Miata's hydraulic system takes them all in stride.

The throwout bearing in a Miata is a special design that's engaged all the time—the bearing face is always in contact with the pressure-plate springs. For this kind of throwout system, it's important that you change the bearing each time you do a clutch job. This is one of those parts you don't want to go in and replace on its own.

Early Miatas had a chronic rattle that emanated from the throwout bearing, as the supplier left a bit too much play in the bearing races. When idling in neutral with no force on the bearing, it would rattle. Newer replacement bearings don't have this problem.

Another friendly noise that came with the early cars is a squeak during idle with the transmission in neutral. This is caused by the junction between the slave cylinder's actuating arm and the clutch release fork. A little grease on this spot will cure the squeak.

The Miata uses a constant-engagement type of throwout bearing—it never stops spinning. Replace it and the front transmission seal (if it is weeping) any time you do a clutch job.

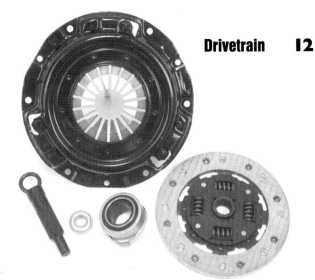

Flywheels

Lightened flywheels are available for all years of the Miata. The stock flywheel weighs in at 18 pounds, the lightened pieces from 9 to 13 pounds. Aluminum versions are available as well that weigh a remarkable 4 pounds. Suppliers for these flywheels include Brainstorm Products, Mazda Motorsports, and Centerforce.

A lighter flywheel will allow the engine to spin up quicker due to its smaller rotational inertia. The engine speed will drop faster between shifts as well. This is one of those finesse items that you might not feel in the seat of your pants, but it will make the car more enjoyable to drive and shift. Racers use them to get the engine up to peak rpm sooner.

The full boat—a new clutch disc, pressure plate, throwout bearing, and alignment tool. Pressure plates age along with the discs (which wear like brake pads), so they should be replaced in any clutch jobs. You can skip the pressure plate, but the labor to go back in to fix a broken one more than pays for the plate the first time. Same goes for the throwout bearing.

Transmission

The Miata's transmission has been universally applauded as the finest-shifting tranny on the market. This didn't come about by chance; Mazda spent countless hours optimizing the shifter feel, paying attention to such details as shift-rod detent notch angles, synchronizer design, and shifter ratios. In addition, stoppers were added to the shift rods to improve the rigidity of the shift mechanism. The result is a buttery-smooth shifter with a short, 45-millimeter throw.

Many vendors offer lightened flywheels. These can be machined-down stock flywheels or brand new units.

The transmission itself came over from the 1989 RX-7, so it has proven itself to have plenty of capacity for even heavily modified Miatas. The ratios were changed to create a close-ratio gear set well matched to the Miata's torque curve.

Beginning in the 1994 model year, Mazda improved the second gear synchronizer to address customer complaints of notchy shifts. A double-cone synchronizer was incorporated, which reduces meshing time and shift effort. The gear ratios remained the same on all gears, although the rear-end ratio was changed from 4.3:1 to 4.1:1. The change in ratio was in response to the higher power rating of the 1.8-liter engine.

Little can be or needs to be done to improve this transmission. That said, all Miatas benefit from the use of synthetic transmission oil. Redline, Mobil, Amsoil, and others sell good examples. Make sure that any oil you use meets the API Service GL-4 or GL-5 rating. The transmission holds 2.6 quarts of oil and is filled from a plug on the side of the transmission housing. Some sort of hand pump (readily available at auto parts stores) is a requirement to do the job correctly. When the oil comes back out of the fill hole, the transmission oil level is correct (make sure the car is on level ground).

Short-shift kits are available that reduce the shift throw even further. Shift effort is slightly increased with these kits, however, and this can affect speed-shifting success when drag racing.

One of the most popular things to change on a Miata is the shift knob. Since this is one of the main parts the driver uses to connect with the car, the tactile feel is very important, and a matter of personal taste. The Miata Club sells the classical shift knob shown, a pet project of the author's, who wanted a simple knob that was a bit shorter in height than the original.

Of course, there are hundreds of different shift knobs available for the Miata, ranging from racy carbon-fiber looka-likes to warm wood sculptures. The thread on the Miata's shift lever is 10 millimeters with a 1.25 pitch. In general, avoid shift knobs that use a generic setscrew for attachment; get one that has an internal thread that matches the lever's. Put a little mild thread-locking compound on the threads if you replace the knob. This will prevent the knob from coming loose at the wrong time.

Limited-Slip Differentials

As a sports car that was going to be raced, the Miata was designed with an optional limited-slip differential. This is a device that prevents one rear wheel from spinning under power uselessly while the opposite wheel sits still. This sort of power equalization is very important during sharp cornering maneuvers and in wet or icy conditions.

For the Miata, Mazda tried something new that works very nicely. The Miata was introduced with a viscous-type limited-slip differential made up of a set of plates connected to each axle that run in a bath of silicone fluid. The plates don't touch, but as one set of plates spin faster than the other, the silicone

firms up under the shearing force and resists the differing speeds. This transmits power from the faster-spinning wheel to the slower one in a smooth, progressive manner. Power is equalized in a nearly invisible fashion, as compared to clutch-type limited-slips that can chatter and vibrate as they lock up.

This smoothness makes a marked difference in a high-speed corner. Due to weight transfer, the inside rear tire becomes lightly loaded and its traction is reduced. As power is applied, this inside tire wants to spin, but if the limited-slip counters this in a rough, on-off fashion (as a clutch-type system may), the outer wheel sees irregular

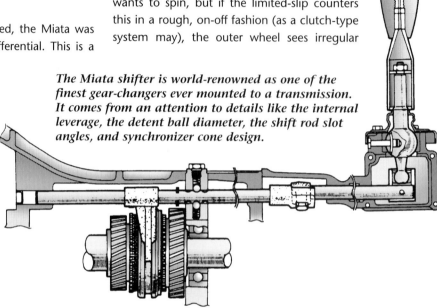

The Miata shifter is world-renowned as one of the finest gear-changers ever mounted to a transmission. It comes from an attention to details like the internal leverage, the detent ball diameter, the shift rod slot angles, and synchronizer cone design.

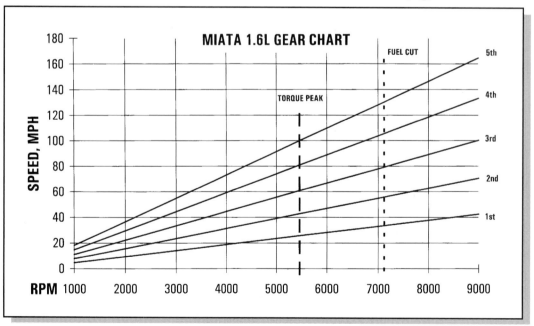

This speed-versus-rpm graph shows how fast you'll go in each gear. This graph is for the 1.6-liter cars with a 4.3:1 rear-end ratio. For the 1.8-liter with a 4.1:1 ratio, add 5 percent to the speed values.

inputs of power and might become unstable. The smooth equalization of power provided by the Miata's viscous limited-slip allows the driver to push harder in corners without being disturbed by jerky torque effects.

In practice, Mazda set the viscous limited-slip to have about a 40 percent lock-up rating—not very high in racing circles, but adequate for most street use. Racers use lock-up ratios in the 80 percent range to ensure maximum power transfer and acceleration. A side benefit to the Miata's viscous limited-slip is that no adjustments are needed for the life of the unit, whereas clutch-type limited-slips need adjustment to account for wear.

Mazda made limited-slips optional on base models, "A" packages, and "B" packages, and there is no way to look at the vehicle identification number and tell if a certain Miata is so equipped. To test whether you have a limited-slip diff or not, jack up the rear of the car so that both tires are off the ground. Spin one tire by hand and observe the opposite wheel. If it turns in the reverse direction, you don't have a limited-slip. If the opposite tire rotates in the same direction, your car does have a limited-slip. Units without limited-slip hardware are called "open" differential.

If you have an open diff in a 1990-1993 Miata, you can install the limited-slip from another car without too much trouble. You'll need to retrofit the entire differential plus the

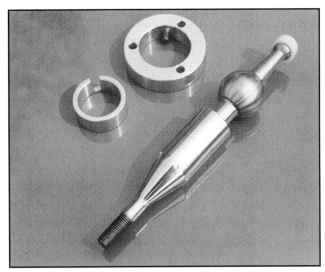

Many vendors offer short-shift kits. While they do shorten the shift pattern, they increase the shift effort slightly, due to less leverage. These are easy to install in about an hour. The entire shifter can be reached from the car's interior.

two halfshafts, but other than dealing with its mating to the PPF, the job is pretty much a bolt-in affair.

Another option is to install a clutch-type limited-slip into your stock housing. Mazda Motorsports sells a clutch-type unit for 1990-1993 Miatas. Installation is not a snap; it

Mazda broke new ground with the viscous limited-slip differential on the original Miata. The power transfer is very smooth, although total lockup is only 40 percent (it is a limited-slip, not a locking differential).

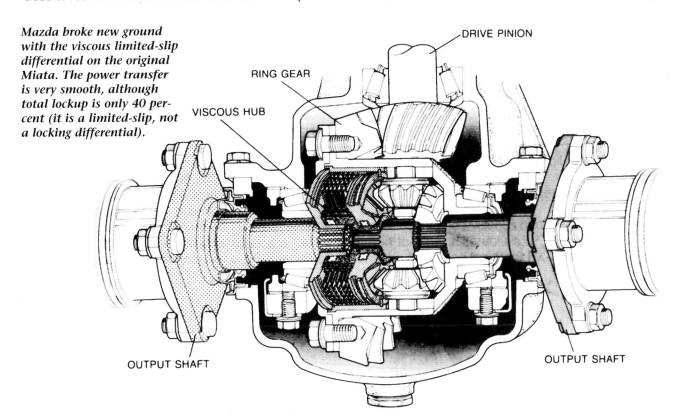

Having a limited-slip differential helps keep the wheel torque nearer to the same value for both wheels, greatly improving acceleration in a corner—essential for a sports car.

involves dropping the complete rear differential out of the car, and while this can be done by the very serious enthusiast, most owners will choose to have a professional shop do the work so that the main ring and pinion gets checked out at the same time. There are also considerations about the alignment and setup of the main ring and pinion, a pretty critical operation. Most shops quote 10 hours for this job, equating to about $500 for the installation labor alone. The 1.6-liter clutch-type limited-slip sells for $918.60 direct from Mazda Motorsports. The part number to order is 9N1A-79-960.

In 1994, Mazda incorporated a new style limited-slip, the Torsen gear differential. Both the 1993 RX-7 and 1994 Miata were introduced with this high-tech diff, which uses a complicated worm gear and thrust washer set to equalize power delivery to each rear wheel. "Torsen" is a trademark name shortened from "Torque Sensing" and is a licensed technology used by various automakers on high-line cars. The Torsen's smoothness of power delivery is unmatched by even viscous-type limited-slips.

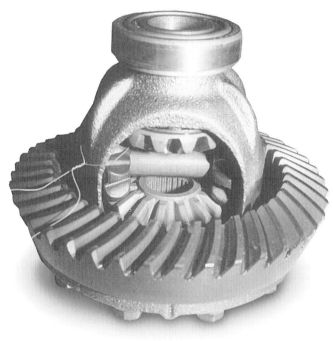

Setting a differential up in its carrier is a tough job—an amateur can do it if he or she gets lucky. In general, it is advisable to have a professional set your rear end up if it is your first time. You can do the removal and installation of the case yourself to save a few bucks.

The differential hangs in a wide carrier Mazda designed to distribute the loads of power application. If you want to put a limited-slip in an "open-diff" car (no limited-slip installed), it is easiest to buy the entire assembly as is from a wrecking yard. You will need the halfshafts, depending on the year of the unit you are buying.

Torsen limited-slips can be found in 1994 and later manual-transmission Miatas (automatics didn't come with them) and are highly valuable as used parts. Not only do they provide greater traction in all cornering situations, there are virtually no maintenance or reliability problems with these bulletproof units. To modify an open-diff 1994 or 1995 Miata for Torsen limited-slip, you'll need to locate a replacement unit from a wrecking yard, complete in its aluminum carrier, which should cost around $900. This will bolt directly into your Miata's rear subframe.

Beginning in 1996, Mazda went to a stub-axle arrangement on the inner end of the halfshaft. If you want to put a Torsen in a 1996 or later car, you can simply buy the differential and aluminum carrier; retrofitting a 1996 or later Torsen into a 1994 or 1995 car means you'll need the later-style halfshafts as well. Any used Torsen out of a 1994 and later Miata can be retrofit to a 1990-1993 car, but you'll need to swap out the differential, the halfshafts, and the driveshaft to complete the installation.

Finally, complicating things even more, in 1997 Mazda incorporated a new Torsen design called the Type 2. This is cheaper to build than the Type 1 and has a higher bias ratio. Mazda Motorsports sells new Torsens for all 1994 and later housings. Owners going the new-part route should opt for the Type 2 Torsen to take advantage of its lower cost and higher bias ratio. The Mazda part number is MM02-27-200A.

Gear Ratios

If you feel the need to change your rear-end ratio, Mazda Motorsports offers a variety of gear sets to do the job. Ring and pinion sets are available in the following ratios: 4.44:1; 4.875:1; 5.125:1. These fit all Miatas. To calculate your theoretical speeds in gears for various rear-end ratios, use the following formula: speed (in miles per hour = (T x E) ((R x G x 1,056), where T = rear tire overall circumference in inches, E = engine rpm, R = rear-axle ratio, and G = transmission gear ratio. Changing the rear-end ratio is generally reserved for road racers who need to match a particular gear to a particular corner. Running out of rpm and having to shift mid-turn can greatly affect your lap times. Some racers have a different rear-end ratio for each track they race, getting a leg up on their Miata competition who may be caught midgear in an important corner.

1213 A company called "OPM" is distributing a clever device that gets shoved inside an open differential. The end result is an instant limited-slip. It does a bit better job than the viscous stock unit, but is not equal to the competition clutch-pack style. It sells for around $700 plus installation.

Mazda Competition sells a clutch-pack-style limited-slip differential for the Miata. This well-proven unit has been around for some time, and is bulletproof and rebuildable (something the new Torsens are not). This 1.6-liter's limited-slip unit sells for $918.60 direct from Mazda. The part number to order is 9N1A-79-960.

Randy Stocker's 1.6-liter Miata. Or is it a 1.8-liter? Randy wanted more oomph for his Solo racer, so he put the bigger Miata engine in his early chassis.

Engine Swaps: Putting a 1.8-Liter Engine in a 1.6-Liter Miata

The ultimate modification to your drivetrain is to tear out your stock engine and put in something else. While this is pretty drastic, it can be a rewarding exercise in the end.

You can put the 1.8-liter engine under a 1.6-liter's hood if you care to. Used Miata engines sell for anywhere from $300 for a high-mileage unit up to $1,200 for a very "new" engine out of a wrecked car. Adapting one of these into a 1.6-liter chassis is not the most straightforward project when you consider that the 1.8-liter engine has a completely different wiring harness and runs off a different computer. There is a way, however.

The 1.8 engine block and head is just 22 millimeters longer than the 1.6 unit, yet will fit in the same motor mounts. Since the transmissions are the same, there is no problem bolting the 1.6-liter bellhousing to the 1.8-liter motor. Also, the starter mounts in the same place, and the 1.6-liter wires fit perfectly. Similarly, the alternator hook-ups fit the same way, so you can use the 1.8-liter alternator in an early chassis. The coolant hoses will fit just right except concerning the 1.8 liter's water-fed oil cooler, which mounts

When considering a change to the 1.8-liter engine, one area you'll need to make a decision about involves the clutch. You can use the entire package from a 1.6-liter, or the entire pressure plate and disc setup from a 1.8-liter, but you have to choose one. It is better to use the 1.8-liter's parts, because they have greater power-handling capacity.

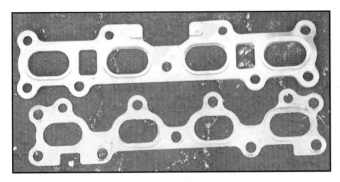

Mazda changed the cylinder head (for obvious reasons) in the 1.8-liter engine. If you decide to fit the 1.8-liter engine in your 1.6-liter car, you can get away with using the newer intake manifold. When it comes to exhausts, you'll have to adapt the new to the old, due to a different gasket surface.

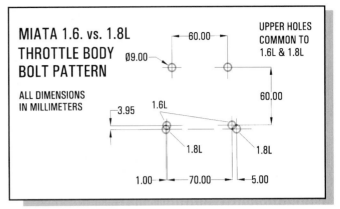

Making an adapter plate or redrilling the holes in the intake manifold is necessary to fit the 1.6-liter's throttle body to the 1.8-liter's manifold. Use this drawing as a guide.

Mazdatrix is a tuning company on the West Coast specializing in RX-7s. It came as no surprise that they put a Miata under the knife and installed a rotary engine in place of the four-stroke unit.

Here sits a 13B turbocharged, intercooled rotary powerplant, Mazda's pride and joy, in place of the usual Miata B6 engine. Major changes were required to the transmission tunnel and drivetrain (the PPF had to be thrown out).

under the oil filter. With a little plumbing it can be hooked up easily.

If you want, you can carry over your 1.6-liter clutch components, but you should use a performance 1.6-liter clutch disc and pressure plate. You will have to use the 1.6-liter flywheel if you use any of the early style clutch components. If your engine comes with a 1.8-liter clutch and pressure plate, then use these units. The 1.8-liter clutch has a bit more torque-carrying capability. The 1.6-liter clutch slave cylinder, release fork, and throwout bearing will work perfectly against a 1.8-liter clutch if your engine comes with one (or against your 1.6-liter clutch and flywheel mounted on the new engine).

Engines are pretty easy to come by, but wiring harnesses are another matter. The cost and complexity of adapting a 1.8-liter engine bay harness to a 1.6-liter's chassis would be enough to frustrate even the best technician. The easy way out it to adapt your 1.6-liter's control system to the 1.8-liter engine. This means using your 1.6-liter's fuel injection harness to fire the 1.8-liter's injectors (make sure your used engine comes with them; the 1.8-liter's injectors flow more fuel, and the bigger engine needs it). There are no electrical incompatibilities to be concerned with; your 1.6-liter's PCM will fire the larger injectors perfectly.

You will be reconnecting the various sensors just as if the new engine were a 1.6-liter, with a few exceptions. There is no EGR function in the 1.6-liter's PCM, so you will leave the EGR valve disconnected (electrically and vacuum-wise). This will not affect the performance of the 1.8-liter in the early chassis.

The crank angle sensor is in a different place on the 1.8-liter engines, so you will have to extend that connector a few inches. This involves four wires that can be simply lengthened

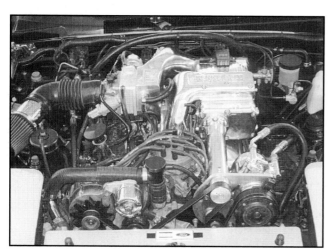

By far the most commercially successful engine swap has been putting Mustang 5.0-liter V-8s into Miatas, as done by Monster Motorsports. Customers bring in their cars (new or not) and leave with a 225-horsepower firebreather under the hood, or in the case of this particular car, a supercharged 300-plus-horsepower monster.

V-6 just for kicks. The Miata Club engineers worked at putting a 1.8-liter V-6 from a Mazda MX-3 into a Miata. Due to fuel management concerns and conflicts in coolant hose routings, it never got much farther than what you see here.

by a 6-inch splice of 20-gauge wire for each of them. Make sure to use a soldering iron and heat shrink tubing—some rainy night out in the country you'll be glad you took a few extra minutes here.

You will need to use the 1.6-liter's ignition coils, since the 1.8-liter unit has a different triggering setup. You'll need to use the 1.6-liter's coil bracket as well. The 1.8-liter plug wires won't reach the 1.6-liter's coil, so grab a wire for the No. 2 cylinder from your old 1.6-liter and use it to reach the 1.8-liter's No. 3 plug.

Because the throttle-body electrical connections are entirely different between the two engines, you will need to adapt your 1.6-liter's throttle body to the 1.8-liter's intake manifold. This will preserve your throttle-position sensor and idle-speed control valve functions in the PCM. The two throttle bodies are the same in diameter (55 millimeters), so no performance is lost. The upper two mounting holes are in the same place, but the lower two have wider spacing on the 1.8-liter, so an adapter plate needs to be made. You can modify the intake manifold by drilling narrower holes (fill the old holes with flush studs, and drill and tap a new pair of holes). You will need to space your 1.6-liter's throttle cable back an inch or so to take up the slack (the 1.6-liter's cable is too long for the 1.8-liter motor). You can avoid this by buying a 1.8 liter's throttle cable (under $30).

You can use the stock 1.6-liter's air-filter box and airflow meter. The rubber crossover tube from your 1.6-liter parts pile will work to connect the airflow meter over to the throttle body. If you want to upgrade your airflow meter to a larger unit, meters from same-year Mazdas as your car can be adapted. Use an RX-7 unit. Don't make this change until your Miata's top-end power is lacking and you've tested your setup for flow (see Chapter 8 on how to test for restrictions). You should raise your baseline fuel injection pressure to around 50 psi, using an auxiliary fuel regulator. This will help to get your air-fuel ratios in line, but you should confirm this with actual measurements (see Chapter 13's discussion on fuel management).

The exhaust headers are different between the two engines. The 1.6-liter's oxygen sensor is mounted in the header itself, while the 1.8 liter's sensor is in the head pipe. For a bolt-on solution, ask for the down pipe (running to the catalytic converter) from where you bought the engine, or purchase an aftermarket header for the 1.8-liter.

Since the 1.6-liter's chassis is lighter and comes with a 4.3:1 rear-end ratio, you will end up with a faster car than a stock 1.8-liter. Zero-to-60 times will run under 8.0 seconds. Randy Stocker (who pioneered this swap) says his greatest problem comes in getting power to the ground through his 1.6-liter's viscous limited-slip differential. An aftermarket limited-slip unit would help.

Forced Induction

The Miata world is a lucky place to live. As much fun as it can be to tear down an engine and put in hot pistons and cams, you just don't have to do this to make a very fast street car. In just a few hours, Miata owners can bolt on a variety of devices that will boost power far beyond that achievable through big pistons and ported heads. A checkbook, some hand tools, and an afternoon in the garage may mean 50 percent or more additional horsepower—reliably.

We are talking about turbocharging or supercharging the engine, of course. Rather than asking simple atmospheric pressure to shove air into the cylinder, a turbo- or supercharger can force it in at an additional 5 or more psi. Adding more air means you can add more fuel while still maintaining the proper air-fuel ratio, and that translates into more power, pure and simple.

Simply put, a turbocharger is an air pump driven by the exhaust gases (think of a water wheel). As the exhaust gases turn one set of blades, another set of blades attached by a shaft pushes fresh air into the engine. A supercharger does the exact same thing, except that it's driven by an engine belt (just like the alternator or water pump) rather than by exhaust gasses.

There are a few different types of superchargers—some compress air inside the blower body just like a turbocharger (these are called "centrifugal" superchargers), while others simply flow large quantities of air with little internal compression (these are called "positive-displacement" superchargers). This is important to note only in that compressing air increases its temperature, which makes it less dense. That, of course, somewhat defeats the purpose. If the air is compressed, an intercooler can be used—this is essentially a radiator for the intake air—to cool things down a bit and regain some of that lost density. Turbos and internal compression superchargers make heat in the blowers. This can lead to hotter and hotter case temperatures, as multiple acceleration runs are made.

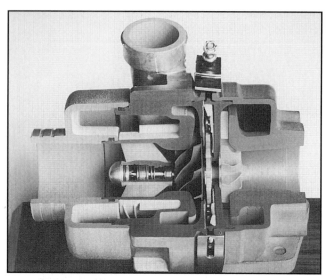

A turbocharger compresses the intake air using exhaust gases to drive an impeller, turning at approximately 25,000 rpm. In most cases, a high-speed center bearing is lubricated by engine oil.

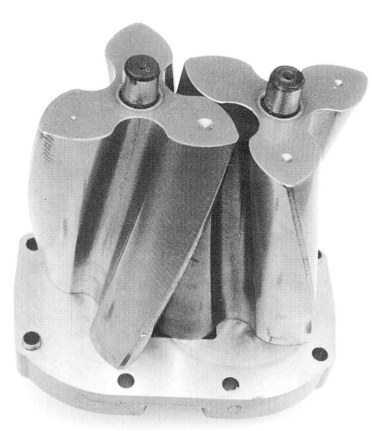

Eaton's Roots-type supercharger uses belt-driven rotors to force air into the engine. Spun at 14,000 rpm, a Roots blower won't take no for an answer—air is moved with each rotation regardless of what happens downstream. For this reason, throttles need to be mounted upstream so no restrictions are presented other than the engine itself.

Centrifugal superchargers are essentially belt-driven turbochargers; they are spun at very high speeds (25,000 rpm or more) and have a nonlinear output to them. Being compressors, the intake air is heated considerably during the process, and thus these superchargers benefit greatly from intercoolers.

Positive-displacement (or "Roots-type") superchargers, on the other hand, move air without tremendous compression. The result is a more linear output over a broader rpm range with minimal heating. Positive-displacement blowers require relatively high rpm to function, ranging from 6,000 to 15,000 rpm. In theory (and general practice), positive-displacement blowers can produce more low-end power than turbochargers, although some turbo kits do a remarkable job of compensating for this design difference.

The Lysholm positive-displacement blower acts like a Roots in that it moves a fixed amount of air for each rotation of the rotors. However, it also acts like a centrifugal blower in that it has some internal compression acting on the charge air. This is why Lysholm blowers benefit from intercooling just as turbos and centrifugal superchargers do (Mazda used a Lysholm blower with intercoolers on the Miller-cycle engine in the Millennia sedan).

Since a supercharger is driven directly off the engine, it will drain some power during use. This is limited to around 10 horsepower for most modern units, which is just a bit more than an air-conditioning compressor. Unless there's something terribly wrong with the engineering, the increased output more than covers the drive losses. Turbochargers also cause a slight power drain—smaller still than superchargers—due to decreased exhaust gas flow, but again these are well offset by the increase in overall output.

No matter the type of forced-induction system used, all of this pressure makes issues of cylinder-head porting and cam duration pretty moot. While the acclaimed Extrudehone polishing of an intake system can increase flow by up to 25 percent, this occurs at peak rpm and wide-open throttle. A turbo- or supercharger can provide over 100 percent improvement in airflow across a wide rpm range. The end result is more power—lots of it.

Boost

The Miata engine responds well to the application of boost. As a general rule, it takes about 4.5 psi of additional intake pressure before you begin feeling much of an improvement in performance, and it goes up from there. At 5.5 psi, power will be up at least 40 percent; at 6.0 some 50 percent; at 6.5 psi with good fuel management, output will be up 60 percent,

Inside the Mazda Millenia's Lysholm supercharger are twin screws that move the air. Like a Roots blower, these blowers like to have their throttle bodies upstream, or heavily controlled if they're downstream. Like centrifugal superchargers, Lysholms have a certain amount of internal compression.

The Autorotor supercharger from Sweden is a Lysholm-design unit serving the aftermarket. BEGI uses this blower in one of its kits for the Miata.

and so on. Up to 12 psi has been pushed into the Miata engine, with a corresponding 100 percent increase in power.

Does all this come free? Only up to a point. After about 6.5-7.0 psi of boost, the stock Miata engine begins to work against itself. The higher heat of the boosted intake charge; the greater effective pressures on the piston, rod, and crank; the limits of the stock head gasket; and so on all work to shorten the life of a stock Miata engine. The turbocharged Mazda 323 GTX engine was tremendously durable at 8.1 psi of boost, but it had a lower engine compression ratio (7.9:1 versus 9.4:1), stronger connecting rods, and so on. The stock Miata engine doesn't have the advantages of these factory-added components, so boost has to be limited or shorter engine life has to be accepted.

The Miata Boost Market

If you're looking to add a turbocharger or supercharger, there are many options to choose from. Various companies have developed all sorts of kits around a wide variety of hardware.

Pressurizing the intake manifold of a Miata is a major engineering exercise that involves various disciplines. In all cases it will affect the emissions and fuel-management systems of the subject engine. If the boost system is well designed, installing a turbo- or supercharger can literally transform your Miata into an even better driving machine. Many of the systems currently on the market have excellent power, good drivability, and impressive longevity records, coupled of course to awesome acceleration capabilities.

On the other hand, a poorly designed system can make the car undriveable, illegal, short-lived, or even downright dangerous. The provider's overall reputation and the experiences of past customers should be the very first things you research when considering a forced-induction kit. Since these kits sell for thousands of dollars, it's highly advisable to find someone else who has already made the investment in a particular system and to learn of their experiences, good or bad. Ask them about the ease of installation, overall product durability and quality, customer support, real-world performance, and final cost.

As a comment on the complexity of designing such a system (especially when involving an OBDII-controlled post-1995 engine), kit manufacturers sometimes have difficulty obtaining California certification. A number of manufacturers have kits that are emissions-legal for just the 1.6-liter cars (BEGI and Nelson, to name two). Sebring supercharger kits are certified for all year Miatas. Some manufacturers have enough business outside of California so that they get away without a CARB certification.

Turbocharger or Supercharger?

Turbo tuners will argue that a belt-driven supercharger has too much parasitic drag to make any real net power. They will also state that superchargers are hard to package and that all the top sports cars use turbos. They will talk about blower efficiencies and how hard it is to make power with a supercharger.

Supercharger fans will counter that the engine's own internal friction is four times that of supercharger drag, so the blower drain is not significant. They'll claim that a turbo's boost delivery is nonlinear and feels "artificial." They'll also point out that turbo lag is an irritating component of any turbo system. Longevity issues and finicky oiling requirements will be raised next, and then the matter of turbochargers' increased back pressure heating up the exhaust valves and increasing detonation. As to the turbocharged sports car claim, supercharger devotees believe that while turbos provide maximum top-end power ratings to dress up the ad brochures, in real-world acceleration, superchargers win out. Turbo opponents will state that twin-turbo supercars use two blowers to mask drivability problems (low-end torque and poor throttle response).

Both camps are right. While you can make up to 7 percent more peak power with a turbo than with a supercharger for a given engine at a given rpm range, superchargers generally create more area under the torque curve (usable acceleration) and produce better street driveability. No matter which side of this debate you happen fall on, most carmakers are moving toward superchargers and away from turbos at the moment. As this creates more high-tech superchargers from suppliers, the aftermarket seems to be following suit.

Superchargers need rotational power and that comes from a belt drive. Here is an example of how Sebring gets the required 10 horsepower up to the blower by using an extension of the stock four-rib belt routing.

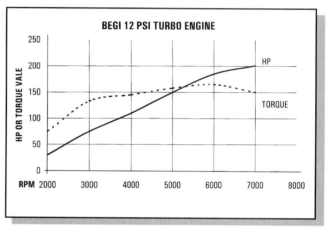

For ultimate peak horsepower, turbos are hard to beat. Here, running 12 psi of boost, the BEGI system puts out over 200 horsepower at peak rpm.

Acceleration Times	0-60 MPH
Forced Induction Miata	6.5
Ferrari 308i	6.4
Lamborghini Miura	6.4
Lamborghini Countach	6.8
Maserati Bora	6.5
Porsche 911SC	6.4

With forced induction, a Miata can equal or surpass the acceleration of some of the great sports cars of the past. Better still, it can also outhandle a number of them.

Detonation and Forced Induction

Before you tax the mechanical components of an engine with too much boost, you'll run up against the detonation monster. Boost creates heat and pressure, which bring the air and fuel closer to its self-ignition point (think of a diesel engine), and the higher pressure speeds up the flame-front propagation, which causes your ignition timing to be affected. This, in turn, affects the timing of the flame front as it approaches the piston head. The result of all this is a knocking or "pinging" sound from your engine when it is under load.

For internal-combustion engines, a single knock or a short "tinkle" from your engine is not particularly damaging, but if you have 15 seconds of detonation in a row, you'll begin heating things up too much. Some sort of metal failure (valve, piston, or spark plug, usually) is going to happen. When you hear a "bag of marbles" knocking down in your engine, that means that detonation is going full song and damage is near.

The knock you hear most often is caused by the early combustion front colliding with the normal (spark-driven) combustion front. Technically, this is "pre-ignition," while detonation proper is caused by the instantaneous combustion of the entire fuel-air mixture and the subsequent pressure front hitting the piston hard and head-on up near the TDC position. The symptoms and results, however, are more or less the same. Ideally, the explosion should hit the piston when it's already on its way down the stroke, someplace around 5-17 degrees after TDC. You can go for higher octane fuel or retard the timing to patch over the situation in marginal cases, but if you want to run significant boost, a more sophisticated approach is needed.

The whole reason you advance a car's timing is to match the combustion with the piston just as it starts the downstroke. The flame front generally meets the piston head just after 5 degrees of crankshaft rotation past top dead center. But since the flame front's traveling speed is fixed over the entire rev range of a

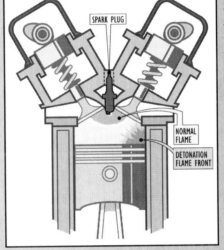

Competing flame fronts collide to produce the "knock" that tells you your engine is detonating. The extreme pressure spike created can crack pistons and blow head gaskets.

normally aspirated engine, as the piston moves faster (higher rpm), you need to anticipate the event sooner.

The flame front travels faster when the intake charge is under boost. Low-rpm driving is done with little or no boost, so the flame front travels at the normal rate. As boost rises, the ideal ignition curve must change to adjust for the faster flame front.

Detonation also occurs on boosted engines during throttle tip-in (when the throttle is just opened) due to the aggressive in-rush of intake air. As the boost air blows past the spraying injector, the most volatile fractions of the fuel are "boiled" off and whisked into the combustion chamber. On a Miata, where the injector also fires against the intake valve when it's closed, the pool of fuel also has its lighter fractions boiled off. These lower-boiling-point fractions have very low octane ratings, sometimes as low as 35. When compared to the 93-octane fuel a boosted engine wants, it's obvious why these fractions start detonating very easily.

The best way to solve both causes of detonation is to have an active knock sensor onboard (as on the 1999 Miata) to retard the timing when detonation occurs. These systems are always seeking the ideal ignition curve, right up against the detonation limit. That gives maximum power for the maximum area under the torque curve.

If you have an older Miata without the knock sensor, you can add one. A company called "J&S" makes an active knock sensor that bolts right on. This is the best way to protect a forced-induction Miata engine. The next best choice is the MSD boost retarder, a simple linear device that takes out 2 degrees of timing for every psi of boost. Sebring sells a special version of the MSD that doesn't start retarding the timing until 4 psi of boost is seen, then takes out 2 degrees of timing advance for every additional psi of boost past that threshold. Either of these devices allows the owner to run 12 to 18 degrees of initial timing, greatly improving the low-end response before boost comes on strong.

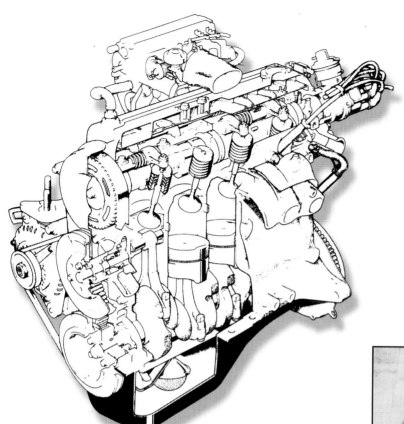

A whole lot of blower on a 1.6-liter Miata engine. Using a Paxton blower from the American hot-rod industry, a Nelson supercharger blows 6 psi into a 1.6-liter engine for 45 percent more horsepower at high rpm.

Mazda learned all about boosting the Miata's B6 engine when it was installed as a turbocharged unit for the 323 GTX. Lower compression, thicker rods, and stronger pistons were some of the improvements they put into this 8-psi boosted engine.

Turbocharger and Supercharger Kits

The first company to mass-market a forced-induction kit for the Miata was BBR, an English company, which released its turbocharger system in 1990. Mazda UK sold these kits through Mazda dealerships, complete with warranty and installation. BBR is a partnership between racer David Brodie and engineer Ken Brittain—a pair that's been tuning turbos and hot rods in England for decades. Some of the smartest ideas for engine tuning have come out of their shops, and the Miata benefited from their attention.

The BBR kits were well engineered and ran 5.5 psi of boost with around 150 horsepower of output, as compared to the stock 1.6-liter's 116 horsepower. In 1991, BBR contracted Mazda racer Jim Downing to distribute the BBR system in the United States. The author became involved in this project and worked through the details of obtaining CARB approval for the kit. Incredibly, the well-designed BBR turbo engine actually ran cleaner than the stock car during the rigorous EPA emissions tests.

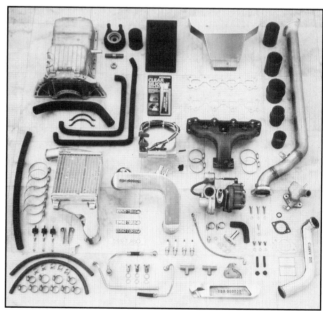

The BBR turbo system is as close as you can come to having a stock turbocharged Miata; it even comes with a Mazda warranty. British dealerships could put this one on your new car before delivery, thanks to an arrangement between Mazda UK and BBR.

Fuel management was handled by an auxiliary computer that plugged into the stock PCM. Boost came in low, reaching maximum pressure at just 2,500 rpm, and the drivability was superb—just like a factory installation. In fact, the BBR system performed similarly to the production 323 GTX motor, although at a lower boost level. BBR included a small intercooler, and Mazda mandated the 5.5-psi cap on boost,

BEGI's Autorotor supercharger kit runs at 10-12 psi of boost, has an air-to-air intercooler and an ignition retarder as standard. It uses a six-rib belt on an auxiliary crank pulley to bring the necessary 20 or so horsepower up to the drive blower.

since the factory would be covering the cars' warranties in England—a clue as to how much boost their engineers felt a Miata could safely withstand.

The BBR kit was well received in the United Kingdom, with over 700 units sold, but it never reached commercial success in America. The BBR turbo kit sold for $2,950 plus around $750 for installation, for a delivered cost of about $108 per horsepower—a bit pricey. The other item that limited its success was that installation required removal of the engine, so that an oil drain could be installed in the side of the oil pan. BBR has discontinued its line of turbos and now only sells Sebring supercharger kits.

Even as the BBR kit was being perfected, various tuners across the country began developing turbocharger installations of their own. Many have come and gone, and only the most advanced were suited to survive. One of these was a company out of Texas called Cartech, which came on the scene early with a series of well-developed turbocharger kits. Cartech's line ran 6 psi of boost and created 173 peak horsepower; Cartech also sold an upgraded kit that included an air-to-air intercooler and higher boost levels; this upgraded version is the only turbo kit currently on the market with CARB certification for 1.6-liter, 1990-1993 engines (EO #D349). The company later changed its name to BEGI. For racers and those looking for maximum power at any cost, there's the BEGI/Flying Miata turbocharger kit, which makes around 209 horses at the rear wheels.

Greddy (a large tuning company out of Japan) currently offers the lowest-priced turbo kit for Miatas. Using a well-sized turbo mounted on a cast exhaust manifold, the Greddy

kit develops around 5 psi of boost (not upgradeable) and gives a 30 percent increase in horsepower. The kit sells for a very reasonable $1,800 and does have an emissions certification. It is an excellent entry-level kit.

Turbochargers are available in many flow rates and sizes, so the barriers to creating a Miata kit center more around the packaging and tuning skills of the developer. Belt-driven superchargers are more difficult to develop for the Miata, due to the fact that few such devices exist that are the right size for a four-cylinder engine. Many blowers are available from Paxton, Vortech, Powerdyne, and others, but these are generally sized for large V-8 Detroit engines.

The Nelson company came on the scene in 1992 with an adaptation of a large Paxton supercharger onto a Miata engine. Although the blower was sized for an American V-8, it fit under the Miata's hood and produced over 7 psi of boost. Power came on in the upper rpm range due to the oversized blower, but performance was strong. This kit offered an emissions certification for sale in all 50 states (EO #D-246-1) for the 1.6-liter engines and increases power by 50 horsepower.

The author had a particular interest in superchargers due to a stillborn plan some Mazda designers kicked around during the Miata's formative years: Supercharging the manual-steering Miata by installing a blower where the power-steering pump usually goes.

Through some dabbling in the shop, a prototype was developed using a Roots-type supercharger made by Eaton. Eaton Corporation, one of the largest automotive suppliers in the world, started manufacturing superchargers for Ford in 1989 for the Thunderbird Super Coupe. Since then, nearly one million of their Roots-type blowers have been installed by GM, Ford, Mercedes-Benz, Jaguar, Aston-Martin, and Holden. Detroit was excited by the Eaton supercharger for a very simple reason: It promised relief from the warranty and drivability concerns the carmaker's experienced with their earlier (late 1980s) turbo installations.

Eaton's smallest blower in the early 1990s was made for GM's 3.8-liter V-6 Buick/Olds/Pontiac engine and featured 62 cubic inches of displacement (that's the volume displaced through one revolution of the supercharger). For positive-displacement blowers like the Roots, Eaton, and Lysholm, size is important, since the blower shouldn't move any more air than the engine can deal with. Nobody races boost gauges or supercharger sizes—the important thing is how much power the final installation makes and how well the blower is matched to a particular engine. With that in mind, the author commissioned Eaton to tool up a smaller blower suitably sized

The Sebring Eaton-based supercharger kit uses the area left by an absent air-filter box to package a 45-cubic-inch Roots supercharger. This kit has been the market leader since its introduction in 1994.

The upstream throttle and bypass manifold leading into the Sebring Eaton blower unit. Thanks to a rear-inlet design and other features, the Eaton supercharger has efficiencies far surpassing the engine-top dragster Roots blowers of the past.

No matter how you do it, if you put pressure against the stock idle-speed control valve, you'll need to install a check valve in the idle-speed control air line to prevent backflow and lost boost. This is a Standard AV-23 (from a NAPA store) air pump check valve from a Ford air pump application—it works great and costs around $20.

for a Miata four-cylinder. What resulted was a 45-cubic-inch blower that could be mated to either the 1.6- or 1.8-liter engine. Eaton went on to suggest a number of further design features specific to this unit, eager to provide a unit that worked in harmony with the Miata.

Since the Eaton blower is a positive-displacement device, the throttle was located upstream of the supercharger—otherwise, upon closing the throttle the blower would be backed up, with noise and mechanical problems as the result. This is acceptable with turbochargers and centrifugal superchargers due to their nondirect pumping nature, but not in a Roots or Lysholm device.

In addition, a bypass system was developed that essentially cut off the supercharger when not in use. By looping the pressurized air back into the supercharger inlet, the supercharger effectively freewheels. This improves idle and part-throttle operation while reducing the drive losses on the engine. These kits are sold under the Sebring nameplate, and over 1,200 units are in use around the world. Sebring kits for all years of Miatas have full CARB certification (EO # D-453) and are legal in all 50 states. Mazda's official tuning arm, Mazdaspeed, has also selected the Sebring kit for its own in-house offerings.

After Cartech changed its name to BEGI, it developed a supercharger system of its own using the Autorotor Lysholm unit. Like the Sebring, the BEGI Autorotor moves the throttle upstream of the blower. Rather than commissioning a tailor-made smaller unit, however, BEGI uses a generic 71-cubic-inch blower at 10 psi and employs air-to-air intercooling to drop the intake temperature. The BEGI Autorotor kit is not emissions-certified, and it uses an extra crankshaft pulley to drive the supercharger. This adds some load to what (particularly on early Miatas) isn't the strongest crankshaft nose in the world, but BEGI is confident in its design.

Briefly put, the Sebring kit bolts on in an afternoon and is sized for the Miata as it was built; the Autorotor is harder to install, may not be road-legal for some applications, and may put more strain on the hardware, but has higher ultimate potential for maximum performance.

When considering which type of turbocharger or supercharger system to use, an owner needs to first consider his or her driving style. Both the Sebring and Autorotor supercharger kits produce gobs of low-rpm power that make the Miata very aggressive in everyday driving. Both have excellent throttle response and instant power at all engine speeds. In addition, a positive-displacement supercharger gives linear power returns: 27 percent throttle input will give 27 percent power application.

Greddy's entry-level turbo system runs 5 psi of boost and bumps power 33 percent. Using as many of the stock intake parts as possible keeps the price down on this Japanese kit.

The latest offering from BEGI uses a Garrett turbocharger and up to 12 psi of boost to make a Miata scream. Note the air filter location and its cold-air pickup for even greater charge density.

This is not the case with turbochargers, which are non-linear in their power delivery. Generally, turbochargers are also less effective at low revs and are subject to varying degrees of throttle lag—a momentary pause between stepping on the gas and getting an increase in power. This makes stoplight drags and hard driving in corners much less predictable. Connecting three curves in a row with a turbocharged engine can be maddening when the turbo lag gets in your way. Turbos decrease throttle response, but increase the "woosh" factor—great for straight-line acceleration. On the positive side, turbos are easier to package and can make more ultimate power than superchargers.

From a tuning standpoint, it's pretty easy to get a Miata into the mid-6-second range for 0-60 times and the mid- to low-14s in the quarter mile. Going any faster than that requires a factor of two: You'll spend about twice as much money, and engine life will be shortened by half.

For example, take the 10-psi BEGI supercharger versus the 6.5-psi Sebring. The BEGI kit produces 144 peak rear-wheel horsepower with the help of an intercooler and ignition retarder, both devices needed to control detonation with 10 psi of pressure. The Sebring makes 140 peak rear-wheel horsepower (measured on the same dyno) with 6.5 psi of boost and no intercooler or ignition controls. Those extra 3.5 psi of boost are making power, but they are also making heat and drag on the belt drive. The net gain is 4 horsepower. The law of diminishing returns starts to creep in after a certain point. For ultimate power gain, BEGI offers a turbocharger that breaks through the 200-rear-wheel-horsepower limit, but picks up turbo-lag and a certain amount of "peakiness." It

also shortens engine life if the car is driven to take advantage of all that extra power. There is no free lunch.

For the real-world user, the peak of the cost/value curve comes at getting the easy power and not trying to be greedy. The Miata's unibody structure and lightweight suspension wasn't designed to carry too much power—175 to 200 engine horsepower is the practical limit for a car you want to keep alive on the road. Much above that and you'll be taxing the engine and drivetrain beyond their design limits. It'll be a blast for a while, of course.

Preparing an Engine for Maximum Boost

As stated previously, the Miata engine will take up to 7-8 psi of boost without complaint. When Mazda wanted to make an 8-psi forced-induction engine out of the same block (the 323 GTX), it made certain important changes to the basic 1.6-liter motor. Many of these parts can be used on the Miata. If you want to build an 8 psi or higher engine, you should invest in heavier-duty components just as Mazda did. Regardless of what a kit maker might claim, the engineers that designed your engine felt it was prudent to beef up certain components once boost pressures got this high.

From the GTX parts bin you'll need the stronger connecting rods and lower-compression pistons. For the cylinder head, use the standard Miata head gasket. It is already reinforced and will withstand up to 12 psi of boost (the GTX gasket won't fit anyway). The exhaust cam of the GTX has a milder duration to facilitate turbo operation, and if you're building the ultimate turbocharged Miata engine, you should invest in one of these to maximize cylinder purging. For

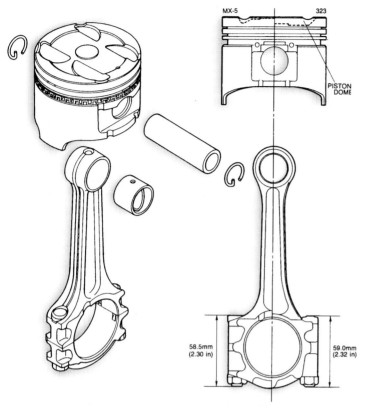

Mazda put in stiffer connecting rods to deal with the 8 psi of boost in the 323 GTX engine. The piston dome was changed as well to reduce compression and avoid detonation. The bearing cap of the rod had a bit more metal to withstand the higher loads without distorting.

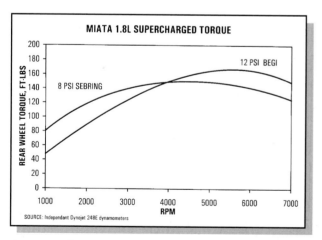

An example of diminishing returns. The 4 extra psi of boost provided by the BEGI turbo system gains a less than proportional amount of torque increase (boost is up 50 percent, torque is up 13 percent). Looking at the total area under the two curves, the two engines have very similar "work" capacities.

supercharged engines the exhaust cam is less critical, although a custom grind with more lift and less overlap will create more power.

Also on the subject of higher boost, Mazda made the determination that stiffer valve springs were needed at 8 psi and above. It's actually possible for the boost on the back of the valves to lift the intake valves off their seats. Even if you don't lift it off, you are counteracting the stock spring's action, thus reducing its effective rate; stiffer springs as used on the GTX are available. For the rest of the powerplant, simply use good engine-building practices. Run the piston-to-wall clearances a little loose (0.006 inches at the skirt) since the piston head will be operating at higher temperatures. Use

	Part name		O.....Interchangeable	X.....Not interchangeable Remark
Cylinder block related	Cylinder head		X	Studs+blind cover positions different
	Camshaft oil seal		O	
	Cylinder head bolt		O	
	Cylinder head gasket		X	Material different
	Cylinder head cover		X	Shape different
	Cylinder block		X	Oil+coolant outlet (for turbo)
	Oil control plug		O	
	Oil pan		X	Shape different
	Oil pan baffle		X	Shape different
	Timing belt cover		X	Shape different
	Front oil seal		O	
	Rear oil seal		O	
Crankshaft related	Crankshaft		O	
	Main bearing		O	
	Thrust bearing		O	
	Connecting rod and cap		X	Weight reduced
	Connecting rod bearing		O	
	Piston		X	Dome design different
	Piston pin and clip		O	
	Piston ring		O	
	Crankshaft pulley		X	One-piece type used
	Rear cover		X	Shape different, sealant to seal
	Flywheel		X	Weight reduced
	Flywheel bolt		O	
Timing belt related	Timing belt			
	Timing belt pulley		X	Tooth type differen
	Camshaft pulley			
	Timing belt tnsr/spring		O	
	Idler		O	
Valve related	Camshaft	Intake	O	
		Exhaust	X	Valve timing different
	Hydraulic lash adjuster		O	
	Valve	Intake	X	Valve margin reduced
		Exhaust	X	Material different
	Valve spring and seat		X	Spring rate different
	Valve guide		O	
	Valve seal		O	
Lubricating related	Oil pump		X	Blind plug in oil level pipe installation hole
	Oil strainer		X	Shape different
	Oil cooler		X	Eliminated
	Oil jet		O	
	Oil filter		O	
Cooling related	Water pump		O	
	Thermostat		X	Opening temperature diff
	Radiator		X	Heat dissipation capacity diff
	Cooling fan		X	Fan motor specification diff

As you go shopping for stronger parts for your Miata, you will find a few GTX parts that will help you out.

a synthetic oil such as Mobil 1 to counteract the high mechanical loads you are putting on the engine, particularly in the piston skirt area. The higher combustion pressures tend to cock the pistons in their bores and oval out the cylinders.

Intercooling

Since boosted intake air comes with higher temperatures, performance can be improved by cooling down the intake charge. The heat hurts in two ways: It expands the intake charge and it primes the combustion process for premature detonation.

Cooling the intake charge makes it denser and less finicky when it comes to detonation. In practice, the cylinder head and intake valve are already running pretty hot in a naturally aspirated Miata. Since the head is full of coolant and caps off the combustion chambers, the intake air gets preheated by running through the aluminum castings of the intake manifold and cylinder head. The intake manifold runs around 220 degrees Fahrenheit under normal operation. For a boosted Miata engine, the intake air can get as hot as 220 degrees before you begin to see detonation creep in. This temperature relates to around 6.5 psi of supercharger boost or 5.75 psi of turbo boost, depending on the system. For boost levels higher than this, the intake temperatures will be getting above the temperature of the intake manifold, so intercooling becomes important.

The efficiency of an intercooler depends on which one a tuner uses. Air-to-air intercooling uses outside air to transfer heat away from the intake air. Since heat transfer is a function of temperature differential and time, an air-to-air intercooler has to be properly located and reasonably large to be effective. If the intercooler is placed behind the radiator, the cooling air has already been pre-heated by the radiator wash air. An intercooler in front of the radiator is much more efficient than one behind the radiator.

The downside of intercooling for some supercharger systems is that putting an intercooler in the intake stream increases the "throttled volume"—the amount of air between the throttle and the intake valve. This applies to systems that have the throttle upstream of the blower. If the throttled volume increases much over the stock value, throttle response will suffer. The larger volume of air has enough inertia that it resists moving quickly when the throttle is opened. Also, the PCM is programmed to expect only a certain amount of time delay between the throttle-position sensor signal and the oxygen sensor's response. Turbos and centrifugal superchargers don't mind large air coolers because they generally have their throttles downstream. Although big intercoolers will still slow down the throttle response of turbo cars, these systems often have enough turbo lag to effectively hide the problem.

A better way to intercool is to use a water-to-air intercooler, where the temperature difference between the charge air and the cooling medium can be kept broad and the internal size can be kept small, reducing throttled volume. Typically this will result in crisper throttle response. Water-to-air intercoolers are easier to package as well, due to their smaller size.

Brain-Storm's new water to air intercooler nestles nicely behind the radiator. This unit has a small overall size and high efficiencies.

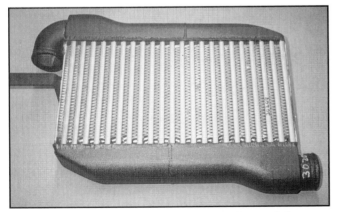

BEGI's air-to-air intercooler mounts in front of the radiator for a cooler position. The downside to going up front for clean air is the added volume and the small pipes that have to be used.

If you're building a high-boost Miata, measure your intake charge temperatures. If you go much above 220 degrees, intercooling can help your goal of making the most power. The Miata's engine is resistant enough against detonation not to need the expense or complication of an intercooler at lower boost levels; if detonation does creep in, an ignition retarder would be a better place to put your money first. But remember, an intercooler does more than just fight detonation. It also makes more power, thanks to the denser intake charge.

Nitrous Oxide

An old trick to make lots of power in an engine is to pump in "supercharger-in-a-bottle," also known as nitrous oxide—laughing gas. Due to a particularly favorable chemical relationship between gasoline and nitrous, the available oxygen is greatly increased when this gas and fuel are mixed in the combustion chamber. Thus, shooting some nitrous into the intake stream has the same type of effect as a supercharger. However, the added oxygen does no good unless you send in some more fuel to go with it. When the recipe is right, you can make all sorts of power. Pretty much the same strategies can cover fuel enrichment for turbos, superchargers, or nitrous applications, which we'll get to in a moment.

Why not use pure oxygen? That's too much of a good thing: The combustion would be too spontaneous and uncontrollable. The nitrogen smoothes things out a bit, giving the flame front time to travel to the piston head in a more predictable fashion. Even so, the flame front in a nitrous charge shoots across the combustion chamber much faster than it does on pure air, so the heat and pressure loads quickly go up to critical levels. If this sounds like a good way to blow up an engine, it can be. In addition to the engine internals, both the fuel and the ignition systems have to be top-notch for a nitrous kit not to become a grenade under the hood. A general rule for retarding the ignition timing is to back off the timing 2 degrees for every 50 horsepower added.

A not inconsiderable side benefit to nitrous injection is that it has a cooling effect on the intake charge. Since the gas is stored as a liquid under pressure in a bottle, it cools rapidly as it converts to a vapor, coming out at about 120 degrees below zero Fahrenheit. This acts as an intercooler all on its own—one reason why the turbocharger and supercharger crowd likes nitrous (apart from being speed-crazy).

The actual plumbing and actuation of a nitrous system are beyond the scope of this book, but many good manuals are available to help you get started if this is the direction you want to go. The Dealer Alternative has experience in putting nitrous on Miatas and can help you get things started.

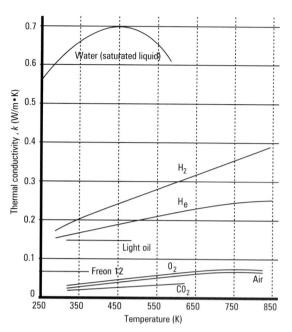

Not only did the good Lord make water the universal solvent, he also made it one of the best heat conductors we have. Compare the thermal conductivity of water to that of air and you'll see the justification for water-to-air intercoolers. This allows the intercooler to be smaller, which is better for packaging and improves throttle response over air-to-air designs.

In general, drivability with nitrous is less than ideal, but the rush is—sort of what a turbo gives you—times two. Still, nitrous is an expensive way to go fast. Most kits use a 10-pound bottle, which costs $35 to fill and will only last about 15 hard runs up the gears, so that's just over two bucks every time you go for the rush. A turbo- or supercharger is a lot cheaper in the long run.

Boosted Fuel Management

The Miata has an excellent fuel map for a naturally aspirated engine. When you add more air (or oxygen in the case of nitrous), you have to find a way to put in more fuel. For a Miata, this falls into a few proven strategies.

The easiest and most popular way is to increase the fuel-rail pressure that feeds the injectors. Stock Miata injectors deliver 20 to 22 pounds of gasoline per hour at 43 psi of rail (or "head") pressure. By increasing that pressure you can increase the flow rate—but only up to a point. The Miata injectors are responsive up to around 85 psi of rail pressure. See the accompanying chart to determine the fuel flow at different pressures for a given injector.

As mentioned previously, the stock rail-pressure regulator limits the pressure to around 43 psi. It also reduces this by

Knowing your fuel pressure is a key part of tuning a high-performance Miata. A standard oil pressure gauge mounted to a bracket and held under a wiper blade makes for an excellent way to measure fuel on the road. You can use a direct "wet" type of gauge in this location safely.

To use an electronic oil pressure gauge to measure your fuel rail pressure, tie into the inlet fuel line going to the fuel rail with some plumbing hardware. Make sure to use sealant tape and hose clamps, because you are dealing with high pressures.

The stock Miata regulator is fitted directly to the fuel rail with an O-ring seal. Before reinstalling it, be sure to rub a bit of motor oil on the O-ring to prevent binding. For most owners, these units are trouble-free.

MSD makes a Miata-specific boost retarder that simply takes out 2 degrees of ignition timing for each psi of boost it senses. This eliminates the detonation caused by timing being too far advanced for the faster-igniting boosted air-fuel mixture. Sebring sells a special version of this product that waits for 4 psi of boost before it starts retarding timing.

about 7 psi during idle (see Chapter 9 for more details on the stock regulator). You can easily put a restriction in the return line and raise the rail pressure up to the limits of the fuel pump, which can push about 80 psi through the lines if it's in good condition. A number of aftermarket tuners sell a static regulator that creates an adjustable restriction in the fuel return line. This raises the pressure at all times, so it is less useful for a boosted engine that operates off boost some of the time. The pressure would have to be set for the maximum airflow condition, making it hopelessly over-rich for the rest of the rpm curve.

The best solution in this case comes in the form of a boost-sensitive fuel regulator. Most of the large Detroit-iron turbo- and supercharger companies use this type of regulator to enrich the engine only during boost. They use a restriction device that's acted upon by a diaphragm that is connected to the intake manifold via a vacuum line, so that whenever the engine is creating vacuum (during idle and cruise), the restrictor is retracted, allowing fuel to flow past without affecting the pressure. When the intake manifold sees boost, however, the upper diaphragm presses down on the restrictor device, raising the fuel pressure. In this way, the fuel pressure is increased proportionally to the boost pressure.

These are pretty clever devices. For 1 psi of boost, the

fuel pressure is raised about 7 psi; for 2 psi of boost, the pressure goes up another 7 psi or so. Thus, as the turbo- or supercharger forces more air into the engine, the injectors keep pace. If the tuner did his or her job correctly, a near-perfect air-fuel ratio can be kept throughout the rpm range. Since the entire system is pneumatic and hydraulic, reliability is high. No electronics are needed to deliver more fuel, which is a nice touch in today's complicated PCM world.

As good as these devices are, though, there's one drawback. For fast-acting turbos or superchargers, there's a lean spot and a hesitation when the engine transitions from vacuum to boost, as the driver cracks open the throttle. For most turbos and centrifugal superchargers, this hesitation is lost in the turbo lag, so it isn't a problem. With some special turbos and positive-displacement superchargers, though, it can be a real drivability problem.

Miata tuners have discovered that raising the baseline fuel pressure from 43 to 50 or so psi effectively covers over this lean spot. This can be done with yet another downstream fuel regulator that permanently raises the system's resting pressure to the higher value. BEGI is generally credited with developing a clever solution in the form of a regulator incorporating both a baseline adjustment and a boost-sensitive restrictor. The nonboosted fuel pressure can be adjusted to a level that cures the hesitation, while the diaphragm and restrictor take care of increasing the fuel pressure under boost.

Regulators of this type, probably the best way to manage the fuel enrichment for a boosted engine, are available from BEGI and Sebring. Both companies include their respective regulators in their turbo- and supercharger kits.

An interesting point to consider is that the stock regulator responds to boost as well. Since it picks up its signal from the intake manifold, when the boost is up, the regulator sees pressure at the signal line. The diaphragm that usually acts in vacuum to lower pressure will now act as a restrictor to the fuel return. This effect will raise the fuel pressure by approximately 1 psi of fuel pressure for each psi of boost, giving some enrichment. On the 1.6-liter engine, for instance, the stock 20-pound-per-hour injector acts like a 22-pound-per-hour injector when the stock regulator senses boost.

Larger injectors can also be installed quite easily. Most Nippon-Denso injectors from another Mazda model will fit in the stock Miata location. The easiest swap is to put the 22-pound-per-hour injectors from a 1.8-liter Miata into a 1.6-liter engine. But while this may be easy, it may not give you the best performance, and increasing pressure to the existing injectors with an auxiliary regulator is even easier still.

The downside of larger injectors is their idle performance and emissions. Since very little fuel is needed at idle, using a larger injector will richen the idle mixture. The oxygen sensor sees this and tries to shorten the duty cycle (the "on" time) for the injectors, but fuel atomization is poor at these very short cycles and you wind up getting droplets of fuel instead of a nice mist. This wrecks idle quality and, more importantly, tailpipe emissions. This is why you see few if any aftermarket suppliers using larger injectors—they can't get an emission certification with them.

Still another old trick is to install a fifth injector in the intake manifold of a forced-induction system and turn it on only when boost is present for a quick-and-dirty enrichment scheme. This is all very easy to do, but drivability is poor even with the best electronic controls. Emissions are difficult to control as well, which is why these systems have now faded from popularity.

Many tuners have played with the various sensors that control the Miata's PCM, but only with limited success. The problem with most tricks of this sort is the limited enrichment they may produce. The actual range of enrichment is not sufficient to compensate for large changes in the engine's

The Sebring auxilliary fuel regulator is used to raise the fuel pressure proportional to the boost increase. The unit uses a two-stage diaphragm and spring setup to achieve the pressure gain. The baseline pressure is also adjustable. Most forced induction Miatas like around 50 psi of baseline fuel pressure.

The heart of the fuel delivery system is the injector. Having your set of four injectors cleaned and matched is a good way to maximize power. If one injector has a bad spray pattern, that cylinder will run lean—and the oxygen sensor may not compensate. In a stock Miata, each cylinder makes around 30 horsepower. Having one off by 15 percent is noticeable.

Miata engines show up in the strangest places. Here, a turbocharged 1.6-liter has been put in an Austin-Healey Bugeye Sprite. Millen Motorsports did the beautiful fabrication work.

breathing ability. Another sticky point is that for some sensors, the PCM doesn't monitor their signal often enough. Thus, the engine can already be at boost before the PCM makes the fuel-delivery change, resulting in hesitation and poor drivability.

In general, the boost lag in turbochargers allows time for the PCM to "catch up," so the delayed monitoring will be masked. If not, you can use a resistor in the water thermister wire to fool the PCM into thinking the engine is still cold (more fuel will be delivered through longer injector dwell times).

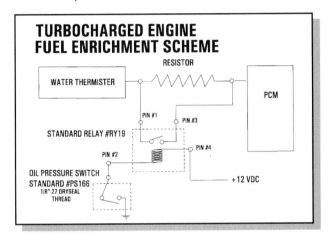

The water thermistor circuit can be used to fool the PCM into delivering more fuel for a forced-induction engine. Since the response time is slow in the circuit, however, this only works on turbochargers on which the blower lag gives the PCM time to catch up.

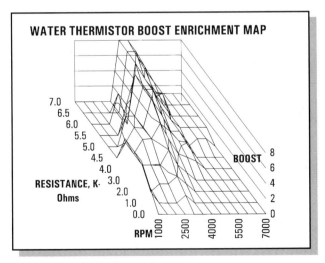

A more sophisticated way to enrich the fuel mixture is to blend in the right amount of water thermistor resistance to make maximum torque at each rpm and throttle setting. This requires a lot of patience and an engine dynamometer.

Before you can figure out the correct resistor for your car, you'll need some means of reading the air-fuel ratio or the oxygen sensor voltage from inside your car while you are driving it. For the do-it-yourselfer, inexpensive monitors are available that read off of your stock oxygen sensor and relay an approximate value for the air-fuel ratio. These are available from various dealers and generally cost under $120. Most have a provision to be mounted to your instrument panel in some fashion so that the fuel-management system can be studied under a variety of conditions. While these cheaper meters are only approximate, they do provide some means of checking your air-fuel ratios over a range of rpm and loads. An alternative is to buy a sophisticated voltmeter, one that has at least a bar-graph display (these can be had for the same $120). Read the bar graph to measure the cyclic voltage of the oxygen sensor. Buy a new oxygen sensor and install it before you start to use one of these devices; old oxygen sensors give false readings.

After hooking up the mixture meter or voltmeter to the oxygen sensor, wire a variable resistor (at least rated for 0 to 20,000 ohms; Radio Shack has these) in the water thermister line. Use wiring long enough that the resistor can be placed inside the car, so your assistant can adjust it while you drive.

Run the car at 6,500 rpm at full throttle (use your left foot on the brake to load the engine and keep it from revving higher). Have the assistant watch your oxygen sensor voltage or air-ratio meter. Have your assistant adjust in more resistance until the mixture is as you want it (14:1 is near optimum for a boosted engine). If you are using a voltmeter, look for a voltage in the range of 0.50-0.6 volts. A fresh oxygen sensor gives off a voltage of 0.45 volts when running right near the desired 14:1 air-fuel ratio. Lower voltages (for example, 0.35 volts) indicate a lean mixture, whereas higher voltages (for example, 0.70 volts) indicate a rich mixture. For a boosted engine, it is better to run slightly rich than lean to protect your engine from damaging detonation (the extra fuel has a cooling effect on the combustion chamber and piston). Also check the air-fuel ratio at 4,000 rpm to make sure you are not too lean at WOT.

After you've got the mixture dialed in, drive back to your work space, and shut off the car. Take your variable resistor out of the circuit and measure the value it was set at (make sure not to bump it after your tuning run). Get a fixed resistor to match this value. Go to the next higher ohm rating if you cannot find one exactly to match. The higher the resistance, the richer the mixture.

In general, up to 6 psi of boost can be compensated for with just the addition of a water thermister resistor (remember, the stock fuel regulator is enriching things as well when it sees boost). Most applications require a resistor of around 10,000 ohms in value. If you go over 20,000 ohms, you run the danger of having the PCM think the water thermister is damaged and the PCM will go into a default mode (in which case the PCM sets everything to the settings for a 180-degree Fahrenheit water temperature).

As a safeguard, always check your spark plug color to determine if you are getting correct combustion. Pull a spark plug (you can just look at cylinder No. 2's) after a run at full throttle at 6,500 rpm that lasts at least one minute (on a new plug). Shut the engine down at that rpm and coast to a stop, then pull a plug to see the color. If it has a nice toasty tan color, you are near the correct mixture. If it is white, you are running too lean; if it is black and sooty, you are running too rich. If the electrode is burnt off, you are running to borrow some money to rebuild your engine.

If the spark plug reading shows a good mixture, the next step is to install the resistor. You could just wire in the resistor permanently, but then your idle and cruise mixture will be far too rich. The clever solution is to plumb in an oil-pressure-light sending switch into the piping downstream of the turbo and then use a relay to trigger the resistor. A generic oil pressure switch grounds its terminal when it sees less than 2 psi or so of pressure. Wire the sending switch and relay so the PCM gets a direct signal from the stock water thermister when you are under 2 psi of boost (switch grounded, relay closed), but brings the resistor into the line at pressures above 2 psi (switch open, relay open, signal routes through resistor). Make sure that the sender switch is grounded. The easiest way to mount the switch is to drill and tap a hole directly into the piping (again, downstream of the turbo). Unfortunately, this resistor method won't work with superchargers that have the throttle upstream since the throttle response is too fast for the PCM to catch up. A fuel regulator is the solution generally chosen for supercharged installation.

On 1994 and later cars, the water thermister strategy can be applied to the intake air thermister with very good results. For engines running up to 6 psi of boost, a simple 15,000- to 22,000-ohm resistor hard-wired into the airflow meter's air thermister line (middle wire of the five that connect to the hot wire airflow meter) will permanently make the PCM think the car is running around at 40 degrees below zero. You can tune the exact resistance needed by your setup using the methodology described in the water thermister discussion. Surprisingly, the idle and midrange off-boost emissions will be fine with the intake-air thermister trick, thanks to the oxygen sensor's wide range of adaptability. The WOT high-rpm

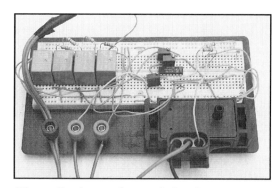

The author's experimental circuit to create a resistance load matching the graph we developed in the previous figure. A MAP sensor feeds a boost-sensitive output to a series of relays that change the water thermistor signal linearly. Steady-state power was great, but tip-in drivability was poor with a supercharger. It worked well on a turbo car—Greddy uses this sort of scheme on certain turbo kits.

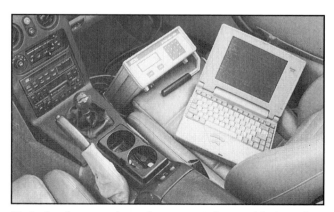

Data-logging a car's performance takes sophisticated equipment. Here, a laptop computer is used to download real-time ignition timing, manifold pressure, air fuel ratio, and rpm, all at 1,000 times per second. The cost of the equipment exceeds the value of the Miata it is hooked up to, but the data it yields is priceless.

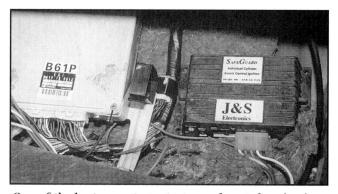

One of the best ways to protect your boosted engine is to install a J&S active knock sensor. This mounts by the PCM (1.6-liter shown) and retards timing whenever detonation is sensed.

Supercharger/Turbocharger Hardware

The actual bits and pieces that go into putting a blower of any sort on a Miata engine involve a bit of fabrication and engineering, so you'll most likely be purchasing a kit already made up for you. Since some excellent kits are available on the market, there is really no reason to make one yourself, even if you were so inclined.

For turbos, one of the main considerations is the exhaust manifold. These are usually cast iron affairs with four exhaust channels running into a central pipe and feeding the turbine inlet. Since the turbo unit has a certain amount of weight of its own and sits cantilevered out away from the cylinder head supported by the exhaust manifold, the manifold must be of sufficient strength to hold that weight without fracturing. This might sound simple, but on a four cylinder engine such as the Miatas, a turbo can see G forces four to five times its normal weight as the engine vibrates in use. Take a look at how strong the AC compressor mount is made and you'll get an inkling of the forces involved in mounting things to your engine.

Not only should the exhaust manifold be strong, it should have good flow characteristics as well. Restrictions here mean less energy gets to the turbine, and thusly to the compressor side. If a kit uses a welded up tubular header, watch out. While they might claim better flow, welded tubular manifolds generally do not last as long as cast iron units.

Since the turbo runs at very high temperatures, it should be placed at least 25mm away from any other component under the hood and to the hood itself, hopefully more. The air inlet up stream will involve your stock air flow meter and an air filter. Obviously these should be as low in restriction as possible. Generally, turbos run the throttles downstream in the stock location, so the plumbing from the impeller outlet to the stock throttle body should be smooth and restriction-free. Make sure to use a check valve such as the Standard AV-23 to prevent boost from leaking out your idle control valve (ISC).

Turbochargers need oil to withstand the 25,000+ rpm speeds of the impellers. Make sure that the supply lines are well-routed and flow sufficient oil for cooling and lubrication. You might want to consider an oil cooler for a turbocharged car (the BBR kit used the oil filter-base unit from the 1.8L and 323GTX). As important as the oil supply line is, make sure the oil drain line feeds correctly to an appropriate spot in the crankcase. A clogged drain line will ruin a turbocharger in short order. As for the entire oil supply, it is recommended that you run synthetic oil (Mobil 1, Redline, etc.) and change it often (3,000 miles) for a turbo car due to the extra stress put on the lubrication system. Turbochargers with water-cooled bearings are superior for longevity and resistance to coking (burning of the oil along the bearing's surfaces), so look for this feature when considering a turbo system. Some turbos have self-contained oiling systems which makes their installation much easier. Turbos generally last 30,000 or more with proper care, specifically good lubrication and a sensitivity to the heat involved. The biggest no-no is to run a turbo engine hard and then to shut it off immediately. Temperatures in the bearing area will skyrocket once the oil flow is shut off. Greddy and others sell turbo-timers that allow an engine to idle for a minute or two automatically before shutting the engine down.

Many turbo kits come with an auxiliary fuel regulator. Make sure that this is mounted in a very secure place away from heat and engine movement. Take care that your fuel lines have gentle bends coming in and going out of the regulator to prevent kinks. Never mount an auxiliary fuel regulator directly to the engine - the vibration of the engine can and usually will adversely affect the regulator's performance.

Superchargers carry similar design requirements in the blower mounting design. The bracketry that holds the blower to the engine should be very stout and well-supported for the same reasons listed above. Downstream and upstream plumbing should be packaged tightly to the engine, with at least 25mm between any chassis component and engine-mounted parts. Heat is less of a concern with superchargers, but you still need to allow for the engine "rocking" during acceleration and deceleration. Brake lines are particularly susceptible to damage.

Supercharger kits use belts to drive the blowers. These are generally reliable if well engineered, but do require regular inspections. Dust on the supercharger or belt idlers is the first indication of a slipping belt.

Some slippage might be unavoidable it you drive your car very hard, but excessive dusting indicates either a loose belt or a poorly aligned pulleys. Do not over-tighten the drive belt as this will stress the supercharger's driveshaft bearings. Autorotor blowers appear to be more sensitive to belt tension, judging from a few blowers that have seized up in the field.

The previous notes about not mounting auxiliary fuel regulators to the engine apply to supercharged cars as well. Make sure that your fuel lines have good clamps at each end, and that you are using high pressure fuel lines (rated to at least 100 psi). Route the fuel lines so there are no kinks or tight bends. As the engine rocks in its mounts, fuel lines can get pinched and shut down fuel flow at a critical moment.

If you use a boost-sensitive ignition retarder or some other electronic devices, take the time to solder any electrical connections. Use heat-shrink tubing (available at Radio Shack) to cover the junctions. Do not use the crimp connectors ("Scotch-loks") typically provided by the vendors to make electrical connections, particularly under the hood. They will fail eventually, usually on some dark rainy night in the middle of Kansas.

The note about synthetic oils apply to supercharged cars as well. Even though the blowers are usually self-oiled, the extra mechanical loads on the engine will be abated some by the use of better lubricants. Superchargers themselves last a bit longer than turbochargers, thanks to the lower operating speeds and temperatures. The Eaton blowers regularly go past 100,000 miles without maintenance.

In the overall scheme of things, you want to make sure that you have not made your Miata less reliable for having modified the engine. This is not a warning about wearing an engine out, this concerns when it just flat stops running. It doesn't matter how fast your car was just before it stranded you on the side of the road - you're still walking home.

From an engineering standpoint, everywhere there is a connection, there is a potential failure point. This applies to joints in the airflow management (cross over pipes, exhaust manifolds, etc.) where clamps, sleeves, or welds can let go. It also applies to electrical systems where wires generally do not fail, junctions do. The simpler the system the better. No matter what claims are made by a vendor, few aftermarket companies make products as high in quality as the Original Equipment suppliers do. Stock Miatas rarely strand owners. Modified ones sometimes do. Particularly for electrical devices, make sure you know how to bypass a device on the side of the road in case something fails.

air-fuel ratios will be spot-on, and good power will be made across the rpm range. For applications running more than 6 psi of boost, the fallback solution of the boost-sensitive fuel regulator works great.

If you want the ultimate in control over your car's fuel-air mixture, you might spring for one of the stand-alone engine computers that are available from BBR and Dealer Alternative. These allow a variety of adjustments for every aspect of fuel delivery (and ignition timing), and if you really know how to tune an engine, you can use these devices to optimize each rpm and throttle setting for your modified Miata. These are great devices, but skilled hands and a laptop computer are required to optimize (or prevent totally messing up) a Miata's performance curve. At nearly $1,000—and that doesn't include all the adjustments necessary to make them work—these piggyback computers are a hefty investment for serious go-fasters only. They are not emissions-legal.

A nice setup for a boosted car is to install a boost gauge and a fuel pressure gauge in place of the air vents in the dash. These are 2-5/8-inch-diameter gauges that fit right in the holes. The pressure gauge is an electric oil pressure gauge. A vacuum/boost gauge is more useful than just a boost gauge.

Racing a Miata

When the Miata was being designed, racing use was always in the back (and sometimes front) of the engineers' minds. No true sports car would be worth its stripes if it could not hold its head high on the track. Nine years later, that careful attention to design has paid off for thousands of racers, many of whom have won national championships or set course records in their Miatas. Whether set up for the occasional autocross or for a serious road-racing campaign, the Miata responds well to modification and good driving.

The following chapter discusses setting up a Miata for either type of racing with the most well-known tips and tricks. Something that is important to emphasize, however, is the driver's skill in handling the car itself. As important as it is to tune the car to the type of racing, it is a rare driver indeed who cannot improve his or her times by attending a driver's school. When budgeting for all of the hard parts and labor involved in optimizing a Miata for racing, save enough green to get yourself to a driving school so you can make the nut that holds the steering wheel as fast as it can be.

Autocrossing

An autocross (or "gymkhana") is a timed racing event in which cars are measured, one at a time, through a course made of traffic cones. The object is to cover the course in the least amount of time without upsetting any cones. Each cone moved costs you points, or seconds added to your time. This is a great sport in which you can drive to the event, run your car, and drive home the same afternoon. The SCCA heavily supports this sport, and it is a great way to enjoy your Miata.

The Miata is predominantly found racing in the stock or near-stock classes. This is very likely a tribute to the car's excellent performance as is, and to just how satisfying the Miata is to race in its original state. The car's double-wishbone suspension and perfect balance made it the ideal candidate for the tight, twisty, and abrupt courses typical of this kind of racing. Autocrosses also don't often demand lots of horse-power; agility and response are prized over brute strength. Miatas have captured numerous national championships in several classes.

Of course, with minor preparation, the Miata's perfor-mance is further enhanced. This prepping includes simple alignment adjustments all the way up to aftermarket com-puter-controlled fuel injection systems. What you can do to enhance the performance depends on the class in which the car competes, but the goal is to create a package that works together; your alignment should work in harmony with your tires, and your tires with your wheels, and so on. The optimum package is flexible enough so that it can be adjusted to meet the demands of every circumstance. It will then complement a driver's skills and produce a competi-tive result.

Stock Class

The joy of stock-class racing is that the time involved is most-ly spent driving, not in preparation. That said, there are many changes and adjustments available to the stock autocrosser. The key to success is to make all the mods and tweaks work in relation to each other, so that the car operates as an improved package, rather than an unbalanced handful.

The Miata is a great handling car right out of the box, thanks to the double wishbones, coil-overs, and disc brakes that have been discussed in earlier chapters. Furthermore, the extreme adjustability of the Miata's suspension allows the owner to tweak it for any driving style and course. This is exactly what most Miata autocrossers do; they set up their own cars to work with their driving styles by fine-tuning their suspension.

The most simple adjustment is the front toe. By simply rotating a tie rod, you can increase the turn-in tendency of the Miata. This change is so simple you can make it when you arrive at a race and then return it to the street setting before driving home. Typical front toe settings for autocrossing range from zero toe-in to 1/16-inch toe-out. As the front loads up under braking, a natural toe-out situation occurs, increasing turn-in response. So if you go to zero toe, the car will actually achieve a good degree of toe-out under forward weight trans-fer when braking and turning. Here's a hint: If you can stand to race with an off-center steering wheel, only adjust one tie rod to set the toe. That will leave the steering wheel cocked at the end of the day as a reminder to return to the street align-ment before heading home. (On the highway, toe-out gives twitchy and unstable handling.) The steering wheel also serves as a guide to recapturing your original alignment.

Setting the rear toe is more complicated, since the

Adjustable shock absorbers allow fine-tuning for track conditions—a must for the well-prepared team.

change is made with the camber bolts, which also control camber settings. Since the rear toe doesn't have as dramatic an effect on autocross handling as the front toe, it's usually just set once and left alone. Any major changes in the rear toe potentially create unpredictable handling, such as rear steer-ing or twitchiness. Leave the rear toe at the street settings until you become serious, but just as a general rule, zero rear toe forms a neutral car, leaving the steering to the front wheels. Rear toe-out produces a rotating tendency that encourages quick turn-ins, but also makes the car unstable under braking as each tire duels with the other to guide the tail end outward. Rear toe-in forms a very stable environment, but drags the rear tires as they drive into each other.

One degree of negative camber in the rear is the norm for autocrossing a Miata. The front camber is usually a little more aggressive, set anywhere from 1 degree negative to maximum negative, which usually arrives at 1.5 degrees. If you plan on keeping the same rear alignment for the street and autocrossing, stick to 1 degree negative and save your tires. Set front caster at maximum to further enhance turn-in quickness.

When aligning for autocross, determine your purpose for the alignment: autocross only, regular autocross as a daily dri-ver, or occasional autocross. This should ultimately decide how aggressive the alignment will be. An all-autocross align-ment, heavy on the toe-out with mega-negative camber, is absolutely treacherous to drive on the street. The car will con-tinuously wander, grabbing cracks, grooves, and puddles.

A four-point roll bar is a legal modification for Solo II and a necessary addition for the SCCA's Solo I, an event in which competitors attempt to turn the fastest lap on a road course. The bars bolt right to the Miata's frame rails outside of the fuel tank.

Changing the front sway bar is legal for the SCCA B-Stock class, and many owners of 1994 and later Miatas add a 7/8-inch or larger front sway bar to control body roll. Once a larger front bar is installed, modifications are needed to compensate for the induced understeer. Driving style can be

modified by introducing trail braking (braking that continues as a turn is initiated) to rotate the car into the turn. Front toe can also be increased for more oversteer, and the front sway bar end links can be modified to control preload on the bar. This allows the driver to further tune the front end. A larger front bar can also help Miatas with open differentials keep their inside rear wheels on the ground by reducing body roll, and the larger sway bar is much cheaper than a limited-slip diff (though not as effective).

If new shocks are in the plan, adjustables are the best bet. They cost as little as 20 percent more than a set of nonadjustable performance shocks, and the adjustability makes that price increase worth it. Single-adjustable shocks are the least expensive option; these usually have one control to dial in the compression damping, while the rebound damping remains constant. The next step up is a double-adjustable unit, in which one knob changes both functions. And if cash is unlimited, you can actually have a shock manufacturer build a shock to your specifications.

There are two primary benefits to adjustable shock absorbers. First, they enable an autocrosser to only stiffen the suspension when needed, so that cruising around on the street isn't a bone-jarring experience. The other reason is the added control over the suspension. By adjusting firmness on the front or rear shocks, a driver can tune the steering characteristics without having to adjust other items that are already satisfactory. Adjustable shocks are just one more way to tweak the Miata's character: Stiffening the front shocks and softening the rears will produce understeer, while the opposite adjustment produces oversteer.

As for wheels in stock classes, the factory alloys are your best bet. Mazda has created some awesome wheels for this car that surpass many purpose-built race wheels. The options for tires are more numerous. If you plan to autocross more than once, it's a good idea to invest in some special autocross specific tires and wheels—otherwise you'll be replacing your street tires in short order.

If you want to win, you'll need to purchase some DOT race rubber. Autocross-only DOT tires are the quickest, with the road-race versions following close behind. When it comes to sizes, the temptation will be to get the biggest available—225/50x14s—but real-time testing might persuade the buyer differently. Although many national-level competitors run 225s, there are still quite a few running 205/55x14s and winning. The larger tire tends to smother the crisp feeling of a narrower width, and it costs more. The stock size of 185/60x14 is also an option, but this doesn't seem to provide as much grip as is desired in autocrossing.

Stock-class autocrossers don't get very much liberty when it comes to engine modifications. Most sanctioning bodies allow alternative air filters, spark plugs and wires, and exhaust from the catalytic converter back. Cotton-mesh-type filters are usually a given for increasing horsepower, but the dyno shows that Miatas actually prefer foam-type air filters. Stick with some 8-millimeter silicone plug wires and stock plugs to deliver the charge. A simple straight-through muffler produces high power and torque, but the noise may not be tolerable for most. If that's the case, go with a Miata-specific cat-back exhaust to eliminate the heft and restriction of the stock unit. The best package, according to the dyno, is a Jackson Racing panel air filter and a cat-back exhaust system.

The stock brakes don't require any work for stock-class autocrossing. Even the stock brake pads work great. They don't need to warm up, and they don't fade in an autocross environment.

Street Prepared-New Contender

It doesn't take much to throw a Miata into Street Prepared (SP) class, but it takes much more to make it a contender on a national level. Most SP classes allow extensive changes to the intake and fuel-delivery systems, exhaust, differential, and suspension, though the inside of the motor must remain unmodified. All the allowed modifications can add up to a bunch of money and even more work. Before this level of competition begins to seem too intimidating, realize that on a regional level, most SP cars are built with an exhaust system, big wheels and tires, springs, shocks, sway bars, and an intake or air filter kit. Most of these items are added to the car just for looks anyway, so why not put them to good use?

The simplest way to organize your suspension setup is to get a preassembled kit from any of the mail-order companies catering to Miata owners. These kits are engineered to work together, and buying all the items at once may also reward you with a discount. Talk to the vendors to decide what exactly their suspension kit was designed for and how much it will impact the car's primary function—daily driver or racer. Taking the suspension up to the next notch for SP autocrossing will require some custom-valved shocks with adjustable spring perches and racing springs. Both Carrera and Ground Control offer these kits for Miatas—and both take very different approaches, so a little investigation is needed to make a decision on which application is appropriate for your needs.

If you have still further aspirations for your suspension, new bushings will complete the package. Delrin is about the toughest bushing material around. Delrin bushings will make for a very harsh ride, but they won't let your control arms get out of line. If you're looking for something more streetable, try polyurethane.

For a fundamental increase in power, the intake on the Miata should be opened up with a free-flow filter, and its primary intake should be located in a cool spot. There are several kits available for this purpose. Most give an increase of 2-10 horsepower. Refer to Chapter 9 for recommendations.

A more serious approach includes abandoning the factory intake and fuel injection system for a full-race setup. A race-car fuel injection setup with velocity stacks, individual throttle bodies, and intake runners for each cylinder is becoming the preferred setup for the job. These systems are easier to tune and maintain than carburetors and work well with the PCM. Manifolds and injection kits of this type are currently available in Japan and should soon be available in the United States. Meanwhile, you either have to pay the hefty price to ship one over or have one fabricated locally. Whether you use the factory intake or go all-out, be sure to smooth out casting marks in the manifold and match ports with the head. The goal is to create a smooth passageway for air to enter the engine.

It takes a fresh engine to properly digest this big dose of fuel and air. This task is best accomplished by a powerplant with good compression. A compression test will identify any leakage, and if there is any, a leak-down test will identify the source as either the head or the block (see Chapter 11). Unless the engine is fresh, some compression will be lost in the head. This can be rectified with a valve job and replacing any pieces of the valvetrain that may be out of spec.

The exhaust system is the final obstacle in the horsepower arena. What's done here greatly depends on previous

A free-flow intake using filters like this Millen unit incorporating a K&N large cone are an easy way to make horsepower at higher rpm, but usually at a sacrifice of low-end torque.

modifications. A poorly matched exhaust can suffocate the engine or open up the exhaust too much, which will reduce back pressure to the point of substantial torque loss. As stated in Chapter 10, most aftermarket Miata exhausts are designed to increase power while maintaining similar torque and horsepower curves. This system should also include an exhaust header, since you'll be spending most of your time at maximum rpm. Look for a header that is created with four equal-length tubes exiting the head into one final collector, possibly with an intermediate four-into-two stage. Also check to make sure the unit doesn't have any clearance problems with the steering column or bellhousing. Once you get the header, consider having it ceramic-coated. This coating will extend the life of the header, dissipate heat, and smooth the interior for improved flow.

The final step in the exhaust system is removing the catalytic converter—the irony of the SP class. Supposedly, the original intention of SP was to create a high-performance machine that was dependable and street-legal, but for some odd reason the catalytic converter got dropped from the equation. So if you're willing to trailer your Miata to the event or drop in a straight pipe at the track, then do it. The catalytic converter is a big cork in the exhaust, and in older cars it usually crumbles internally or becomes caked with carbon, causing a bigger jam.

Controlling wheel spin is the next hurdle. A limited-slip differential is a must when stiffening the suspension and upping the power. With the inherent tight turns in autocross, an SP Miata will find itself spinning the inside rear wheel at every turn without a limited-slip. Used viscous diffs can be had for a reasonable price, while the Torsen diff will provide more lockup for a steeper price. Ultimately, the Mazda factory competition unit will provide the highest performance level, since it was designed for racing.

For years, most SP autocrossers have used 13-inch wheels with 215- to 225-millimeter slicks. But the winner of the 1997 Solo II Nationals used a 16-inch wheel so that his Miata could run a 245-millimeter tread width. If you want to run tires this large, then plan on cutting away some sheet metal and adding flared fiberglass fenders to make room for the wide rubber. An SP Miata with conservative power would perform best with the smaller wheels, since they provide greater torque through gearing. A higher-powered Miata benefits from the bigger wheels, as they increase the track for better cornering.

The Miata certainly has the potential to be a winning SP racer, as proved by Guy Ankey of Tri-Point Engineering, the winner of the 1997 SCCA Solo II Nationals. He transformed

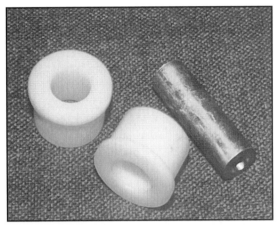

Pictured is a Delrin suspension bushing manufactured by Brainstorm products. These bushings are easily compressed into the control arms, using the simple bushing tool in the opposite illustration. Delrin bushings provide the stiffness of metal bushings without the need for lubrication.

A simple tool for bushing removal is created with some thick washers, a large plumbing pipe, long bolt, nut, and a Miata tie-down hook. Once assembled, an air impact wrench is used to tighten the nut. The bolt head pulls the bushing into the empty space inside the pipe. Use the spare washers to take up the extra bolt space when the nut reaches the end of the threads.

his Miata into an autocross beast and brought home the championship in the CSP class. As Ankey puts it, "This car was built as a race car first and a street car second." Ankey did absolutely everything to his 1990 Miata to build it into a winner, including the addition of a freshened 1.8-liter motor and the previously mentioned 16-inch wheels. That's exactly the commitment it takes to build a winning Miata for national-level SP competition.

Amateur Road Racing

Road racing a Miata is probably the definition of enjoyment. The cars rarely break, are a blast to drive, and are very competitive even without major modification, and parts are cheap to replace. Even the cost of getting a car to dedicate to racing is low, with used Miatas going for less than $5,000. Many racers have one Miata for the street and one specifically modified for track use. If you make the commitment to go road racing, the Miata gives you a few different classes to choose from, depending on your appetite and pocketbook, from showroom stock to the highly modified E Production.

Showroom Stock

Showroom stock is the least-modified way to race a Miata. Modifications were limited to air filters and spark plugs until 1998, when the SCCA decided to also allow cat-back performance exhausts and aftermarket steering wheels. Other mods revolve around safety and include a roll cage, five-point harness, airbag removal, and a racing seat. The reasons for the roll cage and harness are obvious, but the others might surprise you. There's the occasional bumping of cars while on the track, and the last thing a driver needs is an airbag in his or her face while racing wheel-to-wheel through a turn. In the case of a high-G-force impact, factory hinges can potentially fail, which is likely the reason for the SCCA introducing the racing-seat option in this class. A solid race seat removes this potential weakness and provides additional side protection and support.

The Miata R-Package without air conditioning is the Miata to run in showroom stock. This car is the lightest model available and comes with a Torsen differential and Bilstein shock absorbers, making it the true performer of stock Miatas. The later R-Packages (1994-on) have greater horsepower, providing a little more "oomph" against the competition.

Alignment

Alignment is everything in showroom stock. The rules dictate that a competitor must maintain his or her alignment within the specifications as listed in the workshop manual. Driving style and track characteristics govern how the car is aligned.

The SCCA's showroom stock class keeps modification to a minimum, allowing drivers more time for driving and less time spent on preparation.

Zero toe front and rear creates a fast car in a straight line, but makes the stock Miata very twitchy under heavy braking. Rear toe-in of 1/16 inch or more will create a rear wheel drag that stabilizes the car during braking. A small amount of front toe-in makes for comfortable understeer at speed and promotes stability under braking, but dulls the sharpness at turn-in and creates greater rolling friction on straights.

Tires

You'll need DOT-approved road-race tires to compete seriously. These tires are specifically designed for the rigors of road racing and make all the difference in a turn. Competitors are permitted to run 20 millimeters over or under the stock tire size, which is why nearly all competitors run 205/55x14 tires. Although this tire is larger than stock, the compound is softer, so a 2,000-pound car has little trouble heating them up.

Engine

Stock means the engine remains unmodified, but doesn't mean you can't build the perfect stock motor—sort of. When the factory builds an engine, that unit is built within acceptable production-line tolerances. Those tolerances can make a big difference on the dynamometer. If a cylinder head is at the maximum thickness, then that means it's making minimum compression. If the valves aren't seating perfectly, that means they're leaking and losing compression. And if the reciprocating parts aren't perfectly balanced, the engine is putting energy into shaking rather than spinning. You get the idea.

This is where balancing and blueprinting come into play. Essentially, this means building the perfect factory-spec engine. If all the pieces are built to the beneficial extreme of their original designs (for example, the cylinder head is at the

For road racing, aluminum race seats (pictured) provide excellent support at an affordable price. The seat can mount to the factory frame rails to provide adjustability or to custom fabricated rails that provide a lower seating position, contributing to an overall lower center of gravity and more headroom.

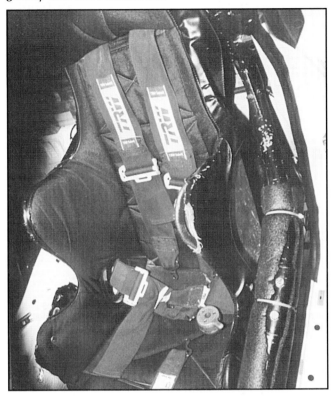

A five-point harness easily installs in a Miata. The shoulder straps wrap around the cage's cross bar. The lap belts bolt into the existing factory seatbelt holes. The crotch belt requires a little more effort as the eye bolt passes through the frame rail. A slot is cut through both sides of the frame rail so that the backing plate will mount flush with the bottom of the car. An existing hole is enlarged to pass the nut through to the eye bolt.

minimum height to increase compression and every reciprocating part is balanced at the lightest weight in the production range), you will have a very fast Miata. Technically you're not supposed to do any of this in showroom stock, but there really isn't any way to prove the motor wasn't built that way at the factory. (Just don't ask what those odds are.) So if you see other Miatas "exactly" like yours cruising by on the straights, now you know why: They must've all gotten lucky and bought cars with the perfect factory motors.

As previously mentioned, spark plugs and air filters can be modified for the stock class. Horsepower gains from alternative plugs is negligible—just check for items that might

cost power, such as improper gap. Foam or cotton air filters have proven more favorable to producing horsepower than paper designs. Clean these filters prior to each race. Race tracks are very dirty places, and all that airborne debris will find its way into your intake, cutting off a little airflow.

Exhaust Systems

Probably the easiest way to make power in these classes is with a cat-back performance exhaust. Choosing an exhaust is the difficult part. Typically, freer flowing exhaust systems create more horsepower at high rpm, but sometimes at the price of torque at lower rpm. The driver's style and the track's design may dictate which unit to build or install.

An aftermarket exhaust might be the easiest solution, since it mounts in the mandatory factory spots, but there's probably more than the customary 4 horsepower from these kits to be had if you buy a custom-designed system. Since the catalytic converter will remain in place, the custom exhaust should retain sufficient back pressure for the engine to produce usable torque. Replacing the stock exhaust with a custom 1-7/8-inch tube using mandrel bends (a bend that maintains a constant diameter in the pipe) will serve well as compromise of horsepower and torque. The custom system should have a constant pipe diameter and a minimum number of turns to reduce disturbance in the exhaust flow.

You may or may not want a muffler in your custom system. The addition of a muffler adds a second source of back pressure downstream from the cat and may result in greater torque output, but at the cost of some high-rpm power. Most mufflers are heavy, however, so you may want to omit it from the system, if you are allowed to under track rules. For most circumstances, though, the newer lightweight composite mufflers (such as Borla's carbon-fiber series) can keep weight at a minimum, while still permitting exhaust tuning and meeting the noise requirements in place at some tracks.

Racing Maintenance

If you're serious about campaigning a Showroom-Stock Miata, then there are some maintenance items to keep an eye on. Suspension bushings will wear, since each race is putting them through more torture than they were designed to see in a lifetime. The rubber bushings are fairly easy to replace, using a long bolt, a piece of pipe, a series of washers, a tie-down hook, and an impact wrench. Also check sway bar bushings and end-link bushings. The bar bushings have a tendency to walk out of the clamps, while the end-link bushings will tear.

After every race weekend, run a compression check or leak-down test, and be prepared to pull the head. If the

A well-prepared team will have all the tools and spare parts necessary, and keep everything in order. It is not always who is fastest that wins; it is usually who is the best prepared.

compression is down just a little, you'll be losing valuable horsepower to the competition, and that will equate to car lengths on a straight. Make sure the valves are seating perfectly and the HLAs are pumping up.

Check the throttle cable and make sure it brings the butterfly fully open when floored without creating torque on the butterfly spindle. Check the shock rods for looseness, along with the shock caps where they mount to the chassis. These are just a few Miata-specific items, but if you're racing a Miata, it will need to be maintained as well as any other race car.

Improved Touring Class

The Miata was introduced into the SCCA's Improved Touring (IT) class in 1996. Because it was placed in IT, the fastest Improved Touring class, there wasn't much interest in building an IT Miata to compete against the likes of Datsun Z-cars or second-generation RX-7s. For 1998, the 1990-1992 Miata was moved to ITA, a class populated with small-bore cars, including the CRX-Si, first-generation RX-7, first-generation MR2, and other late-model economy cars. The IT classes allow major mods to the suspension, intake, and exhaust. A similar class exists as a pro-racing venue known as the SportsCar Speedvision Cup. The developers for these cars are the best bet as resources for prepping a Miata to IT specs.

Safety Equipment

Safety equipment mandatory for IT competition includes replacing the stock driver's seat with a race seat and adding a roll cage and five-point harness.

A coil-over setup with a screw-type spring perch allows the suspension to be corner-weighted. That is, these perches allow the chassis weight to be divided equally among all four corners of the suspension. Also pictured is a steel braided brake line.

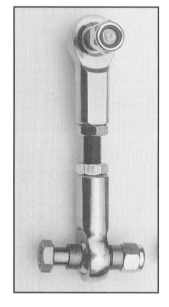

Adjustable sway bar end links allow fine-tuning of the sway bars by permitting minute adjustments for preload. Some end links may also eliminate rubber bushings, creating a quickened reaction time between the control arm and the sway bar.

An aluminum race seat of 0.125-inch thickness provides excellent support without adding weight (thinner seats tend to flex without additional bracing). Custom seat rails should be fabricated to mount the seat to the car's body. These rails lower the seat, provide a firm foundation, add headroom, and lower the center of gravity.

Bolt-in cages are available for a respectable price, but a custom cage will provide increased comfort and improved safety for a specific driver. Bolt-in cages can also be modified by a fabricator to meet any additional needs of the driver, such as a NASCAR-style door bar or extra bracing.

The lap belts of a five-point harness will bolt in place of the factory restraint system. The crotch-belt mount is more tricky. The frame rail runs directly through the center of the driver's footwell, right where the crotch-belt eyebolt should be mounted. Unfortunately, the backing plate can't be placed over the rail, since the rail would collapse under heavy load, so cut a slot through each side of the rail for the plate. First drill the hole for the eyebolt, then grind a slot on each side of the hole through the rail. The backing plate slides through the slots and mounts flush with the floor pan.

Suspension and Chassis

Similar to the SP class in autocrossing, the IT class allows for the replacement of existing suspension components with a coil-over setup. Since the Miata comes with coil-overs already, the change is limited to swapping the factory units for items with adjustable spring perches, racing-grade shocks, and racing springs. Both Ground Control and Carrera developed systems specifically for the Miata in this regard, and the unsprung weight is reduced from the factory setup with these packages, while allowing for corner-weight adjustment. Adjustable shocks are preferable, allowing further tuning of the suspension for a specific track.

A typical sway bar setup for an IT Miata is a 15/16-inch front bar and a 1/2-inch rear bar. Heavier bars introduce flexing at the chassis mounts. If a larger bar is preferred, reinforced sway bar mounts are available from Mazda Competition Parts. Upgrading the bar's chassis-link and end-link bushings to polyurethane or Delrin or adding Heim joints crisps up the feel and reduces the equipment's reaction time. The suspension bushings should also be replaced with Delrin, aluminum, or polyurethane. New bushings limit the amount of lateral movement in the suspension, minimizing any dynamic alignment changes under severe load. Of the four locations available for chassis bracing, a brace connecting the front subframe serves the Miata best, assuming the car already has a rear subframe brace. A 1990 or 1991 won't have come with the rear brace, but these can be updated with a 1992 or 1993 factory subframe. The newer unit contains a brace connecting the insides of the lower control arms.

The quickest tires are DOT road-racing tires, either 205s or 225s; the wider tire trades some straightline speed for additional cornering grip. There are only a few 14x7-inch racing wheels available for the Miata in the correct offset, and they all weigh more than the factory's 1994 and later alloy wheels, plus they carrying a hefty price tag. The extra inch width over the factory wheel doesn't justify the increase in price and weight.

Casting marks at the port end of the intake plenum should be cleaned up for smoother airflow. Same goes for any marks at the throttle-body end.

Griffin makes a high-capacity radiator for the Miata to handle the extra heat loads created by endurance racing in traffic, in which airflow to the grille is sometimes restricted by other cars' wakes.

Racing Power

The first step to making speed for IT racing is to lighten the car. The rules permit removal of the interior carpet, sound-deadening material, center console, heat shields, air conditioner, and parking-brake assembly. Minimum vehicle weight is set at 2,205 pounds including driver for 1998, so if you weigh over 175 pounds you'll probably be racing heavy.

With accessories like power steering and air conditioning absent from the engine bay, there's room to move the air-filter assembly around in search of cooler air. Like the exhaust system, the intake tract has a direct effect on torque and horsepower. In general, a longer tract produces torque and a shorter tract makes horsepower. It's important not to sacrifice too much midrange torque for horsepower, since you aren't allowed to change the gearing and you'll inevitably find sections of a track that require lots of midrange power. Examine the intake for casting defects, and clean up and match the ports to smooth the incoming airflow.

The stock Mazda fuel supply is more than adequate for the engine, making the quest for increased airflow crucial. The other end of the equation is the exhaust system, which should be tuned to meet the individual driver's style and, if possible, the track's characteristics. Just remember that because of the Miata's small engine, it's important not to lose too much torque in search of horsepower. Most road courses have corners where torque is a vital part of successfully executing the line.

While most aftermarket exhaust kits are fine for the street, they generally go against many IT principles by adding weight and sacrificing power for less noise. An equal-length header, a short tube-style muffler, and a downpipe constitute a good working exhaust system for a Miata in IT. This setup minimizes weight, increases flow, produces sufficient back pressure for maintaining torque, and is tunable by swapping out the muffler.

Engine power is easily increased with the modest improvements encouraged in IT, such as balancing and blueprinting. Even with the limited mods allowed, intensive labor is involved in building an IT motor. Each part should be machined to exact specifications, then matched in weight to every other part of the same type. And don't limit the balancing to engine parts—every part that moves is a good candidate, such as driveshafts and halfshafts.

The first step in the building process is the teardown, after which each part must be measured for spec and tested for function. The Miata cams hold up well, but the HLAs take a beating on a high-mile motor. Plan on purchasing a set of 0.040-inch overbore pistons if the goal is to run up front, since this is the one area where internal mods are permitted and the result is more power. Mazda's factory competition arm sells a set of aluminum 0.040-over pistons with rings for the Miata.

The success of the engine buildup relies primarily on attention to detail. The better the job, the greater the reward. A well-machined engine built to exacting specs will be strong, reliable, and substantially more gutsy than the factory motor. Get a factory shop manual from your favorite dealer and follow the specs to the letter. The factory clutch is up to the task of transferring this newfound power to the driveline, but if you need an extra vote of confidence, try an aftermarket performance clutch disk and pressure plate.

Mazda's designers had their own ideas of how a production-based Miata race car would be raced, even back in 1984.

Additional power is released at the front of the motor by reducing the crank load. Racing Beat stocks a lighter, larger-diameter water-pump pulley to reduce the speed of the water pump and lower the overall mass of the crank assembly. Racing Beat also makes a lightened alternator pulley. The Miata came with a double-groove crank pulley for driving the alternator and water pump and the power steering and air conditioning. When the outer groove is removed (along with the power steering and air conditioning), mass is further reduced. Finally, belt tightness has a dramatic effect on crank load. The belt should be just tight enough to drive the accessories—just to the point before it begins to squeal.

At this point you have a good foundation for building a reliable and competitive IT Miata. Use this as a base for continued development of the car and the driver's skill. Carefully read the rules for items that may benefit your specific situation and watch for rules changes each season. Improved Touring is a great opportunity for an amateur racer to experience both the driving and building of a race car without investing too much time or money.

Production Road Racing

Production classes are the next level of race modification beyond IT, using series-produced cars with extensive modifications to enhance performance. The extent of these modifications varies from model to model, with the ultimate goal of maintaining each machine's potential competitiveness within its class. The 1.6-liter Miata is grouped in the fastest class, E Production (EP). Production racing encourages radical interpretations of the vehicle's original parts. Consider this class as an opportunity to achieve a model's performance limits while retaining the core parts that form its identity.

Pratt Cole's 1997 EP National Champion Miata makes a good example of how to build an EP Miata. The first giveaway that this car is an EP Miata is its appearance: large bulbous fenders, super-wide tires, and no windshield. The fenders, hood, trunk, and bumpers are all fiberglass and modified to allow larger tires and to improve the aerodynamics. Bob Boig,

The 1997 SCCA Runoffs EP champion Miata of Cole Pratt sports Mazda Competition Parts' fiberglass kit. This kit allows the fitment of the larger wheels and tires run in Production classes. This Miata also exhibits a state-of-the-art triangulated roll cage. This tructure provides maximum safety and chassis rigidity.

another EP Miata pioneer and runner-up at the 1997 Runoffs, is the originator of the fiberglass kit that is now available from Mazda Competition Parts. All this fiberglass helps reduce the weight, and the reduction process continues with the removal of the entire interior—all this to get the car near the class minimum weight of 2,025 pounds. The windshield frame was removed to reduce drag, and a shortened windscreen was installed to smooth airflow over the cockpit. Only necessary items should decorate the interior, such as a gauge panel to replace the dashboard, a lightweight racing seat, a sprinkling of control switches, and mandatory safety items.

The most important safety item is the roll cage, which also serves as the primary chassis stiffener. On Cole Pratt's Miata, the cage's feet attach to the shock towers and the rears of the doors. From this point the tubes take a triangulated path upward to form a pyramid, peaking just over the driver's head. This is incredibly strong geometry—just ask the Egyptians. Additional bracing was used on the underside for added strength and to reduce chassis flex.

Supporting this rigid structure is a tube-frame suspension. The factory control arms were replaced with tubular units connected to the chassis with Heim joints, rather than bushings. These joints eliminate unwanted alignment changes under load and provide a nearly infinite number of adjustments. The suspension pickup points were moved from the factory location to maintain Mazda's original suspension geometry (yes, it's that good), and the entire rear subframe was recreated using tubes to make room for the differential, which was raised to keep the halfshafts perpendicular with the hubs. Carrera coil-overs with 600-pounds-per-inch springs in front and 400-pounds-per-inch springs in the rear

provide a compliant ride with virtually no roll. The Carreras use a threaded spring perch, allowing the car to be easily corner-weighted for optimum balance. A 1-1/4-inch tubular sway bar keeps the front end level, while a 3/4-inch bar does the job out back.

Panasport racing wheels measuring 15x7 inches are wrapped with Goodyear racing slicks that are 9 inches wide. At 23 inches, the rolling diameter of these wheels is very close to that of the stock wheels—perhaps another tribute to the factory setup.

The engine started life as a standard-issue 1.6-liter Mazda twin-cam and ended up as a screaming four-banger with 14.25:1 compression. The cylinders were over-bored 0.040 inch, and appropriately sized pistons were dropped in. Carrillo rods keep everything connected to the crank, while custom-ground cams drive the valvetrain (the factory cams were welded up and reground, since blanks aren't available under normal circumstances). The rest of the valvetrain was upgraded to withstand the abuse of a 9,000-rpm redline. All this good stuff is now available from Mazda Competition Parts.

If you're serious about winning, have a pro port the cylinder head. If you haven't noticed, most racers worship head massagers as though they were modern-day demigods, and with the ability to create so much power, the worship's understandable. Although the stock injection is legal for EP, a carburetor makes more power. In Pratt's car, fuel is delivered by a 48 DCOE Weber carb with 32-millimeter chokes squirting through a custom intake manifold. On the backside of the combustion cycle, an exhaust header of 1-3/4-inch tubing flows into a single collector before mating up with a 2-1/2-inch exhaust and muffler.

A gaggle of Miatas hounding a lone Honda. Miatas dominated showroom stock racing for the first five years the car was in production, showing the good genes underneath the beautiful shape.

Sequential transmissions are permitted, providing they're mechanically actuated. This is the optimum setup for road racing, but in addition to costing big bucks, this comes with a 50-pound weight penalty. Factory brakes bring everything to a halt per EP-class rules, although racing brake fluid and pads were fitted.

Before you get started, you may want to consider some options. The 1.8-liter Miata is eligible for EP, providing it uses the factory suspension. Even so, Pratt feels that the 1.8-liter, coupled with a modified suspension of stock origin could be a very formidable competitor—and that's quite a statement coming from a National EP champ, not to mention a big compliment to Mazda's design.

Pro Road Racing

There are a couple of professional road-racing venues in which the Miata makes an appearance. The most prominent is the SportsCar Speedvision Cup—which will soon be renamed and/or resanctioned but will most likely remain the same in structure and classification. These cars are allowed similar modifications to the IT-class machines, with engines built to exacting specs and intakes and exhausts tuned for maximum horsepower. Miatas run in the Compact class with the likes of the Honda Del Sol-Si, Dodge Neon, and Nissan 200SX. The Miata recently nearly made its second pro debut in SCCA World Challenge, but that effort was cut short when Ford moved in. Stay tuned…

The most extreme example of a race-trim Miata was completed by Roger Mandeville, the Mazda race-car guru most famous for his championship-winning RX-7s. Mandeville is responsible for the first GTU Junior Mazda Miata, a car largely based on the old IMSA GTU rules, which races in a Puerto Rican sports car series. The GTU Junior began life as a full tube-frame chassis, to which full-race suspension uprights were added. Thirteen-inch discs with four-piston calipers stop it, and Mazda Competition's production fiberglass body, expanded to cover super-large 16x10-inch wheels, covers the tubework. Longtime Mazda engine whiz Dennis Shaw was brought in to tune the powerplant. He massaged the stock 1.8-liter twin-cam until the motor produced a reliable 210 horsepower. Roger mated the engine to a Mandeville close-ratio five-speed with changeable ratios. Complete, this mean Miata weighs in at a lean 1,680 pounds—not much to push around with over 200 horsepower.

Whichever class or style of racing you choose to enter, a Miata does the basics better than almost any car out there. It is bone-reliable, easy to fix when it does break, is very tuneable, is very competitive, and it gives the classic front-engine/rear-drive handling feel that many racers prefer. Hondas can be fast on a track, but few pleasures match the feel of a four-wheel drift through a corner, steering with the gas pedal on a rear-drive automobile.

Appearance Items

One of the best ways to customize a Miata is to put some dollars toward appearance items. This book has been devoted to performance gains, but sometimes you may want a little "show" to match the "go." Over the years, a plethora of body parts and kits have been offered for the Miata, and a complete description of these would fill a book on their own. Here are some highlights:

The most popular body accessories for any Miata are the front and rear lower-lip spoilers. These are available from your dealer and were designed by the same gentlemen who penned the Miata's shape, so they match perfectly.

The aftermarket got into the "mouth-grille" game early on. On a stock Miata, you can see the air-conditioning condenser (or radiator) right through the mouth of a Miata. A front grille covers up the mechanicals and gives the nose a finished look. There are two holes where the license-plate mount bolts in that most vendors use to secure the grille. Most owners pitch the front license plate and bracket (in states where they can get away with it) for appearance's sake. The front tow hooks are taken off as well to clean up the mouth area.

Mazda offers a stripe kit (developed for the 1.8-liter R model) that fits all years of Miata. With the advent of fast-sign companies, many owners simply purchase stripe material from one of these franchises and do the work themselves. Either way, striping goes a long way to personalizing a Miata.

Mazda also offers a rear-lip spoiler for the Miata. This has shown up on special edition cars from time to time. Your dealer can supply you one of these as well, already painted in your car's color. Make sure to adjust your trunk springs (helper springs are available) to compensate for the added weight of the lip spoiler.

A note on color: Mazda spent truckloads of money on making the Miata colors consistent from car to car, and from year to year. They did this because the front and rear

Mazda dealers sell this attractive front lip spoiler. For a Miata that has been lowered, these will scrape now and then, but are resilient enough to take very hard hits without damage.

Mazda's designers made up a rear valance spoiler that finishes the rear bumper out nicely. These were not on cars from the factory due to approach and departure angle requirements for the shipping truck's ramps.

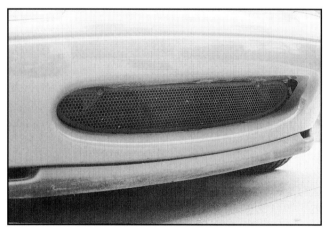

You've got to get a grille. Dozens of different designs are available. If you have an automatic transmission, choose an "open" mesh, because some grilles can cause overheating problems in the summer.

bumper facias are painted off-site, and having the colors match made assembly that much easier to deal with (no repainting). The hardtops need to be matched as well and were also made off-site. The benefit of this is twofold. First, any time you need to touch up your body's paintwork, there's a sure bet that the dealer's paint bottle will match your color very closely (ignoring fading or damage to your car's paint). The second benefit is that the aftermarket can sell prepainted accessories, which some have tried.

The hardest part of getting any body kit on the car, after reconciling yourself to the fact that you will have to drill holes in your car's bodywork to attach the parts, is getting the new parts painted. Most body kits are made of fiberglass, which requires a bit of special paint application on its own. If you buy parts that are made of flexible materials such as urethane (such as your bumpers), you'll need to have the paint shop add a plasticizer to the paint. This will allow the paint to flex without cracking as the parts vibrate and expand or contract with temperature changes.

Hey little Cobra! If you are not bashful about your Miata's performance, you can put on a Mazda R-Package stripe in an afternoon.

Most body kits attach with screws that go into hidden areas. Make sure to paint the backside of the screw and screw holes (if you can get to them) to prevent rust. In general, whatever body kit you put on your car will not be as durable as the steel body structure, so take every effort you can to install the kit in a solid fashion. Many kits come with double-sided foam tape to be used to attach the parts to the body. New, high-tech tapes are so strong that they will pull off the paint before they release the parts, so be careful to get the parts aligned properly before attaching them.

Since front air dams get the brunt of stone chips, a good tip is to have an aftermarket spoiler painted with chip guard (like the lower portions of your door have on them) to make the color stay on. Most aftermarket spoilers are fiberglass, which chips more easily than the stock urethane material, so stone marks become an issue.

Fiberglass comes in two styles: Hand laid-up or chopper gun. The latter has somewhat less strength than the former. In chopper-gun construction, short fibers are shot from a gun

A classic MOMO steering wheel on a Miata makes a great statement and improves the driving feel.

Club Racing Director Rob Ebersol made up his own stripe package, using adhesive vinyl and an X-acto knife. Mazda Competition can supply you with the big MAZDA decal.

The author developed this NACA (the old name for NASA and the inventor of the duct style) duct headlamp lid to get more air into his personal car. Brainstorm Products sells a metal version of this lid. It gets cooler air to the air intake, and it looks sharp.

The Miata's pop-up headlights fell under attack early on. Here is a Japanese solution using high-energy lamps under a smoked plexiglass cover.

Brainstorm Products sells an attractive quad light kit for the Miata that uses high-performance motorcycle headlamps. The height that the headlight lid raises to is reduced by 5 inches.

and combined with the epoxy gel to form the product. In the laid-up process, technicians soak long strips of fiberglass mat in epoxy and lay them inside the mold. Due to the larger mat sections and the layers of mats, this method is stronger. For front air dams, consider the construction used, since you will certainly bump up against a curb someday.

One of the latest full-body kits to come on the market is the Brainstorm Products Italia kit. This is a major collection of body parts and components that radically change the looks of a Miata. If you have a car with some minor front-end damage, you might want to consider applying the repair money toward this conversion.

Putting an Italia kit on a Miata requires some knowledge of bodywork and skill in using body filler. The entire car will need a repaint when you are finished, so you can take advantage of going for that special color this time around.

Aside from the major items, there are a lot of nice little things you can do to make your Miata unique. The Miata's interior is simple and basic as it comes from the factory, and the aftermarket has come up with hundreds of ways to upgrade or change the car's looks.

Starting with the seats, one of the most popular items for earlier Miatas is to upgrade the seat covers to leather upholstery. For around $600 you can order a pair of leather covers for your Miata from Moss Motors, MM Marketing, Brainstorm Products, and others. These are not covers per se, but actually replace the fabric that comes on your Miata. Installation is straightforward, but you can have an upholstery shop do the work for you if you haven't the time or inclination. Removing

Monster Motorsports, the guys putting V-8s into Miatas, have their own way of making a Miata look more aggressive, mostly to cover the larger rear tires needed to handle a V-8's power.

the stock fabric is simple, and the new covers are slipped over the bare seat foam and secured with hook rings. Of course, you need to remove the seats from the car first, but they are held in with only four bolts each. This is a great way to brighten up an older car, and the smell is great.

Steering wheels have recently become a popular area for modification. Moss Motors introduced a wooden steering wheel that retains the stock airbag, an important feature for many owners. For others (who always wear their seatbelts), the stock wheel and airbag are removed and any number of performance wheels from MOMO or Nardi are installed.

Most steering-wheel manufacturers do not make a mounting hub specific to the Miata, so the tip is to order the hub for a Mazda 323 (1989 model). Another issue is the airbag warning light in the dash (or the buzzer that comes on for a short period at startup on 1994 and later cars). On early cars (1990-1993), you can simply jump the two airbag wires together from the steering column and get the light to go out. On 1994 and later cars, most people pull the warning light's bulb out and live with the beep (or kill the beeper as well), although some have had luck with substituting a resistor in place of the airbag. Whatever you do, make sure to handle the airbag itself with great care. If you are changing out steering wheels of any sort, get the airbag off the car (four nuts from behind the wheel's spokes) and get it away from the car. Place it far away from any children or activity—it is an explosive device.

Colored instrument panel faces are very popular (see the Club's 1994 project car in the next chapter). These are easy to install if you have some leftover model-making skills—most require that you pop off your speedometer and tachometer needle. If you go with a light-colored gauge face, you'll want

Mazda's now defunct special projects group called "M2" created this street-competition Miata with subtle tuning changes and a full-cage roll bar. Just the thing for a weekend racer.

Moss Motors sells a classically British three-window top for Miatas. In addition to looking nice, the rear blind spot present on stock soft tops is eliminated.

Russ Silber made a set of side pipes for himself—and for sale to others—that blend the Miata's rocker panels into a classic side exhaust.

to paint the backside of the needles some contrasting color (i.e., red) with model car enamel and a fine brush.

Mazda installed a matching wooden shift knob and parking-brake handle on many of its Special Edition Miatas, and you can reproduce the look yourself with the official Nardi parts from Mazda or others. Moss Motors, MM Marketing, Brainstorm Products, Performance Buyers Club, and others have a vast array of wooden, aluminum, or steel shift knobs to decorate your interior. Full wood kits are available as well for the Miata's interior, if you want to go for a classic look.

One thing you'll need to do, if you haven't already, is to get a set of door-sill scuff plates for your Miata. The companies listed above for shift knobs carry sill protectors, either in plastic or in metal. The door sill of a Miata can get looking pretty ratty after just a few miles of use, so get yours covered up.

On a practical note, your soft rear window needs to be unzipped every time before you lower your top, and it is best not to let it rest naked against the rear shelf carpet. Get a rear-window protector to sandwich your soft window between some protective layers, and your rear window will last much longer. When unzipping your rear window, make sure that your top latches (at the windshield header) are released first. When zipping the window back in, keep the latches loose as well, reducing tension on the window and entire top mechanism.

Speaking of tops, you can get a nifty three-window convertible top for your Miata. This looks great, like the old MGB and Spitfire tops, and it decreases the blind spot common to the stock top. For a luxury look, canvas tops are available. You can even order a replacement top with a glass rear window, an idea Mazda liked so much that they incorporated it into the 1999 Miata.

Chrome accents on an engine can dress up an otherwise dull area. Here is an extreme example of how far you can go. Even the aluminum parts are plated, and braided stainless-steel hoses add the final touch.

A New England company, now out of business, lovingly recreated an Austin-Healey Bugeye nose on a Miata. The molds were bought by a Japanese company, but these kits are not being actively marketed in this country.

You can modernize your instrument panel with a set of colored gauge faces. These are relatively easy to install, but you will revive your model-making skills if you choose to repaint your indicator needles.

Spring company Eibach built a special Miata to show off its performance products. Note the body-colored rocker panels. This is a popular modification that gives the Miata a lowered look.

This body kit, on the Greddy project car, includes new front and rear bumpers, side panels, and an aggressive trunk spoiler.

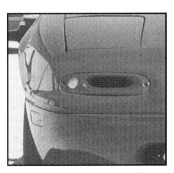

Brainstorm Products tooled up special front-turn-signal housings that double as cold-air induction ports. They give a Miata an even "stealthier" look.

This is a front spoiler from R Speed complete with brake ducts. When ordering a front spoiler, ask about the front clearance on a stock car. If your Miata is lowered, you might end up crashing against the pavement at every driveway.

Racing Beat makes two noses for the Miata. The Type I is mildly aggressive, the Type II (shown) gives any Miata some attitude.

Mazda's design studio built this "Miari" to take up to the Monterey Historic Auto Races when Ferrari was the featured marque. Chopping the windshield made for the sportiest of looks. The car later became the M Speedster shown in Chapter 16.

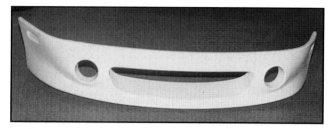

This nose cap from Race Engineering has two holes specifically for driving lights, bringing in a bit of the M Speedster styling.

Brainstorm sells a rear bumper that has been tucked way in for a near-flush look—very clean.

To install the Brainstorm Italia kit, the donor car has to be stripped of many of the stock parts. The rear end gets special treatment, since the new fenders have to be epoxied—rather than bolted—on.

The rear view of the Italia shows a distinct Ferrari influence. Note the large racing fuel cap.

The final result of the Italia kit is something very different than a stock Miata, very Italian. Note the wide tires to fill out the larger rear fenders.

Mentionable Miatas

To give you some scope as to what owners are doing with their cars, this chapter will reprint some of the "Mentionable Miatas" that have been featured in the pages of *Miata Magazine.* This is only a sampling of what can be done with an active imagination and few (or many) dollars, as there are more custom Miatas in the world than we can cover in two books.

First, let's start with Mazda's own project cars, the original Club Racer, the M Speedster, and the M Coupe.

Three Amigos

We had the particularly interesting opportunity back in October 1996 to spend some quality time with the three Miata prototypes: the Club Racer, the M Speedster, and the M Coupe. With three personalities as far from each other as they could be, the comparison makes for some interesting conclusions.

We spent three days with the cars during the Atlanta Miata Games. We had great weather, an important issue since two of the cars do not have working tops (what price glamour?). One of the top men from Mazda's public relations firm, Fred Aikins, had been arranging for this trio of special cars to make it to the Miata Club events around the country all summer long. Many members and attendees were able to see these cars firsthand, and if there was a race track nearby, the cars were usually taken out for a few parade laps. Looking none the worse for their travels, the three cars and Aikins arrived in Atlanta for the final "show" of the year.

These really are unique automobiles, significant on more than one level, much like some of the early Corvette show cars or Ford prototypes from the 1960s. It is hard, just as it might have been then, to realize the importance of what we were playing with. Each of these Miata prototypes was developed by what is one of the industry's most talented design groups—Mazda R&D. Think of the shapes created by this band of designers: The

third-generation RX-7, the MX-6, the 929, the Miata, and others. These are some of the most beautiful cars on the road today, or any day.

This is a group of men and women who take very seriously the art form of car design, a group that made shapes that led some of the major trends in the industry. If you visit the Mazda R&D studios in Southern California, you get a taste of their unseen work. The studio has an old Alfa setting in a corner, a Porsche 356 hiding in the halls, a full-scale mockup of a correct Ford GT-40 that the studio made up just because they liked the shape. Many studios have talented designers. These folks are enthusiasts as well.

It should be no surprise, then, when you see what they have done with their baby, the Miata, when given free rein and a modest budget. The styling prototypes are evidence of their talents. To actually drive these cars is a thrill beyond compare.

Miata Club Racer

The Club Racer, as many of you will recall, was the second darling daughter of the boys at Mazda R&D. The paint was barely dry on the 1989 Chicago Show production Miata when they rolled out this version of what a competition Miata might look like. Starting with an early prototype Miata in

November 1988 (just about when Autoweek scooped the first spy photo of the Miata), the Southern California studio built this car in six short weeks—a phenomenal undertaking. The heavily flared fenders and wide tires were very carefully sculpted to match the Miata's organic theme, and who better to do it than the designers who had done the Miata itself? Project leader Mark Jordan was careful to make this exercise a "production-feasible" model by retaining the stock hood, trunk lid, and doors. The rest is pure macho, with all the aggressive nature you can pour onto a Miata chassis. This car has been universally applauded by press and designers alike from around the world as being a very pleasing modification to the Miata. Even eight years after the lines were penned for this special car, no aftermarket flares or body kits have come close to the simple aggressive elegance exhibited by this unique Miata.

The M Speedster

This car actually started life as the famous "Mi-ari"—a spoof created for the 1994 Monterey Historic Races by Mazda R&D. It is essentially a 1994 prototype (these prototypes get no respect around the design studio) that had its windshield cut down like some fifties hot-rodder. After Monterey, the car became the basis for the most aggressive Miata styling exercise thus far—the M Speedster. "The M Speedster concept car is our idea of what an extremely extroverted and muscular Miata might look like," said Tom Matano, of Mazda R&D. "The M Speedster definitely makes a powerful statement."

It sure looks the part. Hunkered down on its big wheels and tires, the sculpted fenders and shortened "windscreen" make the Miata's proportions all the more aggressive. The overall effect is just "more" Miata-ish in a performance vein. The humps behind the seats hide storage areas for matching helmets. Speed racer would be proud.

The M Coupe

The latest exercise was the refined M Coupe, taking the Miata to a more civilized place than the two former cars. It is also based on a 1.8-liter car's chassis, with the interior receiving a few special touches, such as a cargo bar running behind the seats, special foot pedals and shift knob, and unique door-panel trim. Recently, it has been the recipient of a wood steering wheel that looks right in place. The rest of the car is pretty stock, with the carefully shaped rear quarter panels, doors, and roof showing off the hours taken to style this coupe correctly.

There are actually two Coupes in existence. One is at Mazda's headquarters in Hiroshima, and the other is shown here for us to enjoy. The coupe is a bit heavier than the standard Miata, thanks to the added bulk of the fiberglass roof and the added glass area.

Driving Impressions

You get pretty humble driving around in one-of-a-kind prototypes like these cars. They are priceless, each of them, but they are so easy to drive and so familiar for any Miata owner that it is easy to mistake them for everyday drivers. Only the Speedster gets "in your face"—literally, thanks to its lack of a bug screen.

Fred Aikins asked a few of us to transport the cars from the hotel to Road Atlanta, a 45-minute drive, mostly on highways. It was a brisk morning that made Vince Tidwell glad that he chose the Coupe. Aikins drove the Speedster, and I jumped in the Club Racer, a car I have a special affection for.

I found the Club Racer to be very easy to drive. The chassis is a combination of known tuning practices: Lower and stiffer springs at all four suspension corners, Koni shocks, manual steering with wide 15-inch Panasports and 205/50x15 tires all around. Since the studio started with a base-model Miata, it feels similar to our Club Project Car in the way it drives. Oh, but the engine. You have to love it, all 90 horsepower of it. You see, this car was built on such an

early prototype of the Miata that the engine is not really "correct" as it was built. As an early B6 production model, it has prototype parts all over it, from the air box and intake system to the front cam covers, some of which are 323 parts. It lacks a bit of power in that it was not built to the final Miata 1.6-liter's trim, and the added weight of the fancy bodywork does it no favors.

Traveling in a very expensive convoy composed of these three special cars is a memory to us and those that saw us. It was very interesting to watch people's reactions on the highway as they would pass the three of us. Some would stare at the Club Racer the whole time, others (usually kids) would focus on the Speedster (and on Aikins' hair which was doing some kind of ritualistic dance in the 70-mile-per-hour direct airstream). Others wouldn't get the clue until they saw the Coupe, and then it hit them that these were three cars of similar heritage. "Look ma, thar's the new Corvette."

The Club Racer was an easy ride, but Aikins really was getting beaten up by the wind in the Speedster. I settled in for the 30 miles to the track with Aikins ahead of me, the Coupe leading the line. It didn't matter that I didn't have a radio, as the sweet exhaust note of this car was enough to keep me entertained. Somewhere along the way I noticed a loud whine coming in over the road noise and I began to get worried. Was it a wheel bearing starting to go? Maybe a transmission problem starting to surface?

I accelerated (slowly, with my foot on the floor) up to Aikins in the Speedster and noticed the noise getting louder and louder. As I pulled up beside Aikins, I could hear the noise loudly now as it appeared to be bouncing off of the Speedster's bodywork. As Aikins lifted his foot off the throttle, the noise subsided, and it hit me: I was hearing the Speedster's supercharger whine. I returned to my spot a few car lengths behind Aikins, my heart returning to a normal pace, my ears becoming accustomed to the whine emanating from the hyper-tuned Speedster 20 yards up the road. The thought of having the Club Racer dead on the road in rural North Georgia did not give me pleasure.

On the road, the Club Racer's ride is slightly stiffer than that of an R-Package Miata, and the road feel is great. The input through the MOMO leather steering wheel is direct and precise. The lower center of gravity, and the stiffer springs, keep things planted nicely. The last 10 minutes to the track covers beautiful rolling hills on a smooth two-lane rural road. The Club Racer loved the sweepers, as do all Miatas.

When we got to Road Atlanta, we parked the cars in the display area and compared notes. Vince Tidwell said the Coupe was as pleasant as a car can be, even nicer than a

Miata with a hardtop. Aikins was trying to awaken his tear ducts, his eyes having been long dried out by the wind. He said he now knew what it felt like to be a windshield wiper. I told them I just wanted to get out on the track.

The time for the parade laps came soon enough, and we loaded up to go out on the track. I jumped in the M Speedster this time, making sure to bring my sunglasses. I thought about a hat, but Fred said I'd lose it. I also considered a helmet, but decided against it at the last moment. These were just parade laps, right?

The M Speedster is a slingshot of a car. The seats hold you so firmly, especially with the racing harness, that you feel like you can push the car to its limits from the first roll of the tires. And roll they do. This car is brutally fast. Rather than just make a styling exercise, the boys in the studio had added an Autorotor supercharger boosted to 10 or so psi of boost, shooting through an intercooler. At over 200 horsepower, this car really rips. They put on some good tires and lowering springs to round out the package, and the total feeling is aggressive.

Once up to speed, however, it became apparent that the Speedster was lacking some overall cohesiveness. Whether it was out of alignment (probably) or if the wheels' offsets were overdriving the bushings (also probable), the car did not instill confidence in the corners. It was fast enough, but it sent a few funny signals to the driver that said, "Don't push your luck, Bucko," so I didn't.

Oh, but what a feast for the senses. With the air hitting you smack in the forehead, the turbulence behind the sunglasses was not much better than going glass-less. I now know why early century racers wore goggles. The exhaust roars in your right ear while the supercharger, separated from my ear by 6 feet of air and a thin aluminum hood, whined its whine, ever eager to be put to use. The whole car has a wound-up tension about it, chomping at the bit, asking to be run hard. With a bit more chassis work, it would be capable of blistering laps on the track.

I traded out for the Club Racer and spun a few laps around the course. What had felt solid and planted on the street was beginning to miss the mark on the race track. At the adhesion limit, the car felt a bit twitchy, transitioning from slight understeer to oversteer quicker than I'd like. It was a blast to drive, but I don't think I was going around the track as smoothly as I could. It has a different feel than the Speedster, but the response was the same: caution. Both the hot-rod cars needed a little tuning, or at least less rubber to allow the tires to reach their operating temperatures. The Miata lap records were set at Road Atlanta on 185/60x14s.

Input from the MOMO leather steering wheel is direct and precise.

The seats in the M Speedster hold you so firmly you feel like you can push the car to its limits.

In spite of great seating, the ride in the Club Racer is slightly stiffer than an R-Package Miata.

Finally, it was my turn to drive the M Coupe. If the Speedster is a Miata on steroids, the Coupe is one after a glass of wine. Smooth and quiet are the watchwords when you climb into this last of the Miata prototypes. As expected, both road and wind noise are greatly reduced in this car, and the reductions would be even greater if the roof were made of steel. Other than the 16-inch wheels and tires, the Coupe retains its stock 1.8-liter's chassis. The exhaust system from the catalytic converter back was modified to allow for an under-trunk mounted spare. Sitting in and driving the Coupe, one is first taken by the feeling of spaciousness the rear glass offers, not to mention the improvement in rearward vision. The lateral cargo bar that runs just behind the seats reminds you right off of a Jag E-type coupe, and this car is no less civilized. It would be easy to say this Coupe is no different than a standard Miata with a hardtop, and it is a testament to the Mazda engineers' skill that the hardtop does such a nice job of closing up the structure, but there is more to it than that. The interior space feels different, conversations sound different, and it truly feels like a different car. This is the reason that Jag, MG, Triumph, and others have found customers for coupes and convertibles all along. Something for everyone.

After having driven the two "hot-rodded" Miatas, it was not surprising to find that the Coupe was the fastest through the corners on the track. All it had was great tires, and it seems that is all it needed. In the first session of parade laps, Tidwell led in the Coupe. Other than on the back straight, Vince was losing the Speedster and the Club Racer in the twisties—and these were supposed to be exhibition laps.

Watching the Coupe from the rear gave more witness to the great chassis these cars have—all Miatas. You could watch the rear suspension playing, working, keeping the wheels perpendicular to the tarmac no matter what was thrown at it. It was hard not to become mesmerized by the ballet of the Coupe as Tidwell (no stranger to Road Atlanta) moved about the course. We challenged him when he got back to the pits, telling him it wasn't a race, and his response was, "What's the worry—I didn't go over 80 percent!" To which Aikins and I made a mental note that the two hot rods might be more show than go, at least at this tuning stage. (This reinforces something we've been saying at the magazine all along: It is a lot easier to mess up a Miata's chassis than to improve it. Modifications should be carried out with care and consideration.)

As the sun began to set, we packed up the three cars and headed back to Atlanta. Dicing along the winding two lanes heading home, we saw these cars as they were meant to be. Not race car prototypes optimized for lap times, these were styling models optimized for autumn afternoons and long shadows.

The attraction was undeniable. Each car showed the skills of the designers from every angle. From every new vantage point we saw the character instilled in each individual car's shape. The beauty of these carefully formed bodies in the late afternoon light was magical. Not a coarse intersection or bad reflection could be found. Not only were they great examples of superior car design, they were excellent samples of the craftsmanship skills at Mazda R&D.

We were blessed to have some seat time in these three cars, but at the end of the day the best way to enjoy them was to sit on an old wooden fence and let the sunset's reflection play itself out across the hoods and fenders of these special creations. As everyone contemplates the future of the Miata, looking at these three sisters from the same family gives one great faith. The parents obviously carry good genes.

1990 Miata Club of America Project Car

It used to be that we all knew the stakes for a hot street "rod." You started with a production car, preferably used, and then you put your own sweat and tears into the machine until it said something unique about you, something about your way of thinking. You chose from a list of "approved" parts. Edlebrock, Crane, Hedman, Holley—everyone knew the players without a scorecard. After you made your choices and built your beauty, you had something to be proud of. And, if you did things right, you had a performance machine that commanded respect around town.

Welcome to the 1990s. We are all tooling around in governmentally correct Japanese imports with sanitized four-cylinder engines (at least we get a convertible top!). At first glance, customization is not as easy as it used to be. But

if you dig a little deeper, you'll recognize that our little Miatas can be made into the most serious of hot rods. And we won't have to slow down for corners.

The Club has kept a project car going over the past five years, trying out ideas and dreams from our drafting table and others. We've tried almost everything from SU carburetors to 205-millimeter racing tires, and learned a lot in the process. The final configuration has evolved into quite a nice street car, one that would show its face well at a local drag strip or autocross. As a matter of fact, our project car is faster and has better cornering levels than found with the original Lamborghini Countach, for one-tenth the price. And we can afford to insure our ride.

The basic car started as a 1990 Mariner Blue Miata base model with manual steering, air conditioning, and steel wheels. For reference, a car of this configuration can be found selling for around $9,500 on the used-car market. We paid $15,500 in August 1989 for the car and now have 31,000 sweet but hard miles on it.

Over the years, just about every accessory made for a Miata has been put on this car and taken off. As the magazine's "mule," nothing was sacred, no point of originality spared. After five years of this sort of treatment, certain items gained the right to stay on the car. Some because they truly enhanced the performance, some because they enhanced our day-to-day enjoyment of the car, and some because we liked the way they looked. In some sort of Darwinian process

of elimination, what is on the car now works, and works well.

An interesting observation is that now, just as Mazda planned, a person can buy a used Miata and make it into this sort of performance car for a reasonable amount of money. In keeping with the "affordable sports car" theme, the used car buyer is a large part of the equation. The car you see here could be purchased and built up for less than $14,000. The new owner would have a distinctive automobile, but a reliable car for everyday use. Long-term prospects such as this are just now showing themselves as a big part of the Miata's attraction. Let's go down the laundry list of items on our Project Miata.

Appearance

The most distinctive change made to the car was the wheels. We have had these on for five years and love them. They are Panasport FS 15x7-inchers with a 38-millimeter offset. The hub collar is 54 millimeters, which matches the Miata hubs perfectly.

We chose 15-inch wheels purely for the appearance improvement; it used to be that you had to go to a larger-diameter wheel to get higher-performance tires. Not so today, when plenty of 14-inch tires have excellent handling and cornering performance. You do, however, use a 50-series tire with 15-inch wheels, and these lower-profile tires can have better handling characteristics than 60-series tires used with the 14-inch wheels, although it is not a guaranteed

Over the years, just about every accessory made for the Miata had been put on and taken off the Club project car.

result. Some 60-series tires handle much better than some poorly designed 50-series tires.

A note on lower-profile tires: Since the sidewalls are now "shorter," the ride quality is affected slightly. With today's tire technology, this is less of a problem than before, but you will notice a bit more harshness over tar strips and the like.

As for tires, we have performed two long-term tire tests on this car, starting with Yokohama AVS Intermediates in the 195/50x15 size. These were very nice tires, giving excellent cornering, good wet-weather traction, and good braking performance. The second test is still ongoing with a set of Dunlop SP-8000s with 195/50x15s on the front and 205/50x15s on the rear (the engine modifications warranted the larger rear tires, as we'll explain later). The Dunlops are amazing in all weather conditions and have become our new favorites for Miatas.

The rolling diameter of these two tire set-ups is close enough to the stock tire diameter of 22.8 inches that we were not faced with an inaccurate speedometer or gearing problems. Any tire-wheel combination you choose should be as close to this diameter as possible.

For normally aspirated engines, we do not recommend tires wider than 195 millimeters for a Miata. Wider tires in general will not get as warm on the road, so cornering performance can suffer. We had some vibration trouble with 205-millimeter-wide tires. However, if you are so inclined, you can fit a 16x7-inch wheel with a 205/40 tire inside the stock wheelwells of a Miata.

Back to appearance items. Almost immediately, we put on the Mazda front and rear lower spoilers. These black plastic lip spoilers were designed along with the Miata, but due to the nature of transport trucks and the like, could not be installed at the factory. They are sold as a dealer accessory

and really finish out the Miata's underbody styling. Installation is an easy do-it-yourself sort of job.

We added leather seat covers a few years back and have loved them ever since. The set we have on the project car came from a supplier that is now bankrupt (in every sense of the term), but a few advertisers with more business sense are making similar kits available. Sometimes when our car sits outside and a little moisture gets into the carpet, we can almost close our eyes and believe we are sitting in an old Jag, the smell is so familiar. The only downside? Leaving them exposed to the sun makes the black leather hot—hot—hot. They have held up well over the years, allaying our fears that leather would get torn up in a Miata's interior.

A front grille helped to finish off the front "mouth" of our project car. The one we used is from MM Marketing. Some cars exhibit an overheating problem with some grilles, but we have never had a problem, even with a heavily modified engine in hot Georgia summers with the air conditioning running. Automatic tranny Miatas are more sensitive to overheating with a grille installed, so owners of those cars should avoid them.

The driver's side headlamp cover was replaced with a vented cover. The new lid has a NACA duct molded into it and is prepainted to match our Mariner blue. The duct allows more cold air into the engine's air intake, but we also liked the way it looked. Our Miata now had something distinctive and a bit aggressive to display that bespoke the power hiding within. No commuter car was this Miata; it now looked like it meant business.

The headlights are something new out of Japan. Using four motorcycle headlights, KG Works made up a set of low-profile quad lights for the Miata (or, as the case may be, for their Eunoses). Unfortunately, the lights are very expensive and not strictly legal for use on U.S. roads. Brainstorm Products, the importer, has a DOT-approved set in the works at an affordable price. In keeping with the Miata design theme for round headlights (animals don't have square eyes), these lights are very distinctive. From the driver's seat, the view is all the better with a 4-inch reduction in the height of the headlights when raised.

Convenience Items

The top of our list goes off to the Mighty Products lighted rearview mirror. We have come to rely on this simple little device for mere survival in the darkness of a Miata's interior (1994 Miatas need this more than ever, or something like the Mialite). The lighted mirror uses the factory inside rearview mirror mounting point and comes on automatically with the stock interior lights. This light may sound like a frivolous thing, but it has made night-time driving much more convenient.

We have a window protector installed to keep the soft top's rear window from being scratched when the top is down. There are a few companies offering these now, and they all work about the same. Our only complaint is that when your top is up, lowering a side window blows the unused cover back into the passenger compartment—there is no longer a soft top holding it in place. Our current unit has Velcro tabs on it to eliminate this problem, a nice feature.

Speaking of sound, we have the Clearwater door speakers and amplifier in the car and could not be happier. Even at speeds over 100 miles per hour with the top down, we can hear our favorite tunes. The sound quality and imaging at normal speeds are very good, thanks to these speakers having been custom-tuned to the Miata's acoustics. No off-the-shelf speaker we've tried comes close, and the amp works wonders on the bass notes.

To monitor the engine, we jettisoned the two center air vents to install a vacuum/boost gauge and a fuel rail pressure gauge, both from VDO (2-5/8-inch-diameter gauges). The fuel pressure gauge is actually a modified electronic oil-pressure gauge that we took apart and painted over the word "Oil." On both gauges we painted the needles white to match the Miata's other gauges. We used a green marker to color the gauge light bulbs and wired them to the ashtray illumination light so things would match the stock instrument panel lights. The final effect is very nice, especially at night. Summertime driving is still bearable by using the bilevel air-conditioning position.

We installed a remote trunk release from the Mazda accessory line and found it to be a necessity (it is no wonder that Mazda made a cable-operated version standard equipment in 1992). One of the black shift knobs embossed with the five-speed pattern finished off the interior.

One last thing, we went to K Mart and bought a Lite Minder that buzzes when we leave our lights on. Probably the best $3.50 we ever spent, considering how we like to cruise around with our parking lights on at twilight, trying to look cool. Standing beside a Miata holding a set of jumper cables an hour later in the dark is the full definition of "un-cool."

Engine

On the engine side, we have installed a Sebring Supercharger kit. This is a proprietary-sized Eaton supercharger that easily mounts to the Miata engine. Power is up 50 horsepower, and torque is very strong. The unit has proven to be as solid as a rock and runs hard all day long. The EPA likes the kit, as do our neighbors, who enjoy that it is a quiet unit. Particularly

during Club runs to our favorite mountain roads, the expanded engine flexibility is very welcomed.

We added a EUROX modified engine computer to further increase our power output. The new brain changes the ignition curve and fuel curve at certain points in the map. Our 0-60 times are now under 6 seconds, and midrange pickup is very strong. We have surprised a lot of other cars on the road as they find our car a little too fast to keep up with. Mustang 5.0-liter owners find a Miata's taillights to be a particularly humbling sight.

One staffer made note that we are now within striking range of Tim Allen's Saleen Mustang, which is touted to be the hottest modified car of the year. Taking a historical perspective, we are now faster (0-60) than the Ferrari Boxer, Porsche Turbo Carrera, Lamborghini Countach, Pantera, and many other legendary sports cars, and we still have a 100,000-mile engine and get 30 miles per gallon (not to mention money in our wallets). Spunky might now be the word for our little two-seater from Japan.

For a final exhaust, we now have a Genie system installed, which we are quite pleased with. After four years of aftermarket exhausts that have a nice "performance" sound to them, it is pleasant to have a system that delivers the power without the noise. Using a resonator, the Genie "after-cat" (all new parts after the catalytic converter rearward) system is no louder than the stock setup with just as much power to be gained. Some staffers complained that it was too quiet, but many owners will find this a plus. Being made of stainless steel, it will last a long time as well. The stock exhaust manifold and catalytic converter are back on the car for some exhaust studies we were doing. We had the Jackson Racing header on for a while, and it was a nice improvement.

Racing Beat silicone spark plug wires and cooler NGK spark plugs round out the engine changes. Both have been in for four years now with no perceptible wear.

Suspension

Not much to tell here, just three main ingredients: Koni shocks, Jackson Racing sway bars, and the aforementioned Dunlop tires. The effect is phenomenal, transforming a well-balanced sports car into a serious mountain rocket. The Konis are set at the softest damping rate and at the lowest spring perch setting, lowering the car about one-half inch all around. The Jackson sways are just a bit stiffer than stock and use urethane bushings (stock sizes are 19 millimeters front and 12 or 11 millimeters rear; Jackson sways are 21 millimeters front and 14 millimeters rear, adjustable).

Skid-pad testing with this setup will force you out of your seat and up against the door panel; the grip is unreal. The

Miata's stable character keeps the total feel safe and stable, without off-throttle oversteer or mid-turn twitchiness. As with any suspension changes, we had a full alignment done to make sure we weren't wasting our time. With camber all around set at 1 degree negative, maximizing caster and shooting for zero toe-in, the steering is bright and responsive.

The ride quality is still very acceptable, even for our older staffers on long trips. In many respects, we are not far off from Mazda's R-Package configuration for the Miata. Our setup's ride quality is even preferable to the R's settings to some.

The Big Picture

The total bill? About $4,500 for the parts; our labor was for free. The end result is a completely comfortable highway car that makes no apologies on the track. Call it a Miata with an attitude; we really look for some competition to pull up beside us at stoplights. Just as it was when we first got our Miatas, we now make up excuses to take the car out for a spin. Grocery shopping has become a daily event, just for the fun of ripping through the gears.

The ultimate sports car? To us, it makes a pretty good dent in that goal. It's cheap to run, cheap to insure, reliable, fun, and surprisingly fast. That's all we needed.

Hey buddy, got your pink slip handy?

A V-8 the Easy Way: Keeping It Simple

Miata Club member Les March is our kind of guy. Not only does he know how to swing a wrench, he knows how to get what he wants without dropping a lot of cash. March is of the old hot-rod school that goes for substance rather than appearance, and would rather do the job himself to know it was done right. What March did was put a Mustang 5.0-liter V-8 in a Miata.

March is a 51-year-old supervisor for Calsonic North America, a company that supplies the auto industry with heat exchangers and exhaust systems. He is currently the exhaust prototype supervisor and drives a few interesting

cars, including a 1995 Merlot M-edition Miata. Right away, we could tell that he was an enthusiast with the skills to take on a big project.

Now, putting a Mustang engine in a Miata is not something new to the Miata world. For years, Monster Miata of Escondido, California, has made a nice business of selling turn-key cars with fuel-injected 5.0s in them. What March did differently was to do it on a shoestring budget with thorough and elegant engineering style.

To start with, March found a flood-damaged 1990 Miata that he picked up for a song. The car did not have an engine or transmission—perfect for his project. The water had come up to the console, ruining the stock engine computer and other electrics. The rest of the car was in remarkably good condition with only 15,000 miles on the clock. The underside looked as though it had never been near a dirt road.

With a thorough steam cleaning of the empty chassis, the project was ready to begin. The first step was to order an engine. Rather than start with a dirty old used engine, a brand new "crate" engine from Ford Motorsport was ordered. March chose a 1995-specification SVO 5.0-liter after a few discussions with the helpful folks at Ford. He had the option of carburetors or fuel injection, and had to make a choice. Being raised on carbs, noting the complication a fuel injection setup might add to the project, and adding that emissions in his area are not a big problem, he opted for the carburetors—a classic hot-rodder's choice.

The engine, complete with a bellhousing, came in five days. The total price was $2,376, not bad for a ready-to-run powerplant. Les added a Holley 600-cfm carburetor from Summit Racing and used a fuel regulator to trim down the Miata's in-tank fuel pump. Its peak pressure of 75 psi needed to be changed into a carburetor-friendly 3-5 psi. The regulator also had a return feature to dump excess fuel back to the tank using the stock fuel lines. A low-profile aluminum intake manifold from a 1980s Mustang engine was used to keep the carburetor as low as possible.

When it came time to rig up an exhaust, March began to show his skills as a fabricator and a scrounger. The stock exhaust header on the passenger's side of the engine worked fine, with a bit of work on the collector end, but the driver's-side header didn't clear much of anything. March did a bit of hunting and found that a header from a Ford Explorer that

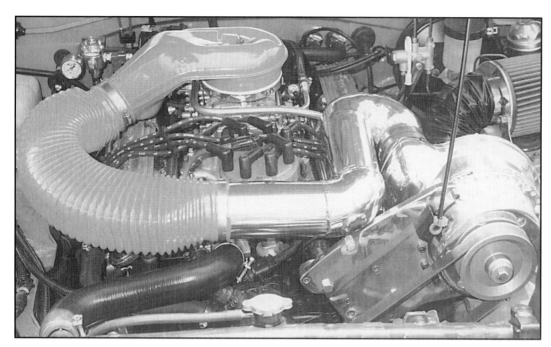

The crisp Miata exhaust note is tuned just a little bit rougher and tougher with the moan of an added supercharger.

worked great. He had both exhaust manifolds Jet Hot coated, which is a ceramic coating that looks great and lasts forever.

A new transmission was acquired, again through mail order. What arrived was a 1995 Cobra T-5 five-speed with a heavy-duty clutch and pressure plate. The total bill for this part of the drivetrain came to $1,340 for all-new parts. The stock slave cylinder in a Miata won't push a Cobra clutch, so a bit of hunting at a Car Quest store resulted in a larger one for $30 that worked fine.

For the electricals, March adapted a used Miata alternator (new ones are very expensive), which mated up with the stock wiring harness correctly. The starter selected was a generic unit from a 1993-1995 5.0-liter Mustang. A Ford ignition coil was needed to fire the standard distributor. The radiator fans and the radiator itself came from a Nissan Altima (March had these on hand).

For the suspension, heavy-duty springs were installed at all four corners ($187) and a front sway bar from a 1964 Ford Fairlane (!) was adapted, since the stock bar interfered with the crank pulley. (March must have one heck of a backyard full of odd parts.) Structurally, March had to do a bit of trimming in the engine bay, but nothing that would affect the overall strength, in his opinion.

The final product is a great-running car that turns heads and burns rubber wherever it goes. March has not had any trouble keeping the stock rear end in good health. Just to add to the recipe, a supercharger was dropped on the car for good measure. He's got something close to 300 horse-

power now, in a car only slightly heavier than a stock Miata.

The main purpose of this project was to develop a high-quality vehicle at a reasonable cost. Despite the goal, March purchased many components new that could have been bought much cheaper used (the going rate for a used Mustang 5.0-liter engine is $600 in the Southeast). March states that the project was not easy, but it made a good challenge. Anyone attempting this sort of conversion needs a well-furnished shop that includes a welder, a cutting torch, various saws, drills, and grinders, and the knowledge and experience to properly use them.

From our end, it looks like a great way to salvage a flooded Miata. Kudos to Les for making his dreams come true and making a Miata that is a bit off the beaten path.

PFS Miata SC:
More Of Everything You Like In a Miata

by Steve Potter

Step on the gas in the prototype PFS Miata SC at 1,800 rpm in fourth gear and in about three seconds you'll know the difference between this car and a standard 1995 Miata. The crisp Miata exhaust note is tuned just a little bit rougher and tougher, and mixed in with the usual sweet Miata underhood mechanical symphony there's the moan of a supercharger, far-away sounding and soft-edged, like a siren's call from a distant island. Really quite musical. And oh, yes, one more thing: The speedometer and tach snap into a clockwise sprint—one that doesn't end until the speedo is reading 100-plus.

Go ahead, push the shift lever up into fifth gear and press the throttle pedal back to the floor. The 1.8-liter four pulls like a bull all the way to the 7,400-rpm fuel cut, at which point you're going an honest 140 miles per hour.

Handling is just as impressive. At the limits, the PFS Miata SC has the same fine balance of a stock Miata, but the limits are so high that you really ought not explore them away from a race track. And it will stop so fast, you'd better glance in your rearview mirror before you test the brakes at full stop.

Now, here's a pleasant surprise. Despite the car's Deep Purple hue, coke-bottle shaped flanks, and aggressive stance, this isn't some automotive equivalent of a Ninja motorcycle, a knife-edge machine that's really only good for getting your jollies on Saturday afternoons. If you find a normal, garden-variety Miata satisfactory as a daily driver, you'll find the PFS Miata SC will be as well.

In fact, with the increased flexibility of its Roots-type supercharged engine, this special Miata is an easier car to drive. No rowing through the gears when you want to squirt into a sudden hole in the traffic, or make a quick pass on a country two-lane. And even though the car circles the skid pad at a neck-bending 1.0 G, the PFS Miata SC has a better ride quality than the R-Package factory racer, and it has very nearly as comfortable a ride as the base car. Noise level is surprisingly low. You'll have no problem hearing the music from the Pioneer FH-P95 four-input audio system that's mounted in the dash, and you could drive the car long enough without fatigue to listen to a whole magazine worth of tunes from the CDX-P606 remote six-disk changer mounted in the trunk.

Meet Peter Farrell, expatriate New Zealander, Mazda factory race driver and IMSA racing champion, high-performance street car builder, owner of Peter Farrell Supercars in Manassas, Virginia, and the man behind the most exciting Miata to come down the road in a long time.

"Like it?" Farrell asked from the passenger seat after I've enjoyed a blast down an isolated Northern California road on a morning last November just before the PFS Miata SC's public debut as the featured car in Mazda's display at the San Francisco Auto Show.

Yes, as a matter of fact, I did. And so did a few hundred street-side auto styling critics, who didn't have the pleasure of driving the car, but still gave it admiring glances as we sped through the streets of San Francisco. This car has terrific curb appeal. When we stopped at traffic lights or pulled over to park, knots of people gathered around it, nodding approvingly.

"I've sold a lot of Miatas in the past five years," said one dealership saleswoman, admiring the car as she circled it slowly. "And for $29,500, I could sell a lot of these." My guess is that she's right.

"Now, tell me all about this car," said the Aussie spokesmodel who'd been assigned to share the rotating platform with Farrell's creation in San Francisco's Moscone Center. "I know I'm going to get a lot of questions." He was right about that. The PFS Miata SC was the hit of the San Francisco show. During the press preview, the Saturday night before the show opened, the PFS car was the center of attention. The next morning the local CBS affiliate did a live video interview with Farrell next to his car. "I've always thought the Miata was a great car," Farrell told the television interviewer. "And most of the people who have bought it, have loved it. But from my perspective, it needed more power. I believe there's an untapped market for a car that has everything the Miata does, but a bit more of it. I wanted to build a version of the car that retains the Miata's balance and charm, but accelerates, brakes, and corners better and has styling that communicates that capability."

Well, this is it, then. "I didn't want to do just another tuner car," said Farrell, who has built more than two dozen copies of his PFS RX-7 Limited Edition, a 360-horsepower version of Mazda's rotary rocket that uses the technology he developed for Mazda's factory entry in IMSA's Bridgestone Supercar series. "I rounded off the sharp edges of my RX-7 race car to make something that would appeal to the driver who wanted a significant bit more than the stock RX-7," he continued, "but I made sure that the car was developed as a balanced whole. That's the same approach I took with the Miata.

"I studied what other people had done with the Miata, and came away with the impression that in too many cases people had just thrown parts at the car, without really considering the whole package. I wanted to address everything about the car, so that the performance was enhanced in every way, but the essential balance that makes the Miata so nice was still intact. And most of the aftermarket bodywork that I'd seen for the Miata didn't appeal to me. The only thing I ever saw that really looked good was the Club Racer that [Miata designer] Mark Jordan did for the [1989 Miata introduction at the] Chicago Auto Show. It had an all-of-a-piece look that I wanted my car to have."

The increase in horsepower comes from a Sebring supercharger kit, with some modification from the PFS shop to fit the particular needs of this application, and a "cat-back" 2.5-inch stainless-steel exhaust system. Chief among the changes to the blower kit is the addition of a massive air-to-air intercooler, sourced from Farrell's RX-7 Supercar racer. "At the 4 1/2 pounds of boost we're running, the intercooler reduces the intake charge temperature to about 10 degrees over ambient," Farrell noted. "That means that we don't have to back the timing off during full boost, and we wind up with more area under the [horsepower] curve. This engine makes 185 horsepower and should last as long as a stock, normally aspirated engine."

Farrell does specify NGK spark plugs, as he has had very good luck with them in racing. He noted that with further development this basic engine package could make in the neighborhood of 230 horsepower. "But that's not what I was looking for here," he continued. "Like I said before, I wanted to maintain the balance of the stock Miata. Mazda designed this platform for a maximum of 200 horsepower, and if we were making much more than that, we'd have to replace the cooling system, the whole drivetrain, and the engine management system, and the price would be near $50,000. That's more than my RX-7 Limited Edition costs, and I don't think there's much of a market for Miatas at that price."

When it comes to the horsepower figures that some aftermarket tuners claim for their products, Farrell can be a little prickly. "I'm afraid they get their horsepower figures from the 'fantasy dyno' and their performance numbers by counting off the seconds in their heads," he said. "I'll stand by the fifth-wheel performance figures for my cars from outside sources like *Car and Driver* and *Motor Trend*. My PFS cars make the numbers that they should based on the horsepower I say they have." (Independent fifth-wheel figures for the PFS Miata SC are 0-60 in 6.9 seconds, 1.01 G on the skid pad, and 140 miles per hour at the fuel cut.)

Handling is improved with PFS Comfort-Sport springs, adjustable shocks, and PFS sway bars, while race-car overall grip is a function of Yokohama 008R high-performance tires (225/50x16 fronts and 245/45x16 rears) mounted on PFS/Fikse ultralightweight modular wheels (16x8-inch at the front and 16x9-inch at the rear). A heavy-duty clutch backs up the uprated powerplant, while a 4.4:1 Torsen limited-slip differential offsets the gearing change from the bigger-outside-diameter tires and restores stock speedo calibration. Record-setting deceleration comes courtesy of Powerstop cross-drilled Miata brake rotors and Hawk carbotic brake pads. Stainless-steel braided brake lines produce a more sensitive pedal feel during all-out braking efforts.

The changes to the coachwork were born from the changes to the mechanical package, namely larger fenders to enclose the big wheel-tire units, and a larger air intake to meet increased cooling needs. The fenders on the prototype (3 inches wider than stock at the rear and 2 inches wider at the front) are all steel, hand-built on an English wheel by former Boyd Coddington fabricator Craig Neff, whose resume includes work on Caddzilla and Chrysler's Prowler concept car.

"This was the only way we could do it," Farrell explained. "The rear fenders are part of the Miata's body structure, and if you cut them off and substitute fiberglass, the car loses a significant part of its rigidity. For the production version of the car we're exploring low-volume steel dies."

The nose of the prototype is fiberglass and bears a family resemblance to the nose on Farrell's RX-7 Limited Edition. Adequate cooling is ensured with an air intake twice the size of the regular Miata's and aluminum ductwork that guides all the incoming air through the intercooler and radiator.

In terms of appearance, these functional coachwork changes have provided a very different visual presentation for the PFS Miata SC. The standard Miata is a very attractive car, and most people would describe its looks as "cute." It has a kind of unisex appeal. The PFS car, with its coke-bottle shape, goes more in the direction of what has been traditionally defined as a "masculine" visual idiom, like the RX-7, the Camaro, or the Corvette. Which is not to say that its appeal will be limited to men. Anyone who likes the Miata, but is looking for more performance and a more distinctive appearance, will be a candidate to own this car.

Speaking of which, how does one become the owner of the PFS Miata SC? Well, for the time being, the thing to do is to contact Peter Farrell Supercars. But Farrell would like for you to be able to buy one from a Mazda dealer, and he's talking to the folks in Irvine about how to make that happen. After all, it's worked for Ford with Steve Saleen, for Pontiac with SLP, for Chevrolet with Calloway, and now for Mercedes-Benz in the United States with AMG, so it shouldn't be out of the question for the PFS Miata SC to appear in Mazda showrooms across the country right alongside the standard and M-series Miatas.

Sources

BBR (United Kingdom; forced induction kits and other parts)
44-0-1280-702389
www.bbrgti.demon.co.uk

Bell Engineering Group (Forced induction kits)
210-349-6515

Brainstorm Products (Broad range of hop-up parts, body parts, and accessories)
1-800-779-3223
www.bsp-inc.com

Butterfly Luggage (Custom-fit Miata luggage)
1-800-851-2620

The Clearwater Company (High-end audio equipment for Miatas)
1-800-96-AUDIO
www.clearwateraudio.com

Crazy Red Italian (Misc. accessories)
916-331-5639
www.crazyred.com

The Dealer Alternative Inc. (Broad range of hop-up parts}
970-464-0878
www.dlralt.com

Dunlop Tire Co.
www.dunloptire.com

Hard Dog Fabrication (Roll bars)
1-800-688-9652

Imparts Ltd. (Misc. tools, parts, and maintenance items)
1-800-325-9043
www.imparts.com

Jackson Racing (Broad range of hop-up parts)
1-800-642-8295
www.miatamania.com

Koni (Shock absorbers)
1-800-994-KONI, ext. 4072

Mazmart (Used Mazda parts)
1-800-221-5156
www.mazmart.com

Miata.net (Website full of Miata information on-line)
www.miata.net

Miata Club of America (Independent membership organization) and
Miata Magazine (Full color bi-monthly magazine dedicated to Miatas)
770-642-4482
www.miataclub.org

Miata World (Misc. accessories)
1-800-832-3292

MM Marketing (Broad line of accessories and hop-up parts)
1-800-666-4282
www.miata.net/mmm

Moss Motors, Ltd. (Broad range of hop-up parts, body parts, and accessories)
1-800-642-8295
www.miatamania.com

Motorsport (Broad range of hop-up parts and accessories)
1-800-633-6331

Panasport (Performance wheels)
310-373-0071
www.panasport.com

Performance Buyers Club (Broad range of hop-up and body parts)
1-800-359-4093
www.performancebuyers.com

Racing Beat (Broad range of hop-up and body parts)
714-779-8677
www.racingbeat.com

Rod Millen Motorsports (Broad range of hop-up and body parts)
714-847-2158

Roebuck Mazda (dealer offering discounts to Miata Club members)
1-800-240-2121
www.roebuckmazda.com

Rogue Speed (Broad range of hop-up parts)
1-888-551-0025
www.rspeed.vivid.net

Sebring Superchargers (Forced induction kits)
1-800-642-8295
www.miatamania.com

Tire Rack (Discount tires via mail order)
1-800-981-3782
www.tirerack.com

WestCo Battery Systems, Inc. (Replacement Miata batteries)
1-800-214-8040
www.westcobattery.com

Zymol Enterprises Inc. (Car care products)
1-800-999-5563
www.zymol.com

Index

160